# WOMEN
# LEAVING *The*
# WORKPLACE

BASED ON INPUT FROM THOUSANDS OF WOMEN NATIONWIDE

LARRY BURKETT is founder and president of Christian Financial Concepts, a nonprofit, nondenominational ministry that provides personal financial counseling and instructs individuals through nationwide seminars. Larry holds degrees in marketing and finance.

He hosts two radio programs, heard on 1,100 radio outlets, and has written more than forty books, including the bestsellers *The Coming Economic Earthquake, Debt-Free Living,* and the novels *The Illuminati, The Thor Conspiracy* and *Solar Flare.*

Larry and Judy Burkett reside in Gainesville, Georgia. They have four grown children and nine grandchildren.

*How To Make The Transition*
*From Work To Home*

# WOMEN
# LEAVING *The*
# WORKPLACE

*BASED ON INPUT FROM THOUSANDS OF WOMEN NATIONWIDE*

# LARRY BURKETT

MOODY PRESS
CHICAGO

# Acknowledgments

I would like to sincerely thank all of the people who made this book a reality. This certainly has been an "unusual" project. I was working well ahead of my deadline and had gone to our cabin in North Carolina to finish the last few chapters when I received a call from my doctor about a test he had run, to determine why I had a nagging soreness in my left shoulder. The tests had revealed a "mass" in my left shoulder (they never use the word cancer).

Needless to say, my work schedule was abruptly halted and, although I didn't know it then, I would not be able to write any more for nearly five months.

Subsequent tests revealed a primary tumor in my right kidney, and in less than three weeks I underwent two major surgeries, in which I had my right kidney and my left shoulder blade removed.

During this time my trusted editor, Adeline Griffith, took my notes and the letters I had selected to use and produced a rough draft of the last chapters and compiled the Appendix.

With the help of our newsletter editor, Chuck Thompson, who assembled information provided by our friend, Connie Brezina, the chapter on homeschooling came into being.

Our career counselor, Mike Taylor, lent his expertise to provide information for the personality evaluation in the Appendix.

So, with combined efforts, the book was ready for my final input when I recovered enough to resume work. To each of these people I want to profess my profound thanks. What a joy it is working with God's people on this earth.

I also would like to say thanks to my good friends at Moody Press—Dennis Shere, Greg Thornton, and Bill Thrasher (not to mention Dr. Joe Stowell)—who have waited patiently while I finished this project (about two months behind the original schedule).

I would be remiss if I didn't give a genuine thank-you to all the women who gave of their time and tears to participate in this project. Without them, none of this would have been possible.

Finally, I would like to say thank you to my wife Judy and our four terrific children and nine grandchildren for standing with me during this ordeal. I confess that I am not the world's best patient.

I love to work, and I love God's people. Heaven's going to be terrific!

# Contents

# Introduction

*"'I know the plans that I have for you,'*
*declares the Lord, 'plans for welfare and*
*not for calamity to give you a future and a*
*hope'" (Jeremiah 29:11).*

More women than ever are seeking to leave full-time jobs and return home to become stay-at-home moms, according to several recent surveys.[1]

At the same time, dual income families still outnumber single-income families three to one.[2]

There is not just one reason more women are leaving the marketplace for home but rather a combination of reasons: There are more working women today and, therefore, more working mothers; juvenile delinquency is alarming parents and drawing mothers back home; and the home business movement has made generating at least some income at home more feasible.

I became interested in the stay-at-home-mom trend years ago when I noticed a significant trend on our daily call-in radio talk show, "Money Matters," on which many women callers were asking questions about how they could leave their jobs and become stay-at-home moms.

Usually their questions were practical and to the point, such as "How can I quit my job when we're just barely making ends meet on two incomes now?" or "How can I convince my husband I should quit work when my job provides our health insurance?"

Most of the callers had a strong desire to be at home with their children, but they could see no realistic way to do so financially.

Sometimes a woman in this situation has the support of her spouse; sometimes she doesn't. All too often the husband's respond is, "It's okay by me if you can figure out how to do it and it doesn't cost us anything." In essence he's saying, "I'll go along if it doesn't alter our lifestyle." Unfortunately, it really doesn't work that way.

## *The Conflicts of Working Mothers*

In recent years most of the Christian community have sanctioned the concept that mothers *should* be at home when their children need them—especially in light of the current juvenile crime wave sweeping our nation. But we haven't done a very good job of teaching young families how to accomplish this without destroying their finances—and sometimes their marriages.

However, because of the thousands of calls and letters we receive at CFC, I have a unique opportunity to see what is happening, on a day-to-day basis, in our society. Women, in general, and mothers in particular, are under

*I will put My Spirit within you and cause you to walk in My statutes, and you will be careful to observe My ordinances.*

Ezekiel 36:27

enormous pressures to balance their families and their jobs. Most of our callers want to be stay-at-home moms, but all too often those who quit their jobs end up with worse troubles than they had before.

So, what are working mothers who desire to become stay-at-home moms to do? Plan well, be realistic, and be willing to sacrifice. I trust this book will shed some light on how to do these things.

Let me hasten to say that this book is not a debate on the philosophical or biblical issues regarding women, and especially mothers, who work outside their homes. This is a book for women who already have worked through this issue for themselves and desire to quit their jobs and become stay-at-home moms. I want to help make that transition possible and help those who are already stay-at-home moms to remain there as long as they desire.

For mothers who have not made the decision to quit their jobs and stay at home, the internal struggle is often so confusing they lose their perspective—including God's direction. If this is true in your case, perhaps the many personal testimonies of the mothers we interviewed will help you to see more clearly God's will for your family.

## Being a Stay-at-Home Mom Is Not for Everyone

Reading through the hundreds of personal testimonies of stay-at-home moms who responded to our survey was a decided blessing. But unfortunately not all were success stories. Some women tried it and failed; some were in worse shape than before; and some lost their marriages. Some of the most heartbreaking letters were from mothers who

At any time we can put the past behind us and begin a new stage of the journey.

—*Ronald E. Wilson*

yearned to be at home but could see no realistic way to do so.

Especially traumatic were the testimonies of working mothers who were looking back to the years when their children were young and needed them the most but now realize it's too late to reach them.

On the other side of this issue are the working mothers who have no desire to stay home. I have tried to present their arguments fairly as well. The feminist movement has had a great influence on how society perceives those women who do not work outside the home. I trust the testimonies of the many intelligent, well-educated women who share their stories will help to undo some of the negative stereotypes that are presented in the media.

In most instances, the testimonies I used in this book are virtually unaltered. To protect the individuality of the letter writers, their style and grammer have not been changed. The letters have been edited to fit the available space; most of the letters were too long to be used in total. Names have been changed and identities protected at the writers' requests. But they are real people with real stories.

*Let us also lay aside every encumbrance, and the sin which so easily entangles us, and let us run with endurance the race that is set before us, fixing our eyes on Jesus, the author and perfecter of faith.*

Hebrews 12:1–2

Women need to read these testimonies because they will help to focus on the critical issues that must be addressed when making this decision. Men need to read the testimonies because the only way a man can ever grasp a working mother's conflicts is by sharing her experiences.

As a financial counselor, my purpose is to help working mothers who want to stay home examine the decisions they must make, prepare for the inevitable changes that will come, and anticipate some of the problems that will result from their decisions.

It's really not all that complicated. What we're talking about here is simply reducing your family's income by half (or more), giving up most of your friends who now think you're a "traitor," and spending your days with demanding kids instead of adults. Piece of cake—right?

As I said, in the preparation of this book I have interviewed many women who have made the transition from the marketplace back into the home—full time. As you will see through their personal testimonies, some had the total support of their families; however, others faced animosity or outright hostility from their families. Most of the respondents said they found the experience of staying home with their children to be the most fulfilling of their lives; others felt like failures and returned to the work force.

In virtually all of the testimonies I found there were some common threads, which I will attempt to isolate and identify whenever possible. Following some of these "patterns" will greatly enhance your transition. Clearly, God has not made any of us clones of other people; but He certainly has made us with similar personalities and temperaments. There are some things we can learn from our peers—both men and women. As the saying goes, "Those who fail to learn from the past are doomed to repeat it."

## *There Are No Guarantees*

As an "aside" I'd like to share a personal observation. Just being a stay-at-home mom doesn't guarantee great kids. I have known some rotten kids who came out of families where their mothers never worked outside the home and did their best to be good parents.

> We must build our faith, not on the fading light, but on the light that never fades.
>
> —*Oswald Chambers*

Conversely, I have seen some great kids come out of homes where their mothers had to work their whole lives. The key seems to be more in the attitude and commitment to being a godly parent than in the time spent at home.

All things being equal, however, it seems clear that children do much better with stay-at-home moms who want to be there and really care.

The sad truth is that most working mothers sacrifice time with their families with little or nothing to show for it. Most of the average working mother's wages are consumed by taxes, transportation, child care costs, and clothing. Even when a working mother's income is large enough to substantially add to the family's budget, the surplus is often consumed by an expanded lifestyle.

## *Earning Income at Home*

*You will call upon Me and come and pray to Me, and I will listen to you. And you will seek Me and find Me, when you search for Me with all your heart.*

Jeremiah 29:12–13

Leaving the formal marketplace to be a stay-at-home mother does not necessarily mean giving up all additional income. In fact, for many women just the opposite has proved to be true. Working at home, they are able to create cottage-industry jobs that match or even increase their previous net incomes.

Obviously this is not true of everyone, but for those who decide to use their "free" time to generate additional income it is quite possible.

The commercial world has created an environment in which the self-employed have greater opportunities than ever before. In fact, it is my belief that by the early part of the next century 50 million American workers will be employed as home-based employees. Rising labor costs, costly benefits, and global competition are going to totally restructure the traditional work force.

Companies are increasingly seeking to employ part-time or contract labor to avoid the high overhead costs of full-time personnel. This is creating some exciting new opportunities for home-based businesses.

Included in Chapter 15 is an overview of home-based businesses, and in Appendix 5 there is a list of resource materials. Everyone has a special skill provided by God that can be marketed successfully. I guarantee it! The key is *motivation:* Do you really want to do it? And also *knowledge:* Do you know how?

I trust I have provided enough of the "how to"s in this book to help those who want to be stay-at-home moms do so.

## The Focus Groups

As with everything I do, I have prayed over this book diligently. My publisher, Moody Press, sponsored three focus groups to evaluate the need for a book on this topic. These groups were made up of three categories: women who had worked and then returned home; women who were still working but wanted to return home; and women who had tried and failed; as well as a few who thought it was a dumb idea.

This was my first encounter with "focus" groups in which people literally dissect an idea and discuss its pros and cons. It was enlightening, to say the least.

I saw women cry because they could not stay home with their children and others who ridiculed them for wanting to. While protecting the confidentiality of those who participated, I will share a few of the observations we gleaned from these groups.

One woman commented, "I sacrificed my children in the pursuit of a career. If I had it to

The riches of God's grace are not only the indescribable joys of the future but gifts we can experience now.

—*Charles Stanley*

do over again, I would eat peanut butter sand-wiches so I could stay home with them."

Another countered, "I would never quit my job. What if my husband left me?" (That's a sad commentary on our society, isn't it?)

When asked if a man could write this book, one group responded, "Maybe, with enough testimonies." But when asked later if Larry Burkett could write it (without them knowing that I was observing behind the one-way glass) they replied, "No way. He's too practical."

That's when I decided to write a "how-to" book and not a "why-to" book.

I have struggled through the laborious task of trying to coordinate my fingers and my brain on a word processor keyboard (they don't always work together) in order to trans-late my thoughts to paper. I have fretted over the idea that the women who read this might think me a "know it all." I am far from know-ing it all. In fact I often wonder if I know any-thing absolutely, except Jesus Christ.

Obviously I am not a woman, and therefore I am disqualified from being a mother, but my closest friend is the mother of our four chil-dren and grandmother of nine. And I have had the privilege of counseling literally hundreds of working mothers over the last 20 or so years.

In addition, as a result of what God allows me to do, I have had the decided privilege of talking with hundreds of mothers via the radio. So I think I at least see the problems—and many of the solutions.

I pray that this book will bless those who read it as much as writing it has blessed me. Without reservation, I love kids, and I am dis-tressed at what we are doing to them in our "me-first" society. Children truly are God's most precious gift to His people, even with the

*You shall walk in all the way which the Lord your God has com-manded you, that you may live, and that it may be well with you, and that you may pro-long your days in the land which you shall possess.*

Deuteronomy 5:33

16

trials and tribulations they bring with them.

Parents have only one chance to raise their children. If they squander that chance, most will regret it the rest of their lives.

I think it was Charles Swindoll who once commented that he had never counseled a dying man who regretted not having made more money, but quite a few regretted not having spent enough time with their families.

I'll close with a thought from Proverbs 17:1, *"Better is a dry morsel and quietness with it than a house full of feasting with strife."*

---

1. "Clocking Out," *Christianity Today*, September 12, 1994.
2. "Picture Is Changing for Dual Income Families," *Investor's Business Daily*, September 2, 1994.

# Chapter One

# Defining the Problem

*"Trust in the Lord with all your heart, and do not lean on your own understanding. In all your ways acknowledge Him, and He will make your paths straight" (Proverbs 3:5–6).*

P rior to the birth of her first child in December of 1982, Barbara had worked her way up in a major airline from flight attendant to flight attendant supervisor and, later, to personnel staff analyst. Her counsel was sought by the airline's legal department as well as station and base managers throughout the organization. She described her position as fun, exciting, and challenging.

Barbara provided more than half of the family's $60,000 annual income. They lived well and enjoyed solid economic security, and her future looked even brighter in the business world. Her company, like most other corporate giants, was actively seeking bright, educated women to promote to executive positions.

After a short leave of absence to have her daughter, Barbara returned to her job at the airline. Then, just eight months after Merita was born, Barbara discovered she was pregnant again. As in the case of her first child, she took a brief maternity leave and then returned to her job. I'll let her tell the rest of her story.

## A Stay-at-Home Mom

"I found myself crying each morning on my way to work as I left my sleeping babies, knowing that I wouldn't even touch them that day until I arrived home at 6:00 p.m. (or later), dragging my tired self in from a very busy workday at the office which had been inevitably followed by a hectic drive across town in late afternoon traffic.

"How well I remember standing at my stove, still in my heels and suit, balancing a clutching baby on each hip, wondering what to prepare for dinner, trying to give my husband the attention he needed by listening to what had happened in his day, and not having a clue about what had occurred in my little girls' minds and hearts without their most loving protective advocate, their Mama, in their lives that day.

"But the Lord knew all of this and it was [Him] who opened my eyes to see the light. I clearly came to know that it was the work of His Holy Spirit's conviction [that] brought me to tears each morning as I left my home and babies behind and made me realize that the lifestyle our family was living at that point in time was not what any of us wanted at all.

"It was in April of 1985 that I resigned from my position [at the airlines] and began my precious work for my beloved family.

*"In our case, our family's loss of my $30,000-plus [annual] salary literally cut our annual income in half. However, when we truly needed something, I prayed, and the Lord always answered. To give you an example, initially, during the toughest times of our adjustment to a lower income, I would anticipate our children's need of clothing, especially during growth spurts and season changes. So, I would get to my knees.*

*"It was truly miraculous how quickly the Lord often answered—and so exciting to realize how ever-present and alive He is in our lives! On one occasion when I had been praying for children's clothing, I received so much (one friend had cleaned out a yard sale of our girls' sizes and had mailed the clothing in huge boxes from St. Louis; other friends 'just happened' to be cleaning out closets and remembered our children) that on one night, when my husband arrived home from work, he literally could not walk through the living room for all of the stacks and boxes of girls' clothes. He just looked at me and calmly asked, 'You've been praying again, haven't you?' After I confessed that I had, I promised him that my next prayer would be for another dresser in which to put all of our new clothes.*

*"This incident is only a small illustration of countless perfectly answered prayers, each one its own beautiful story, every one resulting in increasing faith on our parts and a closer knowledge of Him Who loves us so. In these experiences we have all learned together that we can't give God the glory until we give Him the opportunities to do His glorious work."*

Barbara's story is not unique. Millions of women are opting to leave their marketplace

*Let us hold fast the confession of our hope without wavering, for He who promised is faithful.*

Hebrews 10:23

jobs and become full-time moms while their children are young.

An article in *Fortune* magazine stated that the work force of women 24 to 35 years of age is actually declining for the first time in 30 years.[1]

*Barron's* newspaper carried an article by Richard Hokenson, chief economist for Lufkin & Jenrette Securities in New York, which documented the massive movement of women from the workplace to the home. Hokenson describes this movement as "a demographic sea change. . .the two-paycheck family is on the decline; the traditional one-paycheck family is now the fastest growing unit."[2]

## Exiting the Workplace: A Growing Trend

There is increasing evidence that working women becoming stay-at-home moms is shaping up to be one of the major trends of our generation. This is not surprising, given the deteriorating condition of many families today. The nightly news floods our homes with stories of teens who rob, murder, and assault their friends, families, and neighbors. Much of the blame is placed on the decline in traditional family values and the lack of parental guidance.

Obviously working mothers see this growing wave of rebellion all around them and they are alarmed—and rightly so. A mother's instinctive response is to place herself between the chaos and her children. Simply put, many working moms see their children being raised by others with values different from their own and are alarmed. Most of those we surveyed felt like they were trading "conveniences" for kids.

## No Guarantees of Great Kids

Certainly many fathers are equally alarmed

The family is the cornerstone of our society. More than any other force it shapes the attitude, the hopes, the ambitions, and the values of the child. And when the family collapses it is the children that are usually damaged . . . So unless we work to strengthen the family, to create conditions under which most parents will stay together, all the rest—schools, playgrounds, and public assistance, and private concern—will never be enough.

*Lyndon B. Johnson*
*(June 4, 1965)*

and see the stability of a stay-at-home mom as the only reasonable solution for their families. Let me hasten to say that anyone with any common sense knows that just having a mother around the home will not solve all of our social problems. If it would, we would see all the families with stay-at-home moms turning out obedient, disciplined children; however, in many instances, just the opposite is true. All too often, the stay-at-home mothers, particularly the unwed mothers, contribute to the problems.

But, on the whole, having a caring mother at home will make a significant difference in the social development of children, as many of the testimonies in this book will attest. Even if the children of a full-time mom don't turn out to be missionaries or evangelists, she will know she has done all she can (outside of locking her children in their rooms for 20 years) Obviously there are no guarantees, even for stay-at-home moms; but, the odds are definitely in their favor.

## Trapped in a Job

Many of the baby boom generation mothers had stay-at-home mothers; consequently, many have guilt feelings because they can't be at home for their kids too. In many ways, working moms are trapped by our current financial system. The generation before them had access to low-interest loans for housing, much lower college costs, low income tax rates, and steadily increasing lifestyles. Today most families face a lower real income than their parents, frequent layoffs, a stagnating economy, high income tax rates that punish married couples, and inflated prices for homes and cars that practically demand two incomes.

*I pray that your love may abound still more and more in real knowledge and all discernment, so that you may approve the things that are excellent, in order to be sincere and blameless until the day of Christ; having been filled with the fruit of righteousness which comes through Jesus Christ, to the glory and praise of God.*

Philippians 1:9-11

*He who dwells in the shelter of the Most High will abide in the shadow of the Almighty. I will say to the Lord, "My refuge and my fortress, My God, in whom I trust!"*

Psalm 91:1-2

An economy hampered by restrictive tax rates will never produce enough revenue to balance our budget, just as it will never produce enough jobs or enough profits.

—*John F. Kennedy*
*(December 14, 1962)*

For example: In 1965 the average family worked 105 days a year to pay its portion of federal and state income taxes. Today it takes 129 days. (By the way, in 1965 the average family had one wage earner. Today it has two.)

In 1965 the average home mortgage payment (not counting taxes and insurance) took about 20 percent of the median-income family's budget. Today it takes 35 percent or more.

In 1965 the purchase of a new car roughly equaled 40 percent of the average family's annual income. Today that figure is closer to 50 percent.

Granted, our modern homes, cars, vacations, clothing, and the like are qualitatively superior to those of 30 years ago, but they demand more in terms of family income and, in particular, a woman's time away from home. A lot of women apparently have decided it just isn't worth it anymore. They have come to the realization that they will have just one chance at raising their children. Once that's gone, no amount of money or possessions will provide a second chance.

## How Can We Make It?

As mentioned earlier, the question working mothers are asking is: "How can we get by on one income when we are barely making it on two incomes now?" The answer is twofold: commitment and discipline.

There is no magical way to continue spending $60,000 a year, based on two incomes, when that income drops to $30,000 a year—at least not for very long. I have counseled couples who thought it was possible but ended up in financial disaster. It is possible to drop half of your total income and survive, but only if planned properly.

It would obviously be better to plan every detail of a woman's move from a salaried job to that of a homemaker well in advance, but that is not always possible. I can guarantee you that virtually any woman who has made the move from the workplace to home would heartily encourage other women to be realistic and be willing to sacrifice. Some, like Nancy, did and therefore succeeded.

*"Back in 1989, my husband and I made the decision to put the Lord first in our lives and live our faith. [We] put our priorities in perspective. . . .I can't say enough about [my husband]. There isn't a day he isn't in extreme back pain, yet he never misses work and he is always looking for overtime. He has lifting limitations, so his earning capacity is also limited.*

*"Believe me, when we decided staying home to raise our children was God's will for me, we knew, financially, it would hurt. I was in charge of word processing at a large law firm. We also decided to sell our home in the suburbs and move to the city. . . .We were in debt and with my quitting work we needed to pay off some debt and lower our mortgage which is what we did.*

*"At times it's been worse than rough financially. Without saying anything most times our kitchen is overflowing with food from our church. Our children have an abundance of clothing and this past Christmas our car died. When our church heard of our need they [let] the congregation know and someone donated a car to us! During this past Christmas, our pediatrician felt moved in his heart to ask his church to adopt our family for Christmas, which they did.*

*"After five years, we don't have a savings account or anything materially grand, but God has continually met our needs. He's given us five*

*Children are a gift of the Lord; the fruit of the womb is a reward. Like arrows in the hand of a warrior, so are the children of one's youth.*
Psalm 127:3-4

25

*beautiful children we are raising to one day give back to him.*

*"We are still working on the debt and through one of your [radio programs] I got the idea to offer my proofreading skills to some publishers. Two have taken me up on it. While the income is not steady and I'm just beginning, it helps!*

*"Well that's my story. No regrets, but many loving memories."*

Nancy's situation should be an example of what faith, sacrifice, and commitment can accomplish. Even though she and her husband hadn't planned for so abrupt a change, they still made it work.

## The Child Care Crisis

One of the common concerns expressed by most working mothers is what kind of care their children are receiving. Some women are able to use family or close friends to watch over their children, but our surveys showed this is not the norm. The majority of working mothers are dependent on paid professional services, either in someone's home or a child care center.

To say that many mothers are concerned about the quality of care their children receive while they're away is a decided understatement. With all of the publicity about abusive child care centers, how could anyone not be alarmed? But in reality much of that publicity is exaggerated. The difficulty with most child care providers is disinterest—not child abuse.

Certainly most professional child care centers are well managed and well supervised. But even the best managed facilities are still staffed by salaried child watchers. The exception may be church child care centers where many of the workers volunteer their services. Even then the care they can provide is not the same as a loving, caring parent.

Obviously some of you reading this book are still working mothers, and the last thing a working mother needs is to have someone suggest that her child is in danger at the sitter's or the day school, but since we are trying to define the problems, it is necessary to take a realistic view of our society.

People who keep children in their homes or work at small child care centers are unregulated to a large degree. Very few are screened to ensure they have a heartfelt love for kids and, in truth, some providers confess they cannot stand children. To them it's just a job!

We'll look at ways to help resolve some of the child care conflicts in a later chapter, but for now I'll just give the observations of some working mothers who responded to our survey.

*If you will diligently obey the Lord your God, being careful to do all His commandments which I command you today, the Lord your God will set you high above all the nations of the earth. And all these blessings shall come upon you and overtake you, if you will obey the Lord your God.*

Deuteronomy 28:1-2

## A Day Care Worker's Observations

Terenda, who had worked at a child care center, set out to find a care center for her own child.

*"[Where I worked] we called ourselves the Taj Mahal of day care centers. . . . [In] sharp contrast [to] the day care centers I visited when I was looking for temporary child care. One home I entered, where a lady cared for her child and four others, reeked so strongly of urine that I was nauseated. The toys had a layer of 'crud' on them so thick it could be scraped off with as putty knife. I was surprised and appalled that children were being cared for in such filthy surroundings.*

*"Another situation was a day care center I visited. When I toured the 'baby room,' I saw*

27

God grant me the courage not to give up what I think is right even though I think it [may be] hopeless.

—*Chester Nimitz, U.S. admiral*

*one child who was sobbing uncontrollably and no one appeared to be doing anything to comfort him. When I spoke to the caregiver she said, 'He's new and spoiled. His mom probably held him all the time at home.' Anyone with an ounce of common sense would know that a child, 'spoiled' or not needs a little comfort when thrust into a new, unknown environment. As I left these two places, I clutched my baby close to me and cried.*

*"My work at the day care center opened my eyes to a generation of children who are being lost in the shuffle. As I said earlier, the center where I worked was a premier center, and yet there was still something missing. That something was a mother's constant love and guidance. I loved the children I cared for there, and I feel as though I did a good job nurturing them for the hours we had contact. It was not until my first son was born, however, that I realized the chasm of difference between a mother's love and that of a caregiver.*

*"I'm the only person in the world that has that specific love for my children—I'm their mother."*

## A Teacher's Observations

*"Although my first baby is not expected to arrive for another five weeks, my former job as a kindergarten teacher has given me many reasons to stay home. Each year, after about two weeks of school, I could sort out the children who had stay-at-home moms from the ones who had both (or the only) parent(s) working.*

*"My day care kids were manipulative of others (children and adults), bossy, had a harder time sharing and taking turns, knew exactly what they could do and still avoid a time-out (or would consciously decide what was worth a*

time-out), and would be 'burned out' on school.

"They were tired of the same old rules, time-outs, field trips, science experiments, and routines. They had been in school their whole life!

"Also, children of working parents seemed less likely to get as much sleep, and were much more likely to come home sick. . . .Sometimes, the child would even tell me that Mom or Dad said to have me call them if their child still didn't feel good after certain time, but not before that time because they had a meeting. The parents had more concern for their job than their own child or the 25 other children that were being exposed to whatever their child had.

"My husband and I sometimes worry about living off one income. But we know in the end that God will take care of us, and we definitely feel that God approves of our decision. People often assume that I'm taking a year off from teaching and will return next September. When this happens, I quite honestly reply, 'No, I'm staying home. I don't want someone else raising my kids!'"

*In quietness and trust is your strength.*
Isaiah 30:15

## A Distraught Mother's Observations

"I gave up a very promising career working for one of the top three telecommunications industries to stay at home full time. What led me to that decision? Bruises on my sons behind from the day care provider—that is what made my decision final. I picked my 1-1/2 year old son up from day care to have her tell me, 'I think I may have spanked him too hard today.' I asked what he had done. She said, 'Climbed over my plant bench three time—he didn't spill any dirt or knock any plants off—he didn't play in the dirt either—I lost control and spanked him.'

"I got home that evening and went to change my sons diaper. I was horrified to find bruises

29

on my sons bottom. I cried uncontrollably and held my son in my arms. He didn't understand why mommy was so upset. He just hugged me back. I called my husband in the room and said, 'I'm giving two weeks notice tomorrow and calling Nanna to come stay with him until my job is over.'

"I'll never forget February 22, 1992, the morning I woke him up and said, 'Mommy doesn't have to go to work anymore. My job is right here with you.' He cried and hugged me so tight. I'll always remember that day and the look in his eyes."

## It's Just Better if You Leave

"Every time I left my son I had a gnawing feeling that it wasn't quite right. I sensed that even the most conscientious baby-sitter's care was not equal to my tender love. I knew no one would bother to soothe his cries quite the way I would.

"My resolve to stay at home with my son deepened as I explored the child care options available. Once I took him to an exercise club which also ran a day-care so that I could attend an aerobics class there. . . .a few children sat alone crying.

"'It's better if you just leave,' advised one of the workers. So he can mourn me in a corner too? I thought. But of course today's philosophy is that a child will become 'too attached' to his mother if he is not left regularly with another caretaker. I am amazed that any thinking individual could believe it to be a bad thing for a child to be attached to his mother. I would compare this to a husband who tells his wife that he will be ignoring her so that she won't miss him when he goes to work. Absurd! The loving thing is to spend as much time as possible with the loved one you must leave."

Fortunately there are many loving and caring people in professional child care. But the probability of one or more bad experiences during any ten-year period is very high. Some of these experiences can leave lasting emotional scars on kids. In tallying the problems that prompted many women to quit their jobs and stay home, concern over their children's day care came in first, one hundredfold.

*The mind set on the Spirit is life and peace.*
Romans 8:6

## Bonding

One of the most common concerns expressed by working mothers we surveyed was that of their children developing emotional bonds with child care providers rather than with them. Many working mothers confessed feelings of resentment and hurt when a babysitter would describe their child's first words or first steps. They felt like they had been cheated out of a critical part of their relationship with their children.

One of our respondents wrote, "I've always been fascinated by an event common to most child care centers. Often mothers will transfer their sleeping children to a nursery worker and leave as quietly as possible. As often as not the child will wake up a few seconds later and start to cry. Usually the child is disoriented and could care less about being held by a nursery worker. He or she wants mommy, and nothing less will do."

It also is not unusual for a mother to stop and return to the nursery when she hears her child crying. Exactly how each mother can distinguish her own child's cry out of the many screaming children is one of the great mysteries of motherhood. I would rank that instinct right along with that of seal mothers who are able to locate their hungry offspring among the

The thing is to rely
only on God.
　　　—*C.S. Lewis*

thousands of complaining pups on a beach. It's a special bonding that requires long hours of patient love.

As a practical matter, a working mother is forced to relinquish some of that bonding to others who are available during the day to treat minor wounds, kiss "boo-boos," and comfort hungry, sniffling children.

In a much deeper sense, I wonder what influence emotionally disturbed child care workers must be having on impressionable kids today. That is not to say that there are not emotionally unstable parents, mothers included; there are. Child abuse statistics point to an ever increasing number of irresponsible parents. Perhaps some of those children would be better off if their mothers would work full time; but that's a subject for a family psychologist's book.

In one of our survey groups a mother shared her heartache at hearing her sitter explain in great detail her daughter's first words, first steps, and other little intimacies normally experienced by parents. She said one of her greatest regrets in life was missing the bonding that the other woman had experienced with her child.

Her primary motivation for quitting her job came when her daughter began calling the sitter "Mommie G." She said one evening she stood outside her daughter's room and listened as she explained to her doll that she loved Mommie G. more than Mommie because Mommie G. was with her more. The next day this mother gave notice.

On the other hand, a wise child care worker can ease the pain of the working mother with a little common sense and a quiet spirit.

Cindy shared her testimony about how

much she appreciated her mother's wisdom while caring for her son while Cindy worked. The grandmother never mentioned that her grandson took his first step while Cindy was at work, or that he spoke his first word one day while with her. She allowed Cindy to experience these one-time treasures for herself.

It was not until years later when Cindy was no longer working and had two more children that she discovered the truth. She often had commented how much quicker her second child Grant had walked and talked (compared to her first child Adam)—that is until one day when her mother told her, "Dear, Adam walked just as soon, but I didn't want to spoil the experience for you, so I waited until he did it while he was home with you." That kind of wisdom on the part of other day care workers would go a long way toward easing the pain of a lot of working mothers.

## *Frazzled Mother, Frustrated Employee*

Most of the working mothers we interviewed said one of their major frustrations was the difficulty of trying to balance being a good mother with being a good employee. Too often their priorities conflicted when their roles as employees were pitted against their roles as mothers of sick children or young athletes playing in their first baseball games. They felt guilty when they were not spending an adequate amount of time with their children, but at the same time they felt guilty when they were forced to cut their office time short to be with their children.

Although most employers would not say so openly, they expect their employees' primary allegiance to be with the company. This attitude is reflected in little things like higher pay

*"I will be a father to you, and you shall be sons and daughters to Me," says the Lord Almighty.*

2 Corinthians 6:18

or bigger bonuses to those who put out a little extra—like 60 hour weeks. Mothers (or fathers) who set aside weekends, or actually use all their allocated personal family time, are often passed over for promotions. Around the office it's called "body language," and the real go-getters read it very well.

It's a fact of life that, directly or indirectly, employers feel the job should come first, although some employers try to reach a good balance. But even the most understanding bosses can't resolve the emotional conflicts for the working moms. It's simply hard to function well with a divided mind.

During the research for this book I heard from a great many mothers who were frazzled at work, as well as at home, because of overlapping time conflicts. Some had worked out a system that, in the event of some child-related crisis, allowed them to use a personal sick day or vacation day. But few companies carry enough surplus employees on the payroll to operate with the same efficiency when someone is out unexpectedly; consequently, most women who took emergency time said that they often returned to even greater pressures as their work backed up.

It would be all too easy to blame the employer for being insensitive to the needs of working mothers. But, in spite of the cries of the feminist movement about the need for "protection" for working mothers, the truth is, a company exists to make a profit, and when it can't, it fails; and all the workers lose their jobs, including the working mothers. An employer should do what is reasonable to accommodate working mothers but not to the point of jeopardizing the business.

I believe God uses pressures to help reorder

our priorities. Darlene's story demonstrates that everyone has limits. As Darlene discovered, you can only do so much. When you cross over the line and risk your health, not to speak of your sanity, it's time to quit.

*"About 7 years ago my day started at 5 a.m., almost a mile walk to [the] bus stop, ride a few miles to the transfer point and wait 45 min. for bus #2 [to my office]. [I often] worked through lunch because I had to leave early in order to catch the last bus. I left the bus at a point about halfway between work and home, hiked a mile to the sitter's house, where my husband [had] dropped off our children, age 6 months, 1-1/2 and 4-1/2 on the way to his job. The mile hike [back] with children and diaper bag/stroller had to be rushed to catch [the last bus to our home]. I arrived home with three very tired hungry babies and lots of chores yet to do. After a few months of this nonsense I knew I couldn't take care of my family the way I wanted, nor was I able to give my boss an adequate job performance.*

*"I determined to go from full time to part time. I took a short break, then found a late night/early morning job that meant I was waiting at the door for my husband to come home so I could leave. I was usually home by 6 a.m., so I got a little sleep before I had to walk my daughter to kindergarten. Funny thing. I had a cold almost constantly. I needed a change, so my husband went to a different shift so I could work part time from 8 a.m. to 12:30 p.m. This worked a little better. [When] our car was out of the shop, my husband sometimes drove me. He'd take the car and kids to a sitter, and I'd scrounge for a ride to his job, pick up the car and drive to the sitter later.*

*Many are the afflictions of the righteous; but the Lord delivers him out of them all.*

Psalm 34:19

*How blessed are the people whose God is the Lord.*

Psalm 144:15

*"Throughout this time my heart had cried out to the Lord repeatedly that all I wanted was to be a mom to my kids. My husband's job did not meet our obligations and he was pressuring me to get another job. By that time, October '90, I had had enough. The Lord communicated to me so strongly to stay home with my children.*

*"I'm sure there are women who are called to be moms, and women who are called to have careers. There are many who do both very well. Thanks be to God, who does know each of his children well enough to anticipate their needs."*

In her testimony Darlene went on to explain that she was later diagnosed with cancer, from which she has now recovered; but her family also suffered an even greater tragedy when her seven-year-old son was struck and killed by a truck in their neighborhood. Darlene said that one of the lasting joys of her life is the fact that she had those precious months with her son before the Lord took him home. Just to sit by the pool at the apartment complex and watch her children at play was worth all the financial sacrifices.

*We look not at the things which are seen, but at the things which are not seen; for the things which are seen are temporal, but the things which are not seen are eternal.*

2 Corinthians 4:18

Most assuredly I have not defined all of the problems working mothers face, but I trust that identifying some of the pressures working moms are confronted with almost every day will help others understand and appreciate why so many are willing to sacrifice careers to become stay-at-home moms.

1. *Fortune* magazine, June 27, 1994.
2. *Barron's* newspaper, March 4, 1994.

## Chapter Two

# Planning Ahead

*"Commit your works to the Lord, and your plans will be established" (Proverbs 16:3).*

C hristine and her husband knew from the day they got married that she would stay at home as a full-time mom when they had children. They committed themselves to living on one income, using Christine's income for things like reducing debt and building an emergency cash reserve.

*"Before we were married, my husband and I agreed that I would be a stay at home mom once we had children. We were very blessed to watch your premarital tape on finances. This helped us obtain the goals we desired for our family.*

*"When we married we were about $25,000 in debt plus a mort-*

gage of $37,000. We decided that we would sac-
rifice to rid ourselves of the consumer debt. We
put all the money I made on the debt, after our
tithe and other giving. We also took much of my
husband's pay and put it toward debt reduction.

"God really did a miracle in our lives. I had
just graduated from college before we married. I
had hoped to get a teaching job. . .this would
help us get out of debt. . .God however had different plans. I substitute taught the first year
making about $2200. Throughout that year we
felt led to start a Christian School in our town. I
agreed to work for three years at what ever wage
the school could pay. I made less than $10,000
for the three years, yet we paid off almost all of
our $25,000 debt.

"[I] gave birth to our son at the end of my
third year with the school. Unfortunately the
school had not grown the way we had hoped. We
hired a new teacher for the next year but I volunteered to administrate and work three hours a
day teaching. This was very difficult since I
wanted to be home with my son full-time.
Throughout the year I struggled with what to do
with the school. I wanted to help it survive but
not at the expense of my family. We painfully
made the decision that I would not teach the following year. It was God's school, he would have
to provide.

"That last year I worked was extremely difficult. I had great pressures at work yet my heart
was at home. I loved each of the students, but
my first priority was my son. Because I felt that
so many people were counting on me, it was
very hard for me to quit. I was only able to do it
through God's guidance and strength.

"Looking back I know I made the right decision. God took care of each of my students and
put me where he wanted me to be: My children's

*Momentary, light
affliction is producing
for us an eternal weight
of glory far beyond all
comparison.*

2 Corinthians 4:17

*teacher. I now have my son and a beautiful daughter. We also hope to have other children. We are completely out of debt except for our home and hope to own that soon. My husband lost thirty percent of his wages a few months ago, but it hardly affected us because we have lived on a budget and have no debts. I love my family and the budget that allows me to stay home.*

I wish that all the couples who expect to live on one income were prepared so well; unfortunately, that is not the case. All too often their desire for things sets the priorities, especially when other couples they know are buying new homes and nice cars. Today it's so easy to buy (borrow) based on two incomes. Then, if a baby comes sooner then planned, a would-be stay-at-home mom is forced to go back to work, out of economic necessity.

For many young couples the option to live on one income is eliminated even before they get married. These are the couples who enter marriage with debts on both sides, including but not limited to school loans, credit cards, wedding debts, and an assortment of family loans.

With the best of intentions it is extremely difficult to make the adjustment to one income with too much fixed payout. And, as several women shared, only God is really in control of when children are due. Even birth control pills aren't 100 percent effective in planning the arrival date of children.

In Psalm 127:3 we are told, *"Behold, children are a gift of the Lord; the fruit of the womb is a reward."* Although intellectually most of us know that's true, sometimes those "rewards" can also be trials—especially for stressed-out mothers who are working to help pay off previous debts.

Planning is very important if a working woman expects to make the transition to stay-at-home mom. A common thread throughout the hundreds of testimonial letters from successful full-time moms was that of planning the transition as early as possible. As mentioned previously, those who planned well from the beginning of their marriages were by far the most successful. Many had even planned home-based businesses to help generate income after they made the transition. This area will be covered in a later chapter.

You might well say, "That's good for those who did plan ahead, but what about those of us who didn't but still desire to go back home? What can we do?"

Well, actually quite a lot. The one thing I would hasten to say here, and will say more than once in this book: You should avoid the impulse to just quit your job out of frustration. Your situation may be very frustrating because you have to work a full-time job, manage a home, and raise children, but the financial pressures of an abrupt change without good preparation can be devastating to your finances, as well as to your marriage. The debts and other monthly expenses don't cease just because you quit, and the frustration you may be feeling almost certainly will be compounded by the added pressures of delinquent bills.

That is not to say that enduring a bad situation forever is the right decision either; it is not. It's just that making some lifestyle changes and paying off some bills is a lot easier while you are working.

In our survey of more than 600 working

> When we have limitations imposed upon us we do our best work for the Lord, for then we are most dependent on Him.
>
> —*Kenneth Wuest*

mothers who had decided to return home, almost 60 percent said they had made an impulsive, emotional decision to quit work. But nearly 92 percent said they wished they had planned the move better.

Of those mothers who later had to go back to work, nearly 100 percent said it was due to the lack of planning before they quit.

Rachel wrote us about her preparations to become a stay-at-home mom. We'll pick up her story at the point she and her husband made this decision.

*"We had the opportunity to take your video class on budgeting [at church]. Also about this time we participated in some church classes on improving your marriage. One of the questions posed to all couples was what could be done to better our marriage. I told my husband that I thought my staying home would better ours, even though we have always considered ours a strong relationship.*

*"Not only could I raise our own children, but I saw that my being at home could greatly reduce the stress we experienced with juggling two careers and running a household with two children. We subsequently decided in 1989 to work toward becoming debt free and for me to stay at home once we became debt free.*

*"To become debt free required paying off two car loans, school loans, the mortgage on our principle home and a mortgage on a 10 acre farm with house, garage and barn. We carried no credit card debt. Our debt reduction plan was pretty straight forward.*

*"First we established separate checking accounts for our paychecks. . . .We set up a budget on my husband's salary while my salary was used exclusively for debt reduction and child*

care. In this way we could have time to get used to living on one income before I quit work.

"Even though we bought a less expensive home, however, we did not compromise meeting the needs of our family. We bought a structurally sound home with lots of room and "potential". We are pretty handy with home improvements and managed to correct the shortcomings the house originally had.

"In February of '94 we reached our goal of becoming completely debt free and I left my job to be at home with our 2, no 3 children. Among all this debt reduction, God decided we needed another baby!

"Our finances are not quite what we expected, either. We tithe, pay tuition for the kids to go to a Christian school, participate in my husband's Savings and Investment plan at work, plus put aside monthly amounts for taxes, car replacement, insurance, clothes, vacation, etc. The money left for daily expenses gets pretty lean at times.

"I guess this would not be as much a concern except that we have not yet found a way to set aside funds for college. Current estimates for future (10+ years) tuition are astronomical. I continually have to remind myself that God will provide when (and if!) the time comes. The rapture would certainly take care of things!"

Rachel also shared some of her struggles for "significance" after leaving a successful engineering career and becoming a "domestic engineer"—a situation many women who make the transition can identify with.

All too often Christians rationalize hasty, even foolish, decisions on the basis of "God told me to do it." If God tells someone to do something (and I believe He may well direct a

Pay every debt as if God wrote the bill.
—*Ralph Waldo Emerson*

*We are the temple of the living God; just as God said, "I will dwell in them and walk among them; and I will be their God and they shall be my people."*

2 Corinthians 6:16

mother to quit work and trust Him for the necessary provision), He will provide for all her family's needs.

The evidence that God hasn't directed everyone who says He has is the fact that sometimes their situations actually get worse. God has an individual plan for everyone. It has been my observation that this sometimes involves allowing us to work our way out of a situation of our own making.

Hannah gives a testimony to a principle found in Proverbs 24:3–4: *"By wisdom a house is built, and by understanding it is established; and by knowledge the rooms are filled with all precious and pleasant riches."*

*"From the very beginning of our marriage we have always tried to live on one income. I think that this is a key for women to be able to stay at home. Living on one income has been the major reason why I am able to be at home. It's easy to get used to living on two incomes especially when the wife works when they are first married before children come along. I also worked from the time we were married. I think I got used to that lifestyle of being with other people and getting some of my self esteem from earning a paycheck.*

*"I ended up working until my daughter was about 4–5 months old until I could train someone else and tie up the loose ends of the projects I was involved in. I do feel that I need to earn some extra money per month because my husband makes enough for us to pay our monthly expenses, but not enough to save for larger expenses such as replacing our old cars or house improvements.*

*"Over the past year I have been trying to find something else I can do to work at home. . . .It*

The only way to find the limits of the possible is by going beyond them to the impossible.

—*Arthur C. Clarke*

*If anyone loves Me, he will keep My word; and My Father will love him, and We will come to him, and make Our abode with him.*

John 14:23

*seems as though many home businesses either require some selling of a product or they are not conducive to a mother with two small children who doesn't want to leave the children with a babysitter.*

*"I think it would be great if you could devote part of your book to some how-tos of home businesses.*

*"I feel that there are two main issues that affect leaving the work force: (1) living on one income before having children and (2) making sure the issue of a woman's self esteem is clear—meaning that many women can feel good about a full-time job and paycheck and obtain their self esteem from earning a paycheck, but I think it can keep many women from taking that step out of the work force because working at home can be a very unstructured environment and doesn't usually have many material or tangible rewards (at least not on a consistent basis)."*

## Planning the Transition

If a mother quits work out of exasperation and before adequate planning can be done, some significant changes must be made, and quickly, if the family is to avoid a crisis situation. The steps to follow are the same regardless of whether you are planning to quit your job or have already done so without planning. It's just a whole lot easier if you do the planning before you leave your job.

### 1. Adjust to a one-income budget.

At least three months prior to quitting, adjust to a one-income budget. Actually six months or more would be better, but three months is the absolute minimum.

Your budget also must reflect variable expenses, such as car repairs, property taxes, insurance payments, Christmas gifts, medical bills, and the like. This means you must average these expenses and divide them by 12 to get the average monthly allocation. (If you think that's depressing, just think what it will be like when they come due and you have no funds to pay them.)

You will find a budget outline among the forms in Appendix 1. If you need additional help in developing and maintaining a budget, I refer you to the *Financial Planning Organizer* published by Moody Press. It's available in most Christian bookstores.

Let me assure you that if you cannot adjust to a one-income budget while still working, it will be a great deal more difficult to adjust once you quit.

Obviously there are some expenses that are directly related to working outside the home: clothing, transportation, child care, additional food, and eating out. These are identified in our sample budget and can be substantially reduced or eliminated once the move home is made—that is, if you can divorce yourself from the emotional attachment of extra money for eating out, hairdressers, and the convenience of a newer second car. It may mean selling a second car (assuming there are car payments) and buying an older model. It also may require some periodic family budget reviews so the husband will understand that his "miscellaneous" allowance also will change once you stop working outside the home.

I have included in Appendix 4 a list of questions every couple should discuss, if possible, before the decision to become a stay-at-home mom has been made. It's very important to remember that both of you must be of one mind about this to make it work. Literally,

God's Word calls a husband and wife to operate as one person.

*For this cause a man shall leave his father and his mother, and shall cleave to his wife; and they shall become one flesh.*

Genesis 2:24

It is critical that both husband and wife discuss and agree on the changes that must be made once the second income stops. More often than not these changes involve the little (or big) luxuries that two incomes have allowed, and they're not all that easy to give up. Make up your own personal list from those shown below. These include but are not necessarily limited to:

- annual vacations
- a second car
- eating out regularly
- new clothes (retail purchases)
- regular household help
- babysitters
- private schools.

**2. Set a realistic but definite date to quit.**

It is important that once you have made the decision to return home full time, you do the equivalent of driving a stake in the ground (mentally speaking). Set the time far enough ahead to give your employer fair notice, but be prepared to leave immediately after giving notice if necessary. In other words, don't tell a boss too far in advance who has previously voiced his or her reluctance to stay-at-home mothers, lest you end up out of a job prematurely. Since each situation is unique, you'll just have to use your own best judgment on this decision.

By establishing a definite termination date, it will help you to do some of the necessary planning, such as notifying your children's day care, perhaps selling one car, or even selling your home. Finances should not be the sole determinant of when to quit, but it certainly should be a major factor. If an extra six months on the job will make the difference between staying home ten years or just six months, it's worth the wait.

The key principle that applies here is patience. All too often when we settle an issue in our minds we want it to become so—right now! For some families, a rapid move is possible because they have little or no debt and already are living on just one income. But for most, the time invested in paying down debt and paring down lifestyle will be time well spent.

*The Living Bible* says: *"A sensible man watches for problems ahead and prepares to meet them. The simpleton never looks, and suffers the consequences"* (Proverbs 27:12).

Once you and your spouse have determined that this decision is God's plan for you, allow nothing to deter you from that path, including employers who lay on guilt trips because you're "indispensable." No one ever is.

### 3. Build a cash reserve.

Almost certainly, once you commit your family to a one-income budget, something will happen to create a crisis. It may be a car repair, a medical expense, or any number of other unplanned expenses. If you can build a reasonable cash reserve while working, it will help smooth over some of the rough spots that may occur in the first few months after you quit.

Ideally, you should try to save enough for about six months of operating expenses, but I realize for most young couples that is not really feasible—at least if the wife is to quit her job in the reasonably near future. But whatever you can lay aside will help.

*Rest in the Lord and wait patiently for Him; do not fret because of him who prospers in his way.*

Psalm 37:7

No matter what, a portion of your family's income should be saved, even while living on one income. Saving is a good discipline and virtually the only way to avoid the use of credit for most families (except for God's intervention).

I would encourage you to think of debt as the archenemy of stay-at-home moms. If your budget is tight, even a small amount of debt, and especially consumer debt, will wreck your finances and push you right back into the job market. If you can't afford to pay cash for something, don't buy it! If a debt is created because of an uncontrollable problem, like a medical expense, let your Christian friends and family know of your needs, and be specific! There are many people who are willing to help with a current need but are not inclined to help pay off credit card debts.

The letters we received from stay-at-home moms were full of testimonies of God's faithfulness in difficult financial situations.

Remember the promise from God's Word that opened Chapter 1: *"Trust in the Lord with all your heart, and do not lean on your own understanding. In all your ways acknowledge Him, and He will make your paths straight"* (Proverbs 3:5–6).

### 4. Establish a schedule for a typical day as a full-time mom.

To some degree, the routine of getting up in the morning to get to work on time is a good one. One of the things many women who leave the marketplace have to resist is the tendency to think that because they are home all day there is more than ample time to sleep in, have a leisurely breakfast, and still get everything they have planned done; it just isn't so.

Just as people who have inherited a sizeable

amount of money have squandered it by thinking they could never exhaust such a huge surplus, if you're not careful, the same thing happens to your surplus time.

It may sound corny to say that a stay-at-home mom should use a daily planning calendar like those in business do, but it's a good thing to do. Businesses invest millions of dollars in individual time management aids because they have been proven to work. Your time at home is also valuable; in fact, it is your single most precious commodity and a nonrenewable resource.

If you do nothing else, I encourage you to make a daily priority list of things that you want to accomplish. Too much regimen can be legalistic, but too little can lead to slothfulness.

As the Proverb warns, *"A little sleep, a little slumber, a little folding of the hands to rest—and your poverty will come in like a vagabond"* (Proverbs 6:10–11).

*Chapter Three*

# Sacrifices

*"Offer to God a sacrifice of thanksgiving, and pay your vows to the Most High; and call upon Me in the day of trouble; I shall rescue you, and you will honor Me" (Psalm 50:14–15).*

The decision to leave a paying job and return home is clearly going against the tide of our society. Not only will a stay-at-home mom face discouragement from those who don't agree with her decision, but a single-income family also runs contrary to "official" government policy. I say that because our government has built the tax system around the need for two incomes per family. In fact, government tax policies often dictate two wage earners per family.

As the marginal tax rates of our country have climbed, they have absorbed more and more of the primary wage earner's income. In 1965 state and federal taxes took about 24 percent of the wage earner's income. But as government services expanded, the need for more tax dollars did likewise. Today, median-income wage earners pay an effective state and federal tax rate of almost 30 percent. With two wage earners, the percentage is even higher.

## Inflation Takes a Bite

During the same period of time, prices have more than doubled. A wage earner currently making $30,000 gets to keep about $20,000 after payroll and income taxes reduce it. That $20,000 has been diluted by inflation so that it is just $8,000 in spending power, compared to 1965. The family actually nets less today than they would have 30 years ago; thus, the pressure for the wife to go to work is applied through income dilution.

An additional factor is that today there are more "things" to buy than ever before. Once two cars were a luxury, for the rich; now they are a "necessity" for most families.

I grew up in the generation of the fifties and started a family in the sixties. I remember well that there were not all the distractions (attractions) that are available to families today. Very few couples we knew in the sixties took their kids to Disneyland (Disney World didn't even exist). They didn't take winter skiing trips, eat out regularly, buy new cars on credit, or own large homes. Although credit was available for housing, and sometimes cars, credit cards were virtually nonexistent, and school loans were not even a consideration.

I can remember trying to get one of the few credit cards available, the American Express card, and couldn't qualify because my income was too low. Today almost anyone can qualify for a variety of credit, which opens up a whole

The man or woman who concentrates on "things" can hardly be trusted to use those "things" for the essential good of mankind. Only those who have guided the development of their spirit as well as their mind are really. . . qualified to use wisely the things that man's reason has enabled him to fashion out of nature's raw materials.

—E.S. Fields

new vista for spending more than you make.

I say all of this to make a point: If you intend to buck the trend and return home from the workplace, in most cases it will require a great deal of discipline and sacrifice. Leaving the work force can be done, and millions of women are doing it; but "things" must be put in the proper priority. Material things are a lot of fun, at least when they're new but, as Eileen shares, they must be controlled.

*"The material sacrifices we've made don't really seem like material sacrifices. I would love to have a beautifully decorated dream house some day, and we're working it into our plans, but it certainly wouldn't be worth it now with two active, noisy, messy pre-schoolers (with possibly more to come).*

*"We own two previously used cars, a small commuter car which [my husband] car pools with to save gas money on his 50 minute commute into Washington, D.C. each day, and an old Toyota Camry with 115,000 miles on it. It will have to last at least two more years until we have enough saved to pay cash for a reliable used station wagon, and if my car doesn't last, we'll learn to live with one car. Most of our kids' clothes and toys come from yard sales (my number one hobby!).*

*"Our biggest challenge seems to be to keep our grocery bill below the budgeted $425 a month - we don't always succeed. We don't take big vacations - mostly we visit family out of state, or take day trips. [My husband] has to stay out of computer software stores, I have to stay out of craft stores, and we both have to stay out of book stores, or we get into lots of trouble!*

*"We've tried to be creative with gift-giving instead of automatically spending money . . .*

*I will instruct you and teach you in the way which you should go; I will counsel you with My eye upon you.*

Psalm 32:8-9

*homemade gifts or "coupons" for services account for many of the gifts we give. We spend less than $50 total on our children at Christmas —most of the gifts come from yard sales. We trade babysitting with a neighbor instead of paying the $3-4.00 an hour to a teenager.*

*"We try to keep homemade pizzas and casseroles on hand in the freezer at all times so we don't end up calling [for delivered pizza] when I'm too tired to cook dinner."*

The reward of a thing rightly done is to have done it.

—*unknown*

It is interesting to note that testimonies like Eileen's and most of the others really speak of alternative rewards, rather than sacrifices. For those who grew up in my generation, most of what are called sacrifices today were considered luxuries then. I guess it's just a matter of perspective.

## It's Time to Be Realistic

This is the point where it is critical to be totally realistic and honest as a couple. Unless the husband's income is in excess of $50,000 annually, there will be some sacrifices if the transition from workplace to home is to be successful. Even for those with incomes above the $50,000 level, some lifestyle changes will be necessary, depending on what their present spending level is, but generally the adjustment is easier.

For those below the $30,000 level, the sacrifices probably will include basic things like entertainment and recreation, annual vacations, buying prepared foods or clothing at retail outlets—even the kinds of gifts they can afford.

Let me reemphasize here that a budget is absolutely essential to control spending. And a budget is more than just a record of what had been spent; it is a plan for how much you can spend on a monthly basis in every category. If you attempt the transition from two incomes to one without a good functional budget, the likely result will be debt, arguments, and an involuntary return to the work force.

Sacrifice is a relative term for most people. For one family it means not buying a new car every couple of years. For another it means shopping garage sales for clothes rather than retail outlets. Often, for women leaving the work force to be full-time moms, it can mean all of the above and then some.

Jill told about some of the sacrifices she and her husband chose to make to enable her to become a stay-at-home mom.

*Without faith it is impossible to please Him, for he who comes to God must believe that He is, and that he is a rewarder of those who seek Him.*

Hebrews 11:6

"*I was an elementary school teacher for eight years following college graduation. My husband was in various college programs during this time, so I was the sole breadwinner. I completed my masters degree in order to earn a better salary and take the pressure off of my husband to make a hasty career decision. However, after seven years (and my nearing 30), we felt it was time to start a family. I became pregnant in the fall and started to look forward to the birth of our first child, being a mother, and staying home the next summer.*

"*As God would plan it, my husband found a job in his field of interest and I gave up a contract for the next school year. Although I had always wanted to be a stay-at-home mom (as my mother was) and felt that it was best for our family, it was difficult to pass up the second income—and the school loans, second car, and first home that it could have covered for us. We were in agreement on the issue, however, and have never regretted it.*

55

"The next three years of apartment living with one income were generally comfortable and we made ends meet as best we could. My husband changed jobs again in hopes of getting ahead, but we basically lived from pay check to pay check. I tutored during the summer months and occasionally did some baby-sitting, but felt that going back to work would complicate our lives too much, be costly, and be against my convictions.

"When we were expecting our second child, we felt that it was time to purchase a house. We had little money saved, but with generous gifts from both sets of parents, we were able to make a sizeable down payment and purchase a modest home in a decent neighborhood. I loved being at home with our children and being a homemaker in every sense of the word.

"In [an] effort to save money, we didn't replace our [second] car (we had been loaned) after an accident, I made necessary items on the sewing machine when possible, and started selling and purchasing clothing through consignment shops, garage sales, etc. Since my husband needed the car for work, I didn't get out much during the day (which was a blessing in disguise since I couldn't spend money shopping!).

"As other people often say to me, 'It must be nice that you can afford to stay at home,' I do my best to kindly let them know that this is _not_ the case, but that we as a family make the situation work. We give up expensive vacations, costly clothes, a second car, frequent eating out, a bigger home, etc., but we get much in return, as we are forced to be a close family.

"My husband still does not make more than $25,000 a year, so we are by no means on 'easy street.' Yet, we still have been able to tithe regularly at church, pay our bills, and save a few dollars each pay check. We are basically content *and know that God will continue to provide for us as He has so bountifully in the past, as we seek His will for our family and give Him the thanks."*

As I read Jill's testimonial, I thought of the woman described in Proverbs 31:10-11: *"An excellent wife, who can find? For her worth is far above jewels. The heart of her husband trusts in her, and he will have no lack of gain."*

Before closing this discussion, I would like to restate some advice offered by the vast majority of women responding to our survey: Be realistic about the necessary adjustments that must be made; be of one mind (husband and wife); be disciplined with your finances (live on a budget); and, most importantly, trust God to provide for your needs. Good advice!

The following is a noninclusive list of sacrifices that were common to many of the hundreds of women who responded to our survey when asked, "What sacrifices have you made to return home?" The list is ordered by the number of responses received.

*Whatever we ask we receive from Him, because we keep His commandments and do the things that are pleasing in His sight.*

1 John 3:22

## 1. Eating Out

The vast majority of women said they had significantly changed their eating-out habits. Most of their budgets simply could not absorb the cost of such entertainment. Many had substituted homemade meals for fast food. Eating out generally was limited to special occasions like birthdays. In most cases, the transition was harder if the children were a little older because of the expectations they already had acquired.

Once the decision was made and a realistic entertainment food budget was established, eating out ceased to be a high priority. It would

57

be interesting to see when the kids grow up if they have fewer health problems than the average teenager of today, as a result of better nutrition. I personally think they will.

## 2. Shopping

Many of the women acknowledged that they had acquired habits while they were working that included periodic shopping sprees to "perk up" their spirits. With more limited resources at their disposal, they found they had to virtually stop browsing the shopping malls. Many said that they were less tempted to buy indulgences even when they could afford to do so (that's called good stewardship).

## 3. Gift Buying

Few people keep good enough records to actually know how much they spend on Christmas, anniversary, and birthday gifts; that is, until they no longer can afford to do so. Without question, most families are shocked to discover how much they spend on gifts.

If you set up a separate gift category in your budget, you will develop an accurate record. Even more important is the need to establish a specific budget amount and stick to it. Most of the stay-at-home moms we surveyed simply set a budget for each category of gifts and determined (after some fits and starts) that they had to stick to it.

Usually this meant picking up bargain gifts throughout the year at super discounts, shopping garage sales for Christmas toys, and sending cards to friends and family instead of buying them gifts. Virtually all testified to some feelings of guilt initially, but later even their families supported the notion that there had

*You have need of endurance, so that when you have done the will of God, you may receive what was promised.*

Hebrews 10:36

been too much gift giving anyway.

The women we heard from had many great ideas to help the stay-at-home mom cope with the pressures of gift buying. One of the most common was to develop a hobby and turn it into a small source of income to be used just for gifts. That way, if the money was available, the gifts could be purchased; if not, then friends and family would get the hobby crafts as gifts. I can honestly say I appreciate the home-crafted gifts I receive more than I do store-bought items; they reflect the love that went into making them.

## 4. Christian or Private Schools

Many working mothers commit a sizeable portion of their incomes to private education expenses, especially Christian schools. One of the most difficult decisions for many stay-at-home moms is whether to give up Christian schooling for their children. Some who decided to keep their children in Christian or private schools eventually were forced to go back to work. For others, private education costs have necessitated at least a part-time job, a home-based business, or greater sacrifices in other areas of the budget.

I can't emphasize too strongly that private schools, Christian included, are a major source of single-income families' debt. If you sincerely believe God wants your children in a Christian school, trust Him for the provision; don't borrow to keep them there.

### *Homeschooling Option*

Many stay-at-home moms opt to home-school their children rather than sacrifice their goal of being home full time. The vast majority of women said that initially they were fearful

> *Do not fear, for I am with you; do not anxiously look about you, for I am your God. I will strengthen you, surely I will help you, surely I will uphold you with My righteous right hand.*
>
> Isaiah 41:10

> A wise [woman] adapts [herself] to circumstances as water shapes itself to the vessel that contains it.
> —*unknown*

that they could not do an adequate job of teaching their children at home themselves. But as you will discover in the homeschooling chapter, all but a few found that they could not only teach their children, but they could do a far superior job when compared to public or private education (see the national statistics in Chapter 16).

It is important to note that homeschooling is not for every mother; nor is it for every child. Most mothers can do a good job homeschooling their children, but I have personally known some who lacked either the discipline or the temperament to homeschool.

For those who cannot afford to continue their children's private schooling, and for one reason or another decide not to homeschool, the choice then boils down to public schools. Public schools, particularly in small communities, can be a viable option for many families, if handled properly.

I recall a woman (we'll call her Shirley) I counseled with several years ago who made the decision to be a stay-at-home mom and faced this problem. She knew that without her salary there was no realistic way her children could continue in the Christian school they attended. Actually she and her husband were not totally satisfied with the school anyway.

She looked into homeschooling but decided that she had no peace about teaching her children at home. Perhaps it was because the homeschooling movement was in its infancy back then and had little organization or materials available. But it also may have been God prompting her to pursue His plan—not hers.

After praying about this decision, they withdrew their children from private school and sent them to a public school. She said it was

Do not anxiously hope for that which is not yet come: do not vainly regret what is already past.

—*unknown*

one of the most difficult choices they had ever made. Their friends, their pastor, and their parents all pleaded with them to reconsider. She confided one time that she felt like a leper in her church circle because she was "sacrificing" her children on the altar of secularism.

It was the support her husband provided that gave her the strength to check her children out of their Christian school and into the public school.

The experience was horrible. The children returned home each day with tales of being bullied, harassed, and ridiculed (even by some teachers) for having attended Christian schools all of their lives.

This mother was totally distressed. Shirley believed she had obeyed God in returning home, but the children were suffering as a result. She said she was sorely tempted several times to return to work, put the kids back in their former school, and consider the experiment a failure. But something inside kept telling her the decision was right—in spite of the negative consequences.

Out of desperation, as the situation at school continued to worsen, she decided to go to the school and assess the problems for herself. What she saw appalled and alarmed her. Several of the classes she visited were in chaos, with kids stomping around the room and defying all attempts to control them. The teachers were frustrated and irritable, with classes that often numbered thirty students. The teachers were overwhelmed.

Shirley asked why the school system didn't provide more teachers or at least some teacher aides, to which all the teachers replied: a lack of funds.

Then an idea struck her. She had some time

she could volunteer to aid the teachers and she believed some of the other mothers who didn't have to work all day might also. So she approached the principal with the idea of organizing a mothers' volunteer group. He jumped at the chance, and in spite of some reluctance on the part of some of the teachers, Shirley began to call each and every mother who had children in the school.

When it was all said and done, she had organized more than 100 volunteer parents who would contribute from four to twenty hours a week in the classrooms.

In addition, she convinced several businesses in her city to help enhance the classroom facilities by donating a variety of things—from money to computers.

Shirley continued this ministry until her youngest graduated from high school. Then she went back to college, earned a degree in counseling, along with a graduate degree in special education, and went back into the school system as a counselor to children with learning disorders, many of whom were creating the problems in their classes.

For Shirley, public education was God's plan for her children. She was needed to help advance the schools in her area for the next generation of kids.

### 5. Domestic Help

Usually the need for a housekeeper or other domestic help is generated by the fact that a woman is working a full-time job outside of the home. But when a mother elects to return home and no longer can afford the domestic help, it can be a sobering experience—especially for young women who never have had to be a full-time homemaker.

To many readers, giving up domestic help may not seem like a sacrifice (since you don't have it anyway), but to those who can afford it and have to give it up, it is a sacrifice. But this is really a small price to pay for the privilege of seeing your children grow up under your care rather than having your domestic help raise them.

## 6. Privacy

Perhaps nothing is more difficult for the stay-at-home mom to give up than her privacy. Even under the best of circumstances, when you're with children virtually all the time, privacy becomes a treasured commodity. As many of the women who responded to our survey confirmed, the lack of privacy is a sacrifice common to almost all moms who have made the transition back home.

Kay had been working for several years before she decided to stay at home. For her the greatest single sacrifice was her privacy. As any mother knows, children can become all consuming, especially if they are insecure about their relationship with their parents. Kay, an engineer, found that her child, and subsequently other children, can really spoil the best-laid plans. I'll skip to the last page of her letter.

*Let the peace of Christ rule in your hearts, to which indeed you were called in one body; and be thankful.*
Colossians 3:15

*"I must admit . . . I sometimes have some frustration with my new role of 'domestic' engineer. As a chemical engineer I did well career wise. I also was able to have lunch with my husband nearly every day, had the company of adults, and was able to have tangible results from my work on a frequent basis. All this came with a nice paycheck.*

*"I have traded the business environment for one where I do tasks that are never noticed*

*(except by my husband) unless they are not done (laundry, cooking, cleaning) and they must be repeated over and over. I am constantly called upon to referee, arbitrate, discipline and generally "train up" two very competitive and bright kids, and of course play with, feed, clean up after, discipline, clean up after, teach, console and clean up after a one year old.*

*"I seldom have adult company and I never have lunch with my husband! Add to this my own desires to 'accomplish' something tangible each day. I often find myself frustrated. I have a list of things to do that are outside daily house-keeping duties. I get a real sense of accomplishment any time I can mark one off as complete.*

*"On the other hand, when a lot of time passes between completing tasks, I have to admit that it bothers me. I need to enjoy my family and my life one day at a time. I know I need to be more patient and that my reward for staying home for our kids may not always be obvious, but it is still hard."*

*Blessed shall be the offspring of your body. . . . Blessed shall you be when you come in, and blessed shall you be when you go out.*

Deuteronomy 28:4, 6

In the final analysis, the sacrifices that many stay-at-home moms make will seem pretty insignificant 10 years from now. After all, what difference does it really make that you aren't able to take a skiing vacation or trade cars every couple of years? Actually, not very much. But the investment in the lives of your children will pay dividends well into the next generation.

I can honestly say that I never heard a mother express regrets about the material things she gave up in order to be home with her children. However, I have heard many women say that if they had it all to do over again they would sacrifice any and all material possessions to stay home with their children.

Regret is insight that comes too late.

—*unknown*

Being a full-time mom will not guarantee happy, well-adjusted children, but at least you'll know you have done your very best.

No one is rich enough to buy back the past.

*—unknown*

# Chapter Four

# I Want To,
# But I Can't

*"Seek first His kingdom and His righteousness;
and all these things shall be added to you.
Therefore do not be anxious for tomorrow; for
tomorrow will care for itself" (Matthew 6:33–34).*

The transition from job to home always requires some sacrifices, but it is possible if planned properly. Sometimes the
odds against it seem overwhelming: debt, indulgences, and uncooperative spouses appear to be unconquerable. Perhaps in a
human sense they are. But in God's power, nothing (no thing) is
impossible. Perhaps to hear from others who presumed the move
from job to home was impossible (but made it anyway) will
encourage you to keep on praying.

Many working mothers who responded to our survey had similar comments about the impossibility of leaving the marketplace.
They said they would like to stay home, but felt they couldn't.

Most went on to explain that they believed no amount of financial sacrifice would make staying home possible, unless they were willing to live in a tent and apply for welfare.

Some of the situations were heart breakers. One woman in Iowa told of her daughter who has multiple sclerosis and their only source of insurance comes from her job. "If I quit work," she wrote, "my daughter will not get the treatment she needs. It would be the equivalent of condemning her to die." She went on to say that she had investigated the possibility of getting Medicaid if she were not working, but she discovered that her husband made too much money to qualify.

Another woman in Kentucky shared that her husband worked in the construction industry and was very prone to long periods without an income. Her job was their only source of income during these periods. "Even with my income," she said, "we can barely keep up with our bills. I would love to be able to stay home with my children, but it's simply not possible."

I'm sure that many of you reading this book can tell your own stories about why it seems impossible to be a stay-at-home mom, even when the desire is there. But, in reality, the choice to return home full time may be difficult; it may have to be delayed; but it is never impossible, or at least it shouldn't be.

I can already hear the murmuring among those who feel like they are trapped in a job while their hearts are at home: "Easy for you to say. You're not a working mother." To that I will give a hearty "amen." But the testimonies of hundreds of stay-at-home moms who made the transition in spite of the odds witness to the fact that nothing is impossible if God is in it.

I often look back to Judy's and my early

*I can do all things through Him who strengthens me. And my God shall supply all your needs according to His riches in glory in Christ Jesus.*

Philippians 4:13,19

For those concerned about children growing up in poverty, we should know this: marriage is probably the best anti-poverty program of all. Among families headed by married couples today, there is a poverty rate of 5.7 percent. But 33.4 percent of families headed by a single mother are in poverty today.

—Dan Quayle
(Standing Firm)

marriage years and think how blessed we were compared to today's young couples. To be sure we had it hard financially since we were married very young (Judy was 16 and I was 19). Often while I was in college we had as little as one dollar a month for entertainment and recreation. Our big indulgence was a trip to the local zoo where we bought a quarter bag of peanuts to feed the monkeys. We were on a first name basis with almost all of them.

But our big advantages were: a lack of unrealistic expectations, the fact that nobody would lend money to us, and an almost total lack of peer pressure.

We only had one car, but that was all my parents ever had, so I didn't expect to own two. Our car was nearly ten years old when I bought it, but at least I was able to pay cash for it. No one expected us to be able to buy a home because we couldn't qualify for even the most meager loan, so we were content in rentals for our first years of marriage.

When Judy was pregnant with our first child it wasn't even a question if she would quit her job and stay at home. In 1962 I don't think we even knew any working mothers. I'm sure there were some but not among our circle of friends.

It was assumed, and I accepted the fact, that I would change from being a full-time to a part-time college student. There were no government-backed college loans and no family to support us, so I accepted the reality that college would take five or six years, rather than four. Why? Because, even as a non-Christian I believed that our children needed their mother—more than we needed her income.

I realize that by even saying this I probably will offend some women who are trapped in

*They cried out to the Lord in their trouble; He saved them out of their distresses.*

Psalm 107:13

jobs that keep them away from their children, but that is not my intention. As I said, we were fortunate to live in an era when stay-at-home moms were the norm. There was not the availability of credit that now traps young couples into two-income commitments.

I grew up in a generation when we could roam our neighborhood streets without fear. My children grew up in similar neighborhoods, but they were the last generation to have that freedom. Now many homes are empty most of the day and elementary age kids (so-called latchkey kids) are left to their own devices for hours a day. It's little wonder that as teens they are unruly and often violent. The mischief they cause at ages 8 or 10 turns criminal at 15 or 16.

If you have the desire to stay at home you need to *believe that there is a way*. Often the transition cannot be made immediately, as discussed previously, but it can be done. There are some basic steps to making this "wish" a reality.

*Be transformed by the renewing of your mind, that you may prove what the will of God is, that which is good and acceptable and perfect.*

Romans 12:2

1. Make a commitment to get out of all consumer debt, and under no circumstances use credit cards to "supplement" your income. The rule is, if you can't pay your new charges off every month, destroy the cards.

   There are organizations like ours and the Consumer Credit Counseling Service that can help you work out a repayment plan with your creditors and help you to stick with it. Often it is possible to arrange a reduction or elimination of the interest charges to expedite repayment. You'll find the appropriate information in Appendix 2.

2. Develop a budget based on your hus-

band's income only. Any spending that doesn't fit into your one-income budget simply has to be eliminated. Often this means putting the house up for sale, selling one car, or (horrors!) selling the bass boat or motor home.

To live on a budget will require both spouses to work together. If one of you is not willing to do so, obviously it will not work. I can't promise that a reluctant spouse will come around. I've seen many who have and some who haven't. The most you can do is discuss it openly and honestly. If that's impossible, find a good counselor. Often your pastor is a good resource, or perhaps he will know of someone who can help.

Sometimes there's nothing like hearing from another reluctant spouse who "converted" to budgeting to sway your reluctant mate. But, if after all of your best efforts your spouse is still intractable, you must simply turn this area over to God and get peace about it. After all, you can only do what you can do. God can and will intercede to protect your children.

3. Leaving the work force does not necessarily mean stopping all of your income. With the current trends toward home-based businesses, many women have actually been able to increase their net income at home (see Chapter 15 for more information on home business).

Start looking now at possible business opportunities that can be done out of your home, and develop one while still employed.

> The only thing people understand about money matters is that it does.
>
> —*unknown*

> Far better it is to dare mighty things, to win glorious triumphs, even though checkered by failure, than to take rank with those poor spirits who neither enjoy much nor suffer much, because they live in the gray twilight that knows not victory nor defeat.
>
> —*Theodore Roosevelt (1910 speech)*

*The kingdom of God does not consist in words, but in power. What do you desire?*

1 Corinthians 4:20–21

Even the most uncooperative husband will come around once he sees you are able to generate income while staying home. It can be done! Later I'll share some remarkable testimonies from moms who have done it; many of them thought it would be "impossible" for them too.

# Chapter Five

# The Struggle for Significance

*"There is one who pretends to be rich, but has nothing; another pretends to be poor, but has great wealth" (Proverbs 13:7).*

*I*t is amazing what a word of encouragement spoken at the right time can do to help someone's self-esteem or, to the contrary, what a word of discouragement can do to defeat someone who is already suffering from self-doubts.

Allow me to share a personal experience. I remember sitting through many high school classes wondering why I was always behind in math and science. I rarely did well on tests and often was singled out by teachers who accused me of being lazy. They would point to my high IQ tests (back when they still revealed such things) and say, "I know you have the ability; you're just being lazy." That really angered me and made me rebel against all

What lies behind us and what lies before us are tiny matters compared to what lies within us.

—*anonymous proverb*

In the false shackles of feeling worthless, you cannot appreciate the liberty that is yours in Christ.

—*Charles Stanley*

teachers, much to my own detriment.

Then a high school algebra teacher, Dan Blackweller, asked me to come in after school one day. I was certain he was going to lay into me too, but he didn't. He said, "Larry, you have a lot of potential, and I would like to help you develop it. I think you're a visual person in an auditory world." In other words he had correctly assessed that I learn better by seeing than by hearing.

Mr. Blackweller taught me how to take notes of lectures and how to outline written course material. As a result I went from a low "C" student to an "A" student. But more than anything else, I remember that Mr. Blackweller had offered me a word of encouragement at a dark time in my life. It is abundantly clear from our surveys that working mothers who opt to become stay-at-home moms need that encouragement too—no matter how strong they appear to be from the outside.

Even women who appear to be strong and self-reliant suffer from a lack of confidence if removed from their safe environment, such as the workplace, as Paula attests.

*"I had a high paying job when I got pregnant with my second child. My first child was 11 years old and because he was still at home I only worked 6 hours a day as it was. That way, I was home when he was and I was almost a stay-at-home mom. But when I got pregnant, my husband and I decided it would be best for me to stay at home full time to raise [the baby]. We didn't see the sense in having a child only to let someone else raise it.*

*"The transition was from one world to another. Our lifestyle changed in every respect. Although my husband earned a good salary, it*

*wasn't enough for any of the luxuries we had been used to. But the greatest adjustment for me was in 'learning to be home.' It took me a whole year to get into my new routine. And somewhat longer than that to feel my 'value'—I have a very supportive husband who only encouraged me during all this time.*

*"Even though we went from eating at restaurants any time we felt like it, paying our bills the day they arrived and shopping at [the best stores] to eating out rarely, usually paying our bills in the grace period and shopping at yard sales and thrift stores, I haven't a single regret. These are the only young years my children have—while I have the rest of my life to work."*

Our survey data shows a "pecking order" for significance, based in great part on personality types. There are four basic personality types: D, I, S, C.

D personalities are Dominant people; I personalities are Influencing people; S personalities are Steady people; and C personalities are Conscientious (perfectionist) people.

Obviously no one is just one personality type. We are all blends of many attributes, but generally we tend to be more of one type than another. I have found that gender is basically irrelevant in respect to personality, and there are as many Dominant women as men and, conversely, as many Steady men as women. In our society, Dominant women have been taught to suppress their natural tendencies and Steady men have been taught to conceal what society regards as a weakness in men.

Understanding who you are and what personality type best describes you will help to make the transition from the workplace to home a lot smoother.

*Prove yourselves to be blameless and innocent, children of God above reproach in the midst of a crooked and perverse generation, among whom you appear as lights in the world, holding fast the word of life.*

Philippians 2:15–16

I am a High D. We are goal-oriented and project-oriented people, who hate to do repetitive tasks. We are quick to make decisions (the old saying goes "often wrong, but never in doubt"), and we get most of our self-satisfaction as a result of getting jobs done, rather than from the applause of others (though everyone appreciates praise).

The High D women who become stay-at-home moms must set specific goals and time schedules and be careful not to order everyone around. Self-esteem is rarely a problem for most High D personalities, but they tend to get bored easily.

If I could offer any advice to the Dominant, decision-making mother who opts to be a stay-at-home mom, it would be to direct your energies into areas that allow you to utilize your creative abilities, such as a home-based business. We will discuss these options in a later section.

High I, Influencing personalities, on the other hand, often are called "people persons." They get their sense of self-worth from the recognition of others, especially their spouses and close friends. If you're an Influencing person, you need the care of a strong support group, the praise of an appreciative husband, and kids who truly like having mom at home.

Influencing people can usually be spotted: Almost everything they, their children, or their spouses have ever done is displayed prominently in their homes. This personality type talks a lot, makes friends easily, and is great at promoting ideas and products. High I people assuredly need social contact.

The caution I would give all Influencing personalities who leave a job to return home: Keep your expectations realistic. Kids don't

Marilyn expressed gratitude for having had enough economic security herself to make the choice she did, raising our children, doing volunteer work, and helping her husband's career. She asked that stay-at-home moms be accorded the same respect for their contributions as women in the work force.

—*Dan Quayle*
(Standing Firm)

always show appreciation, especially when you become their primary authority. Also you may have a High D (Dominant) child who is demanding, bossy, and unappreciative. Maybe that's why God wanted you at home: for your child's sake, not for yours.

And remember, opposites attract, so you probably aren't married to a High I who will praise everything you do instinctively. Communication and understanding are the keys to your self-esteem. If your relationship to Christ is right, you won't need the constant approval of others.

As Betty wrote, her life as a stay-at-home mom is fulfilling in a totally different way today.

*"I am [my husband's] counsel, his top aide, his confidante, and his partner. I teach our children here at home and keep the home fires burning at all times. I am the family's purchasing agent, economic advisor, taxi-driver, encourager, prayer warrior, insurance claims representative, chief correspondent, and number one cook-and-bottle-washer.*

*"I had enjoyed that part of my career in which I had been privy to important business decisions being made. It had meant a lot to me that I was significant enough for regional managers and vice-presidents to come by my office to just chat or discuss current personnel matters and decisions. I liked the power of reporting to corporate officers and knowing that my small opinion might have been considered.*

*"Therefore, you can imagine the traumatic adjustment of my suddenly finding myself exclusively at home, reporting only to an oft-tired husband and two toddlers. Why, it was my own sociological version of culture shock, to say the*

*least! However, again, the Lord graciously inter-
vened, and as He helped me to bathe my transi-
tioning ego in His Holy Word, to which I turned
more and more often, I slowly began to be transformed into the wife and mother He had created
me to be.*

*"Now, nine years later, as I carry on in such a
rich life that I often claim to be the wealthiest
woman in the world, I know that this work at
home is indeed the most important that I could
have chosen. Jim and I both strongly believe that
our children's precious personalities and quick
wits, their strong characters, and their much evident senses of security and well-being are directly attributable to the Lord's convictions of our
hearts to bring me home - where our children
and I belong."*

*The Lord is my rock
and my fortress and my
deliverer, my God, my
rock, in whom I take
refuge; my shield and
the horn of my salva-
tion, my stronghold.*

Psalm 18:2

High S, Steady personalities, are the glue
that holds our society together. If you are an S
personality, consider yourself blessed by God.
The S personalities of the world get things
done; they rarely worry about things they can't
change; and they readily adapt to whatever circumstances they are in. On the other hand,
they tend to delay necessary decisions and will
suffer circumstances they could change rather
than risk any confrontations.

Based on our surveys and testing, it is my
opinion that it is the Steady-type moms who
always are remembered so fondly by their children. After all, having such a mom is very
much like having your own personal servant.
Steady personality moms tend to do too much
for their children, even to the point of making
them so dependent that they don't function
well on their own. As in all things, there must
be balance.

S (Steady) personalities, much the same as I

(Influencing) personalities, need lots of support, but they aren't as talkative about it. It is vital if you are an S to verbalize your hurts, especially with your spouse.

As a High D (Dominant) personality, I usually look for a secretary who is a High S. Why? Because I need someone who will make me aware of the feelings of others around me. However, since I get most of my input through written communication and rarely remember verbal input, I also need someone who is detailed and writes things down. So, I need a High S, who is a detailist.

The C, or Conscientious, personalities are normally people we call perfectionists. If you are a High C, but a Low S, personality, life at home can be terrorizing unless you allow God to temper your attitudes. Conscientious personalities resist change and hate clutter, both of which are almost impossible demands with small children. However, you can use your perfectionism to an advantage if you learn to control it and "go with the flow" a little more.

It is my belief that the contentious woman described in Proverbs 27:15 was probably a perfectionist who expected everyone else to be as detailed as she was. If that is your expectation as a full-time mom, life really will be miserable for your family. There are some reasonable compromises that can be made for the sake of peace in the home.

While High D moms need to concentrate on being more sensitive, High C moms need to accept a little disorganization as a fact of life. Otherwise they'll spend their entire day yelling and picking up after their kids and driving everyone crazy.

I have been accused of being an arm chair psychologist. Not so, but I've seen enough

Insist on yourself; never imitate. Your own gift can present every moment with the cumulative force of a whole life's cultivation; but of the adopted talent of another you have only an extemporaneous half-possession. That which each can do best, none but his Maker can teach him.

—*Ralph Waldo Emerson*

*A constant dripping on a day of steady rain and a contentious woman are alike.*

Proverbs 27:15

examples, as well as evidence, from our Career Pathways test of more than 16,000 individuals to know that personality attributes play a major role in determining attitudes and behaviors. Understanding who you, your spouse, and your children are will greatly enhance your self-esteem as a stay-at-home mom. To help you with this, I have included two copies of an abbreviated personality survey in Appendix 3.

By no means do I want to imply that this self-contained personality survey is comprehensive, but we have tested it sufficiently to know that it is reasonably accurate. Actually I have included two copies because it is just as important to know how and why your spouse responds as he or she does. Each of you should complete a survey. They are marked for husband and wife.

As I said before, I am a High D (Dominant) personality but with an almost equal High C (Conscientious/Perfectionist). That means I am quick to judge the work of others. I have been told that General George Patton and Attila the Hun probably had the same profile.

Just like everyone else, I appreciate praise, but I am not primarily motivated by it. And, unfortunately, I don't always remember to give praise where it is due. But with the Lord's help and constant reminders from my wife and family, I am doing better.

## A Husband's Self-Esteem

While reading through the letters that came in, I noticed a recurring comment from many stay-at-home moms. They mentioned how much it had helped their husbands to see themselves as the breadwinners. Most of the women said they never had thought about it much while working; and, since working was a fact of life, there was not much that could be done about it anyway. But once they quit and the family was primarily dependent on just one income, they noticed a difference in their husbands.

The difference was difficult to define. Most said they sensed that their husbands had become the head of their home. In God's economy that's an ego builder for men. Regina wrote:

*"It had been nearly three months since I left my job. What an incredible summer I have had with my children! Although many of my working friends swore I would be bored and begging to go back to work, there hasn't been a dull moment. We swim, go to the library, play at the park, and pack picnic lunches for an afternoon at the zoo. We also play house (I sometimes get the coveted role of 'baby'), read, go to the Thursday kiddie matinees, and play regular school and Sunday school.*

*"Although they miss their friends from daycare, the girls are so much happier now that I am a 'real Mom' as Erin so eloquently puts it. Behavioral problems have virtually disappeared. Plus, I start my laundry and housework at 8:00 a.m. instead of at midnight.*

*"Not only are we living nicely on one income, but we are able to afford extras, like sending [my husband] to the Promisekeepers meeting in Boulder, Colorado, and installing new siding on our house. Also, we were able to increase the amount of our monthly offering at church.*

*"The best part of all this is my relationship with my husband. [He] is very happy with the 'new, improved' me. Our relationship and our faith is stronger than it has ever been. It's almost as if we never experienced the problems caused*

*The eyes of the Lord move to and fro throughout the earth that He may strongly support those whose heart is completely His.*
2 Chronicles 16:9

by my work-related stress. Also, I think it does something for a man's sense of self-worth to know that he can support his family by himself."

And now, . . . Holly's brief note says it all.

*"I am so grateful to my husband for the protection and the provision he gives to our daughter and me. He is so good to bear whatever a professional man feels when he is driving a 10 year old car to the job while other employees have newer vehicles. He curbs his own 'wants' to keep us from debt and financial irresponsibility. He does without to keep pressure off us for two incomes. He has worn the yoke, enduring without complaint, the pressure of not being able to afford some things. He has kept the value of my being at home."*

## An Excellent Wife: Who Can Find One?

Before closing this chapter I would like to share a personal observation. Over the last 20 years, I have counseled many men who confessed their lack of self-worth, and even resentment, over the fact that they were not the primary providers for their families.

It's too easy to say, "They just need to accept the fact that times have changed." Times do change, but basic biblical principles do not.

In my humble opinion, a woman who will build her husband's esteem by placing her trust in his ability to provide—even if she has to shop at garage sales for her children's clothes after becoming a stay-at-home mom, meets the criteria set forth in Proverbs.

I realize there are some irresponsible men in this world and, consequently, some jeopardy goes along with this decision, but the vast majority of husbands and fathers are honor-

*Now God has not only raised the Lord, but will also raise us up through His power.*

1 Corinthians 6:14

*An excellent wife, who can find? For her worth is far above jewels. The heart of her husband trusts in her, and he will have no lack of gain.*

Proverbs 31:10–11

able, hard-working providers who deserve the esteem that comes with being the breadwinners of their homes.

# Chapter Six

# Is Your Spouse Supportive?

*"A gentle answer turns away wrath, but a harsh word stirs up anger" (Proverbs 15:1).*

O n our stay-at-home-mom survey we asked, "Did your husband support [your decision] or object to you quitting your job?" Ninety-two percent said their husbands heartily supported their decisions. But that still leaves 8 percent who either objected or flatly opposed the loss of their wives' incomes.

There are a myriad of reasons why a husband might object to his wife, and mother of their children, quitting her job to stay at home.

The first and most obvious reason: "We can't make it on one income."

The second reason: "We would have to give up all the little

extras that make life livable."

The third reason: "I just don't agree that our children would be better off with my wife at home." (This is particularly true if the husband came from a home where both parents worked and he has never known another lifestyle.)

More than any other single factor in the last several decades, the feminist movement of the sixties and seventies weakened the perceived value of stay-at-home moms and promoted the ideal of a working woman's worth. This concept meshed perfectly with the liberal agenda of devaluing the family unit in general. Feminists presented stay-at-home moms as the equivalent of an oppressed minority.

This same liberal mentality has promulgated the use of taxpayers' money in an attempt to solve all the social problems of America. In reality, this philosophy further undermined the family by raising the tax rates and pushing more women into the work force. The burden put on families through these incessant tax increases, to support "entitlement" programs, has removed a major entitlement: a mother's right to stay home with her children if she wants to.

The massive amounts of money necessary to fund welfare, urban "renewal," and other social experiments didn't just happen to coincide with the feminist "liberation" movement. It was part and parcel with the great "sexual revolution."

Does this mean there was a planned conspiracy to force women (and mothers) out of the home and into the office? That's hard to say with any degree of certainty, but the result has been just that. It's sad that the feminists believe full-time mothers are an oppressed minority in need of liberation.

The children are the losers and are not rep-

*Let everyone be quick to hear, slow to speak and slow to anger; for the anger of man does not achieve the righteousness of God.*

James 1:19–20

resented in this great liberation movement. One must assume the feminists believe that with social programs like Head Start in place children are better off as wards of the state while their mothers work. More than once, leaders of the feminist's movement have espoused the idea that, indeed, children would be better off under the care and supervision of "professionals," rather than full-time mothers who are throwbacks to the Ozzie and Harriet era.[1]

Therefore, it is not surprising that many men raised in the sixties and seventies support the idea that wives should work—and even expect them to.

The Christian community has done little to counter the working-mother movement. And, in fact, Christian families have about the same ratio of working wives and mothers as non-Christian families do, if our surveys are reasonably accurate. More recently, a significant trend back to full-time moms has developed, but working mothers still significantly outnumber full-time moms.

But, as I said earlier, the issue of whether mothers should work will not be resolved in this book. So, the question then becomes: "What can a working mother who wants to stay home do when faced with a reluctant or recalcitrant husband?"

For those who are married to Christians, the appeal should be made from a biblical perspective. For those who are married to non-believers, most likely the decision will boil down to the finances of the situation. I first would like to address the Christian spouse.

## *The Biblical Basis*

Without getting too theological, I'd like to link some biblical concepts together that deal

This is a free country. Within very broad limits, people may live as they wish. And yet, we believe that some ways of living are better than others. Better because they bring more meaning to our lives, to the lives of others, and to our fragile fallible human condition. Marriage and parenthood should be held up because between husband and wife and in fatherhood and motherhood come blessings that cannot be won in any other way.

—*William J. Bennett (1992 Rep. Nat'l. Convention)*

with husband/wife relationships.

Therefore, by scriptural definition, the following principle applies: A husband and wife are to be one—respecting each other as partners. If a wife has prayed about her decision to return home and feels a peace from the Lord about it, and the husband cannot point to some specific principle directing her not to do so, he should yield to her spiritual discernment in this issue.

Conversely, a wife and mother who wants to continue working, even though her husband would rather have her return home, must also provide a clear biblical justification for continuing to work.

I firmly believe that a strong biblical case can be made for mothers not to work outside the home while there are children at home. But what about the other side? Can a case be made for the mother working outside the home? Very possibly.

If financial commitments have been made based on two incomes and there is no conceivable way they can be met by only one working spouse, the commitment to honor a vow is the paramount principle. We are told by Solomon that God requires us to honor our vows. *"It is better that you should not vow than that you should vow and not pay"* (Ecclesiastes 5:5).

Simply put, a working mother needs to make the necessary adjustments in spending to pay down some of the debt before quitting her job. This will help to defuse the argument of her reluctant husband—that they cannot afford for her to quit.

In countering the arguments of a reluctant husband, one thing is evident in the hundreds of letters I reviewed: Both husband and wife must be willing to accept the changes in

*For this cause a man shall leave his father and his mother, and shall cleave to his wife; and they shall become one flesh.*

Genesis 2:24

*Live with your wives in an understanding way. . .and grant her honor as a fellow heir of the grace of life.*

1 Peter 3:7

lifestyle that result from the loss of one income.

All of the logical arguments (biblical or otherwise) for a mother to stay home with her children are basically irrelevant if the husband has his mind set against it—just as would be true if the husband wanted his wife to return home and she were set against it. So I clearly recognize that the arguments presented here are for the benefit of women *whose husbands are part of a team* looking for the best possible solutions.

If you are married to a man who simply cannot be persuaded by any logical arguments (biblical or otherwise), you need to be realistic. After you have made your feelings known and have presented all the available facts, if your husband is still intractable, you need to turn this area over to the Lord and let Him do the convincing, in His timing. Many a reluctant husband has been redirected by a godly wife who simply trusted the Lord to change her husband's heart.

## We'll Be One Income Short

What about the argument, "If we can't live on two incomes now, how would we ever make it on just one?" The truth is, you can't. . .unless some changes are made. As we discussed previously, it really is a matter of priorities. Are the conveniences and indulgences made possible by two incomes more important than the investment that a mother can make in the lives of the children? All too often in our society the indulgences win out.

Eric wrote to share his experience as the husband of a stay-at-home mom. He concluded that once the adjustment was made they hardly noticed the difference. Most of us could

> *He has granted to us His precious and magnificent promises, in order that by them you might become partakers of the divine nature, having escaped the corruption that is in the world.*
>
> 2 Peter 1:4

testify to this truth. Nicer homes, fancier cars, and expensive vacations make virtually no difference in the social development of children.

*"When Jennifer became pregnant, we were both working full time. Our combined incomes came to over 50 thousand dollars per year. It was her conviction to be a 'stay at home mom'. I reluctantly agreed to her staying home part time—after all, we were the typical fresh out of college couple, who, when we got a bunch of money, knew how to spend it! We had a new house and two new cars—and of course we had to have our weekly date!*

*"After Brianne was born Jennifer cut back to three days a week at the hospital. It took some discipline, but we managed fine. I began to get an attitude check about priorities after going to a Youth Conflicts Seminar and got a financial attitude check after reading your Financial Guide for Young Couples. God put it in my heart to get out of debt in two years.*

*"I believe He spoke greatly through your book, but He had also put a great desire to preach and minister in me. I desired greatly to go to Seminary, but knew our debt load made it nearly impossible.*

*"We started 'tightening our belts' more and paid the last car note about a year later. God sold our house (I didn't do anything but pray and put a 'For Sale by Owner' sign in the front yard) and we were on our way to Seminary— completely debt free. There was just one problem: Brianne was four years old and my crazy wife got the nutty notion to stay home with her FULL TIME!*

*"You must understand the magnitude of this: not only would I have to find a job that was able to keep us alive, but we also had to pay for Seminary. Jennifer and I both had our minds set*

*to not borrow any money to do this, but frankly, I was very skeptical—I was counting on her working at least part time!*

*"We moved and God provided me a job two months later (we had saved up enough to last us two months). Jennifer opted to stay home and homeschool Brianne. After two years of Seminary I am making 7 thousand dollars less than I was back home (28,000/yr); Jennifer is at home; we are debt-free; we pay for Seminary (except books, which are provided by our home church) in cash; we have a 'rainy days' savings of approximately 600 dollars (so far); and we even get to eat out pretty much when we want!*

*"Yes it can be done—praise God!*

*"A <u>Big P.S.</u> — We also give over 10% of my gross pay to the church and donate to two other ministries!"*

More often than not, our problem is not a lack of money, it's a lack of faith. We are told by James, *"You do not have because you do not ask"* (James 4:2). And he goes on to say that sometimes we ask with wrong motives.

Asking God to provide the resources to allow a mother to stay home with her children is a right motive. Remember God delights in doing the impossible.

Nicole, one of the women who responded to our survey, told of her struggle with her husband. He was so adamant about her continuing to work that he threatened to leave if she quit.

*"I struggled with the guilt of packing my children off to a sitter every morning. Then I just decided that if God didn't change my husband's heart I would continue to work and learn to accept it. It was a long difficult struggle.*

*"Often I would cry all the way to the office*

*As many as may be the promises of God, in Him they are yes; wherefore also by Him is our Amen to the glory of God through us.*

2 Corinthians 1:20

*91*

*where I worked. But after a while I began to feel a peace about my position. I just prayed that God would be the protector of my children. 'After all,' I told myself, 'there are millions of mothers who work and their children seem to do okay.' But when I would pick up my children and sometimes they would be crying over some incident at the day care, my heart told me that being home would be better.*

*"But there was simply no other choice available to me, and every time I mentioned it to my husband he would storm out of the room. The thing that hurt most was that he told me he wouldn't have married me if he had thought I wasn't willing to pull my own weight. Often his parting words were, 'Sure, I'd like to stay home and loaf too, but if I have to work you have to work'.*

*"This went on for nearly another year until our youngest daughter started school. Then one evening while we were eating she asked a question about sex that no six year old should have even known. My husband nearly choked at the graphic question, and asked her, 'Where did you hear about that?' She replied, 'Oh some of the boys at day care showed us. . . .'*

*"My husband's attitude went from wild rage to remorse. That night he said, 'You were right. It's time you came home. I can't believe I've been so blind'.*

*"I have been a stay-at-home mother for nearly two years now, and I love it. We don't take the long vacations we used to, and we don't trade cars (or trucks) every two years, but our children are doing so much better now. Tell all the mothers: You can't lose by waiting on the Lord."*

## A Word of Caution

Several of the women who responded to our

It is necessary to learn from others' mistakes. You will not live long enough to make them all yourself.

—*Hyman Rickover, U.S. Navy admiral*

survey gave some stern advice: "Know your spouse well before undertaking this decision." Some of them told of additional conflicts and even divorces because of the changes in lifestyles after they quit work.

One of the most common warnings was to look for the danger signs and not be naive about the current trend in our society. Some men (and women) simply are not willing to sacrifice their lifestyles for their children, even if they know it's the right thing to do.

This especially seems to be true in situations where the husbands agree (mostly to avoid an argument) but are not really committed to the process. Rather than be totally honest and admit they don't want to make the adjustments, they go along but harbor resentments.

Several women, looking back, said there were some key indicators they ignored, such as comments like, "Okay, if YOU can make it work"; or, "I don't care if you quit work, but don't expect me to give up my (bowling, drinking, fishing)."

*Not one of us lives for himself, and not one dies for himself; for if we live, we live for the Lord; therefore whether we live or die, we are the Lord's.*

Romans 14:7–8

It is unfortunate that there are some pretty self-centered people in this world. I pray that you aren't married to one, but sometimes even the best of people are; opposites attract. The struggle of working a job while your heart is at home is very difficult, but being a single parent is a lot worse.

If a husband is not willing to make the necessary adjustments in lifestyle that will allow his wife to stay at home with their children (assuming that is her desire), a woman should take that as a sign of greater problems and seek spiritual and marital counseling first.

As Jesus said in Luke 16:10: Anyone who is not trustworthy with money is simply not trustworthy (paraphrased).

I hesitated to address so many negatives, but I felt I would be remiss not to address the dark side of leaving the work force over a spouse's objections.

Alexis wrote us the heart-wrenching story of her husband's betrayal. Probably he eventually would have left the marriage anyway, but because she had left her career the situation was made worse.

*"[After] our first child was born I stayed home for about four years. My husband would tell me how much he enjoyed my being home, but deep down he didn't.*

*"I wish I would have gotten the stars out of my eyes and really understood what my husband was trying to tell me before we were married. He wanted things—a house—a car, etc. I wanted a family, family togetherness. After ten years of marriage my husband never really got what he wanted.*

*"When I stayed at home with the kids deep down he didn't like it. When I went back to work he wasn't happy because he said I wasn't making enough money for someone with a degree. He went back to school to get his master's degree. . .met a woman. . .told me he was in love with her. . .and started spending his time with her. I was about eight months pregnant. As I write this he has filed for divorce. The baby is 3 months old. And I am looking for a job.*

*"I feel like no one really respects stay at home moms. When you have a job people look up to you, but when you do the same job at home people act like you are lazy.*

*"I hope you ask women to really be sure they understand their husbands before they make the move . . . and may God use [your book] to bless women to have understanding and wisdom*

*Under His wings you may seek refuge; His faithfulness is a shield and bulwark.*

Psalm 91:4

94

*(God's wisdom) to make the best choice for their families."*

I'll pick up a letter (the last page of a four-page letter) from Kimberly, who told of her heartache after her husband also left.

*"I'm sure I don't have to tell you how difficult it is to enter the work force again after a 13 year absence. I can never replace those lost years, lost earnings and career opportunities. I cannot even pick up where I left off. Entry level, minimum wage jobs are all that I can expect.*

*"If I am blessed again with an opportunity for love and marriage I will not put myself in that position of jeopardy again. I know it will be a burden on my family life not to be a work-at-home wife and mom. But since I cannot count on the laws to protect me, I must protect myself and any who are in my care as best I can. Any women who think this could never happen to them are especially at risk."*

Fortunately, this is not the norm; it is the exception. To balance this negative perspective, I would like to share one of the many responses we received from supportive husbands of full-time moms. As Rick testifies, God still speaks to men too.

*"When our sons were ages 8 and 5, my wife Deborah was working. With our combined salaries we were doing pretty well, making ends meet and saving for the boys' education. We had about $20,000 put aside for their elementary and secondary education with plans to save more for college.*

*"One day Deborah said she felt God was leading her to quit her job and stay home with the*

*boys. My first reaction was pure horror. I am a statistician and was able to quickly figure out that not only would there be no college in our boys' future, but we would go $5,000 in the red annually without Deborah's salary, even with a frugal budget.*

*"We were already tithers and were active members of a church. We went to see the pastor and, to my horror a second time, he said he thought we should trust God: Deborah should quit her job to stay home and raise Joshua and Jason.*

*"Despite the loss of [Deborah's] income, we continued to tithe. That's when God began to do miracles. On one occasion we were within 24 hours of having our home foreclosed. We had told no one. That night the assistant pastor of the church handed us a check for $200. He said God had told him we needed it. We needed exactly $200 to make the mortgage payment.*

*"On another occasion, we had about $1,000 in debts that urgently needed to be paid. We told no one. An elder of the church handed us a check for $1,000 saying much the same thing the assistant pastor had said.*

*"Having Deborah at home with [the boys] made a tremendous difference in their development. Joshua was a very slow learner before then. He repeated every grade in school, even though he was attending a private [Christian] school. He began to improve his school work with his mother at home. Despite our tight budget, we kept him and Jason in a Christian school with the money we had set aside for their education. We refused to touch that money for any other purpose and it paid off.*

*"And what of college? We had no money for college, but we didn't need it. Joshua decided on his own that he wanted to go into the Army. The Army later paid for nearly all of his higher edu-*

*Thou art my hiding place and my shield; I wait for Thy word.*

Psalm 119:114

*cation. Jason's grades were so good that he earned a full academic scholarship for four years of college. He graduated from college with high honors and has taken post-graduate courses too.*

*"I wonder if things would have turned out so well if Deborah hadn't stayed home with [our] children."*

I think I need to share at least one more testimony—just for those husbands who have that nagging doubt about giving up their wives' "security." Kevin says that God is security enough.

*"My wife and I were married in 1984. . . . .and both worked. We failed to do many of the things you recommended—we did not save a significant amount of her income, did not live on a budget, or practice good stewardship of the resources God had blessed us with.*

*"We were the typical young couple with two nice incomes and no children. We drove new cars, had nice new clothes, the latest consumer technology, and basically spent money on what we pleased without too much thought. To our credit, we did not run up any significant amount of consumer or credit card debt. [My wife's father] taught her not to rely on credit - I'm glad!*

*"[Because of a major bank failure in our area] local real estate values plummeted. We were shocked to discover that the house we still owed $69,000 on was only worth $36,000. We were stunned. Needless to say, we spent much time in prayer. We made the decision to sell the house and pay off the debt. We did have just enough money in savings and stock to cover the difference. It left us with nothing to buy a new home with, however.*

*He who trusts in the Lord will prosper. He who trusts in his own heart is a fool, but he who walks wisely will be delivered.*

Proverbs 28:25–26

"*In the middle of this dark hour, God sent a ray of light—Patty learned that she was pregnant. Immediately we were faced with a decision. Should Patty continue to work after the baby was born? We really needed the money. In our hearts, we both knew the right answer was no—Patty needed to be a stay at home mom. The Lord blessed our commitment to keep Patty at home. She was able to work through her 8th month of pregnancy. We saved every penny she made [and] made a down payment on the rent house we were living in. God provided me with enough income to meet our needs. We saw miracle after miracle happen in our lives.*

"*I can say that we've learned some wonderful lessons. God has taken care of us and honored our commitment to keep Patty at home.*"

---

1. "How the Feminist Establishment Hurts Women," *Christianity Today*, June 20, 1994.

## Chapter Seven

# What a Working Mother Is Worth

*"The Lord your God will prosper you abundantly*
*in all the work of your hand, in the offspring of*
*your body. . .for the Lord will again rejoice over*
*you for good . . . ; if you obey the Lord your God*
*to keep His commandments and His statutes"*
*(Deuteronomy 30:9–10).*

There have been many stories written about the financial worth of a wife. If only the direct financial value of her services is calculated in terms of cleaning, cooking, sewing, delivering, and shopping, the net value usually totals about $20,000 a year. But when children are involved, her worth goes up dramatically.

You can hire cleaners, cooks, drivers, and sitters at some hourly rate, but you can't hire the caring, compassion, and devotion of a mother at any price. When is the last time you heard of a housekeeper who sat up all night with a sick child? There may be a few, but you couldn't hire them for $20,000 a year. The bottom line is, a mother is worth a lot more to her family than most employers can ever afford to pay.

As I mentioned earlier, many working mothers are merely substituting hours on the job for hired help, transportation, child care, clothes, and entertainment, with little or nothing left over for their efforts. I rely on objective data to support theories, so I used our survey to learn what it costs today, in real dollars, to replace a stay-at-home mom. The results were surprising.

The survey we took involved 801 homes across America. Since costs vary considerably by area of the country, I used the median figure (one half above, one half below). All figures are in current dollars. The families represented here include a husband, a wife, and two children.

## Costs of a Working Mother

1. Child care costs: about $300 per month for one child; $450 per month for two. This figure does not include lost wages when a child is sick, additional medical expenses associated with group child care, or the additional fees that always seem to be associated with children's groups (gifts, trips).

2. Transportation costs: $250 per month, including car payments, maintenance, and gasoline costs. This cost presumes a working mother drives her own car at least three days per week, the average age of the car being about five years old.

3. Work-related clothing costs (articles of clothing directly attributable to working an outside job): estimated cost about $50 per month.

4. Additional eating out costs: estimated at $80 per month. As most working mothers well know, there is a fatigue factor that comes along with managing a home and a job. This is often manifested in hurried meals, eating out a lot, or ordering in pizzas.

   One observation shared by many of our respondents is that many working women, who see little or no net financial return for their time, feel like they deserve to eat out once in a while; and they're probably right.

5. Domestic help: Estimated at $25 per month (not many working women hire domestic help).

6. Miscellaneous expenses (laundry, lunches, office gifts): $60 per month.

Obviously there may be other expense categories for individuals, but we have limited our evaluation to items that recurred most consistently in the survey.

*Do not be anxious for tomorrow; for tomorrow will care for itself. Each day has enough trouble of its own.*

Matthew 6:34

The composite total of additional expenses for a working mother with one child came to approximately $765 per month. The total expenses, after income taxes, come to approximately $900 per month, assuming that the child care expense is either tax deductible or subject to the tax credit provision of the IRS code.

All other expenses, except child care, are paid with after-tax dollars. The additional earnings of a working wife also may push the family into a higher tax bracket; this variable was not included.

If we assume the median income of a working mother is $14,500, that means a net return of slightly more than $300 per month for her labor. Based on a 40-hour work week, a working mother nets about $2 per hour (average) for her time![1]

Forget the child labor laws; we have mothers who are working for Third World wages to support our tax system, child care providers, and new car dealers.

If that same working mother were available to use her services at home to reduce the family's food bills, shop at discount stores and garage sales for the kids' clothes, and reduce her family's income into a lower tax bracket, it is quite possible that she would net more savings for her family than the income she generates. Unfortunately, where debt is at issue, the creditors won't accept non-cash cost reductions, so many women are trapped into working to make the debt payments.

I was sincerely impressed with the ingenuity of many of the women who responded to our survey, particularly as it concerns reducing family expenses. One mother said that she had worked out a plan with her family doctor (and later the dentist) in which he would accept her services in the form of redeemable coupons for child care, piano lessons, and even lawn care in exchange for professional services. Any coupons they couldn't use themselves were resold to other doctors they knew. Without realizing it, this mother had created a new form of money: barter credits.

Several of the women who responded to the survey have found bartering to be a good alternative to paying cash for some of the services their families needed. There are many other alternatives available, if you have the time and ingenuity to explore them. Home-based businesses are being promoted as a new computer-

> It takes a certain level of aspiration before one can take advantage of opportunities that are clearly offered.
>
> —*Michael Harrington*

age phenomenon; but in reality, generating income from a part-time home business is as old as the book of Proverbs—perhaps older.

We will discuss home businesses later, but let me say that virtually any stay-at-home mom is able to generate some income through a home-based business; and, most women often can replace their lost wages over a period of time. After all, $300 a month (net) is not a large-scale enterprise.

Even for two-income families with six-figure incomes, often the bottom line is that a mother is working to pay taxes and to support a higher spending level.

In an article in the *Chicago Tribune*, financial analyst Michael Englung of MMS International, a San Francisco forecasting firm, noted that even in families where the primary wage earner makes $100,000 and the secondary wage earner makes $50,000, nearly 80 percent of the second income is consumed in taxes, child care, and transportation.[2]

That seems a pretty pathetic return for the demands an employer makes on a $50,000-a-year employee, especially a mother.

Another interesting side note was reported in *U.S. News & World Report*. A Loyola University five-year study found that husbands whose wives stayed home received 20 percent higher raises than men whose wives worked.[3]

Another study by Frieda Reitman, of Pace University in New York, found that men with MBAs whose wives stayed home got 25 percent higher raises than those whose wives worked.[4]

So, effectively, the wives who continued to work did so for little or no actual wages. Human nature being what it is, compassionate employers tend to pay more to those whose needs are greater.

I confess that, as an employer, I not only tend to do the same thing, I consciously do so. I believe in paying everyone fairly and always try to do so; but if I know that an employee is the sole provider for his or her family, I will always lean (emotionally) toward paying that person more. Why? Because I know what it costs to live and raise a family today.

*Is your eye envious because I am generous? Thus the last shall be first, and the first last.*

Matthew 20:15–16

Is that totally fair? I believe so, based on Christ's teaching in Matthew 20:1–16, the parable of the workers in the vineyard. As long as everyone is paid fairly, and what was promised, it's acceptable to pay some workers more generously. Union leaders might not agree, but single-income families surely do.

Perhaps another perspective of why men whose wives don't work get paid more is because they are freer to concentrate on their jobs. Sometimes, with both parents working, schedule conflicts arise, forcing the husband to keep a more rigid schedule; and having both parents working affects business travel schedules, as well as business entertaining. Like it or not, in the real world, all of these are factors in making salary and management position decisions.

## The Real Worth of a Stay-at-Home Mother

Statistics from most studies tend to support the idea that, in general, working mothers net little for their labors away from home. But I believe the real financial worth of a full-time homemaker is far greater than even these previously quoted figures reflect.

Let's make the assumption that the services of a mother had to be hired at current market rates and see what she is really worth to her family.

1. *A live-in nanny.* I called several friends who have hired live-in nannies in various parts of the country and found the going rate (for legal workers) to be about $10,000 per year plus room and board. Generally speaking, that does not include regular meal preparation or housekeeping.

2. *Housekeeping.* The average hourly wage for a housekeeper is about $8 an hour. Based on an average work week of 30 hours per week, a full-time housekeeper costs approximately $14,000 a year, including payroll taxes.

3. *Private tutor.* Almost without exception, school-age children do significantly better if they have access to a tutor (normally mom) at least four hours per week. Most stay-at-home moms spend more time than that, but we'll call it four hours for fairness sake. At an average rate of $10 an hour, that's about $2,000 per year. (We'll throw in the bedtime stories that mom gives before naps at no cost.)

Without confusing the issue with a lot of other minor expenses, I can easily calculate that replacing a full-time mom with hired help would cost in the neighborhood of $26,000 a year.

In truth, many of the affluent families I talked with said they were unable to get reliable domestic help at any price. Most had either resorted to hiring illegal aliens, which is unlawful, or they hired foreign domestic help in the U.S. on temporary visas.

One single parent, a physician, said he was so desperate he even advertised in foreign newspapers that he was looking for a full-time

*Delight yourself in the Lord; and He will give you the desires of your heart.*

Psalm 37:4

nanny, and he would be willing to marry her, if necessary, when her work visa expired.

Interestingly enough, two of the women responding to our survey were just such mail-order brides. They said the arranged marriages were working out just fine.

I would say to any husband of a working mother, if you're settling for her average net income of $3,600 a year, you're getting a bad deal. She's worth a lot more than that to your family in direct costs; and that doesn't even take into account what she could save through better shopping and food preparation, if she had the time.

Connie gives an excellent description of the real worth of a full-time mom.

*This is the confidence which we have before Him, that, if we ask anything according to His will, He hears us. And if we know that He hears us in whatever we ask, we know that we have the requests which we have asked from Him.*

1 John 5:14–15

*"I knew that if I had children I could only do my best for them if I was at home. I was a secretary and assisted my husband on the farm for several years before becoming a mother of two children. I quit work. . . .These were very difficult years though because the finances simply were not there, and we almost lost everything by borrowing money to cover our debts.*

*"We could have had government programs assist us, but chose not to. . . .We had been listening to Larry Burkett . . . and had come to the conclusion that it is better to depend on God. We began to trust in God for our financial needs. We were already tithing since we thought God wanted us to do it and had managed to do that through the financial troubles.*

*"We began to pay a little every month on each bill. We did without colas and eating out, nothing extra was spent. The garden produced wonderfully and I canned everything I could. Also lots of other people gave us produce from their gardens and I canned that too. By the end of a*

*year everything was paid off.*

*"I was at home with the children all the time. I prayed with them before they left for school on the bus. We did devotions from various books, discussed everything together. Because I did not work out of the home I spent two [sometimes more] days a week sitting in [my son's] class- room assisting the teacher. I also became involved in the Parent Teacher organization at our school and helped run the book fair and volunteered to help the music teacher so my children saw me quite often at school. All of these things take time that many working women in constricting jobs simply do not have.*

*"I taught children at church camp and so pre- pared Bible lessons with crafts and handwork coordinated. This paid for all of us to attend camp since we could not have afforded to go otherwise.*

*"The secret to what has happened in our lives . . .I was willing and my husband was willing to let God be the Lord of our lives and to let Him use our talents to make a special place for our children to grow up loving Him. God has blessed our lives and our work and multiplied it well to meet our needs.*

*For in Him all the fullness of Deity dwells in bodily form, and in Him you have been made complete, and He is the head over all rule and authority.*

Colossians 2:9–10

*"When I asked my children what they liked best about having a stay-at-home mom, they both said my being there when they got home . . . .Some working mothers are not able to be there for their children."*

Obviously we also could concentrate on other aspects of a stay-at-home mom, such as meeting the emotional needs of her family, avoiding the stress that takes its toll in health and mental well-being, or the benefit of know- ing that the children can stay home when they are sick instead of going to a sitter or school on those marginal days. It is hoped that these spiritual and emotional benefits will be amply represented throughout this book in the testimonies of the people who provided them.

I'd like to share one last testimony before closing this chapter. I used an excerpt from the following letter in a previous chapter, but I wanted to use all of Gail's letter because it reminds me of Proverbs 19:14: *"House and wealth are an inheritance from fathers, but a prudent wife is from the Lord."*

*"I was an elementary school teacher for eight years following college graduation. My husband was in various college programs during this time, so I was the sole breadwinner. I completed my masters degree in order to earn a better salary and take the pressure off of my husband to make a hasty career decision. However, after seven years we felt it was time to start a family.*

*"As God would plan it, my husband found a job in his field of interest and I gave up a contract for the next school year. Although I had always wanted to be a stay-at-home mom (as my mother was) and felt that it was best for our family, it was difficult to pass up the second income—and [being able to pay for] the school loans, second car, and first home that it could have covered for us. We were in agreement on the issue, however, and have never regretted it.*

*"We had little money saved, but with generous gifts from both sets of parents, we were able to make a sizeable down payment and purchase a modest home in a decent neighborhood. I loved being at home with our children and being a homemaker in every sense of the word.*

*"In effort to save money, we didn't replace our car after an accident, I made necessary items on the sewing machine when possible, and started*

*selling and purchasing clothing through consign-
ment shops, garage sales, etc. Since my husband
needed the car for work, I didn't get out much
during the day (which was a blessing in disguise
since I couldn't spend money shopping!).*

*"[When] other people often say to me, 'It must
be nice that you can afford to stay at home,' I do
my best to kindly let them know that this is not
the case, but that we as a family make the situation work.*

*"We give up expensive vacations, costly
clothes, a second car, frequent eating out, a bigger home, etc. but we get much in return. I am
fulfilling my God-given responsibility with our
three children at home. I have time to walk them
to and from school, go to the playground, read to
them whenever they want, take care of them during illnesses, volunteer at school, etc.*

*"My husband still does not make more than
$25,000 a year, so we are by no means on 'easy
street.' Yet, we still have been able to tithe regularly at church, pay our bills, and save a few
dollars each pay check. We are basically content
and know that God will continue to provide for
us as He has so bountifully in the past, as we
seek His will for our family and give Him the
thanks."*

*He sets the needy
securely on high away
from affliction, and
makes his families like
a flock. The upright see
it and are glad.*

Psalm 107:41–42

1. "Living on One Salary Means Planning and Sacrifice,"
   *Washington Post*, September 25, 1994.
2. "Your Money," *Chicago Tribune*, September 28, 1994.
3. "Working Mom and Daddy Penalty," *U.S. News and
   World Report*, October 24, 1994.
4. Ibid.

# Chapter Eight

# Stay-at-Home Fears

*"God has not given us a spirit of timidity, but of power and love and discipline" (2 Timothy 1:7).*

One of the questions asked of our survey group was, "What caused you the most concern or fear about quitting your job and returning home?" When the answers were sorted and evaluated, two areas stood out.

1. *Loss of health care benefits.* This was far and above the greatest concern of women whose jobs provided the primary health care benefits for their families. For those surveyed who were still in the marketplace, it was a major factor in their decisions to continue to work.

2. *Unforeseen financial disasters.* Even under the best of circumstances we all have some unforeseen financial disasters.

These can be as simple as a car breaking down or as complicated as the loss of a job. Under normal circumstances financial worries can cause anxiety, fears, even fights; but, for a family that has made the decision to live on one income, the potential crisis looms bigger than life.

We are told by Paul in Romans 8:28 that *"All things work together for good,"* and that is true. But most of us can only appreciate that when we look back on a crisis—especially a financial crisis in which our families' security was threatened.

In reality, my wife and I have had a few of these crises along the way, as have virtually every other couple. I can say honestly that we survived the crises and later realized that our greatest fears were over things that might happen—not those that did.

God promises that if we trust Him He will give us peace in the midst of chaos. I can personally testify that God's peace is there when we need it, but rarely is it provided in advance. There is a cliché about God's intervention that is full of truth: "Never late, rarely early."

Good planning can help to avoid most financial crises, but only faith can overcome the fears about them.

Our emotions, including our fears and anxieties, are a part of our human makeup. None of us can totally eliminate them, but the more we face them and plan appropriately, the better we can manage them.

*Having been justified by faith, we have peace with God through our Lord Jesus Christ, through whom also we have obtained our introduction by faith into this grace in which we stand; and we exult in hope of the glory of God.*

Romans 5:1–2

## Irrational Fears

I used to dread, even fear, flying. It wasn't so much the possibility of dying I feared. I was claustrophobic as a result of a childhood expe-

112

rience, when I nearly drowned in an underwater cave in Florida (where I grew up). Before becoming a Christian I rarely flew. Then after becoming a Christian, wouldn't you know, God sent me out to teach and air travel became an absolute necessity.

I didn't particularly enjoy the stress of having to fly, but God knew what was best for me. I still believe that flying in a metal tube is an unnatural act; but, I have flown hundreds of times over the past 20 years, and now I can even enjoy it—except in very bad weather.

When I faced my anxieties, they evaporated. It was the fear of being enclosed, not flying, that I was suffering from. God says that He has not given us a spirit of fear but of joy.

Don't let Satan rob you of the joy of being a full-time mom if you believe that is God's best for you. Without question, many women who decide to leave the work force and return home do so with some fears and trepidation—especially in the area of finances. The vast majority of those fears are exaggerated. The rest are totally manageable with God's help.

*Be anxious for nothing, but in everything by prayer and supplication with thanksgiving let your requests be made known to God.*
Philippians 4:6

Each of us has been equipped by God to handle differing degrees of stress and even different kinds of stress. A situation that seems to devastate one person, like a job loss, can be handled with ease by someone else. But conversely, the person who handles a job loss with ease may fall apart during a health crisis.

I recall a couple I was counseling whose financial difficulties were so severe, and the pressures so great, the wife was on the verge of collapse. Her husband said, "I just don't understand why our debts stress her so much. We have a child who has brain damage as the result of an accident, and she always has handled that situation well."

Sometimes it's the type of stress involved. Other times it's all the stresses added together. Still other times it's simply the fear of the unknown.

The one thing I realize, after years of counseling, is that even the strongest of Christians have their weaknesses, and there is nothing unspiritual about admitting them. In fact, few people will seek counsel from "perfect" individuals. Real-life situations need real-life people to appreciate and understand them.

I find that the vast majority of people can handle the situations they face if they understand them and know the limits they can expect. For instance, many people who owe back taxes fear that the IRS can take their homes and send them to prison. Often they worry to the point of near collapse. They panic when the phone rings, for fear it is an IRS agent; and an official-looking government letter strikes panic in their hearts.

I have been through this many times and I know the limits of the IRS's authority. Except in the case of fraud, they have virtually no criminal authority. They are a creditor, much like other creditors—only bigger and more demanding. Best of all they are bound by a law called the Taxpayers' Bill of Rights, which severely limits their bullying ability.

Once it is explained that the IRS is bound by a very specific set of rules too and taxpayers can only be imprisoned after being tried and convicted of blatant criminal fraud, most people feel instant relief.

Similar restrictions apply to creditors who often harass debtors and hospitals that threaten to withhold treatment from those who still owe them money. Each are severely limited by our consumer protection laws.

*Behold the eye of the Lord is on those who fear Him, on those who hope for His lovingkindness.*

Psalm 33:18

That is not to say that bills shouldn't be paid or taxes remitted; they should be. But most fears are created by the unknown. Once the truth is known, the fear abates. That's what I hope to do in this chapter: abate some of your internal fears about quitting the work force and returning home.

## *Medical Disasters*

As I said, the most common concern expressed by the women who participated in our survey was being without medical insurance and, subsequently, having some kind of health disaster. Many women today work primarily to provide health insurance for their families.

There is no question that a medical crisis can quickly become a financial disaster. It is not unusual today for a relatively simple hospital procedure to cost thousands of dollars. Gone are the days of $500 baby deliveries. Now a normal delivery can cost thousands of dollars for the hospital alone.

A couple of years ago I went through a relatively simple eye surgery on an out-patient basis. When all the bills were accumulated, including the anesthesiologist (who earned about $80 a minute for his time) my medical bills totaled nearly $6,000—for 40 minutes in the hospital! At these prices, families have good cause for concern.

The threat of losing the family's health care coverage keeps many working mothers on the job. Approximately 25 percent of the working mothers we surveyed said they would quit and return home if it were not for the fact that their family's health insurance was a part of their job package.

Those who had children or a spouse with

*Do all things without grumbling or disputing; that you may prove yourselves to be blameless and innocent, children of God above reproach in the midst of a crooked and perverse generation, among whom you appear as lights in the world, holding fast the word of life.*

Philippians 2:14–16

preexisting conditions felt they were totally trapped. They had no other choices and often expressed resentment that welfare mothers had better benefits under state-provided Medicaid because they had no husband at home.

There is no simple answer to the health insurance issue at this time. I am convinced that eventually our political leaders will address this issue and pass laws making health insurance transferable from job to job and available to those with preexisting conditions. But for the time being, a mother in transition from the office to home has very few options available.

1. *COBRA provisions.* Under the Consolidated Omnibus Budget Reconciliation Act (COBRA), an employee can maintain a company-provided health insurance policy after leaving employment for up to 18 months, provided he or she pays the company's insurance premium cost plus 10 percent. In most instances, this is a substantial amount of money and is beyond the reach of modest-income families.

2. *Private policies.* If there are no major preexisting health problems in the family, private health insurance is an option. Again, the major factors are qualifications and cost. Most private policies waive all benefits for preexisting conditions for one year or longer without medical treatment. In some cases the companies will refuse coverage entirely.

This problem could be resolved easily through legislation. If health insurance companies were required to accept all applicants, even if the preexisting conditions were not insured for the first year, the costs could be spread over their healthy clients. This system is utilized with great success in large company group insurance plans. Contact your state insurance commissioner's office and suggest options be provided prior to the next election.

If the option of private insurance is available to your family, selecting a major medical policy that pays only for in-hospital care is the least expensive way to go. (I used to say it is the "cheaper" way to go, but when health insurance is involved normally there is no cheaper way.)

Selecting higher deductibles also may make the insurance more affordable. The less risk the insurance companies have to assume, the lower the rate you'll have to pay. I recommend checking the annual *Consumer Reports* magazine, insurance edition, for a recommendation on the best and cheapest policies. You can usually find a copy of this magazine in your local library.

3. *Part-time work coverage.* Some employers offer health care benefits to part-time employees. This may be an option for some mothers who absolutely must have health care insurance. Usually large-group insurance plans do not have pre-existing conditions clauses, thus eliminating this limitation.

However, I need to be totally honest and

There is this difference between the two temporal blessings— health and money; money is the most envied, but the least enjoyed; health is the most enjoyed, but the least envied; and this superiority of the latter is still more obvious when we reflect that the poorest man would not part with health for money, but that the richest would gladly part with all his money for health.

—*Charles Colton*

say that the vast majority of employers do not offer health insurance benefits to employees who work less than 30 hours per week. In fact, in today's cost-conscious environment, many companies hire part-time people just so they don't have to pay health insurance benefits for them. But it never hurts to ask.

4. *Special group insurance.* As of this writing, there are at least two Christian organizations that offer health benefit packages to Christians at a cost substantially lower than commercial companies.

a. The Christian Brotherhood Newsletter, based in Barberton, Ohio, is a voluntary association of Christians who pledge to pay for the health care costs of its members. They have several thousand families participating, and they have been in operation for more than 10 years at the time of this writing.

The current costs average about $225 a month per family. Some preexisting conditions are excluded; others are not. This decision is made by the members. Only nondrinking, nonsmoking Christians are considered for membership at this time.

My daughter, who is a single parent, has her health coverage with the Christian Brotherhood. Her current cost is $75 a month, and that's a bargain by any standard.

b. The Good Samaritan is an insurance company specializing in coverage for Christians. Unlike the Brotherhood Newsletter, this is an insurance company with specific and guaranteed benefits (as

*The steps of a man are established by the Lord; and He delights in his way. When he falls, he shall not be hurled headlong; because the Lord is the One who holds his hand.*

Psalm 37:23–24

opposed to voluntary contributions). The costs are slightly higher than the Brotherhood insurance plan but significantly lower than most commercial health insurance plans.

Addresses for the Christian Brotherhood Newsletter and the Good Samaritan plan are in Appendix 2.

For families who cannot afford insurance and cannot qualify for any other type of coverage, such as Medicaid, when they make the transition from workplace to home, it comes down to a decision of trusting God for their needs. If the Christian community were functioning as God intended, we would take care of our needy—especially those with medical needs—but, unfortunately, this is not always the case.

Remember though, God is still in control. If home is where God wants you to be He will provide.

Marcia tells of her experience in trusting God in the face of what appeared to be insurmountable odds.

*"I was teaching elementary school and working on my Master's degree when I became pregnant. My husband and I (in our secular wisdom) decided that I would work and he would quit his job, return to college and take care of the baby after it was born. My husband did quit and was in his second semester of his new course work when our daughter was born.*

*"During my maternity leave I realized I wanted to raise my daughter myself. I didn't want to be a mother just 2 or 3 hours a day (from the time I got home from work until she went to sleep). I wanted to make sure she knew she was loved and valued. I wanted to be there to experi-*

*Everyone who comes to Me, and hears My words, and acts upon them, I will show you whom he is like: he is like a man building a house, who dug deep and laid a foundation upon the rock; and when a flood rose, the torrent burst against that house and could not shake it, because it had been well built.*

Luke 6:47–48

*ence every first step, smile, food, word and accomplishment she had. But, my husband had no job, so I felt trapped. I felt like I had no choice but to go back to work.*

*"While I was struggling with these feelings, I began participating in a Bible study course at my church called 'Experiencing God'. During this study, the Lord spoke to me. He told me I would be able to stay home if that was his will. He would provide for my family.*

*"I told my husband, family, friends, and co-workers that the Lord told me to quit my job, stay at home and he would provide for us. My family thought I had become a religious fanatic, my friends thought I was nuts, one of my co-workers said I was an idiot.*

*The Lord is my helper,*
*I will not be afraid.*
Hebrews 13:6

*"But my amazing, wonderful husband said 'If you say the Lord spoke to you, I believe you,' and we took that wonderful step of faith together.*

*"On the day that I resigned my teaching position, my husband had no job. We had no income, no health insurance, no savings, nothing. Just faith in God. Four very long weeks later, my husband received a phone call. He was offered a permanent substitute position at a nearby middle school with complete family health coverage. He took it.*

*"The salary was not enough to pay our bills every month but God always provides a way. Every month we receive money from some unexpected source. One month a woman called me on the phone and told me the Lord had spoken to her and told her to send our family $180. Every month the money comes in different ways, but it is always there. God provides for all our needs. Not our wants. We have cut back on a lot of things we thought we needed. Now we realize we actually* need *very little.*

## Fear of Being Without

As realistic as the fear of being without health insurance is in our high-cost society, very often other fears are totally unfounded. But, as a twist on the old saying goes, "Reality is in the mind of the beholder." I know that many women, evaluating the option of staying home, wonder if they and their families will literally starve. I can assure you, even though Christians are sometimes slow to respond to needs, they will not allow a family to starve knowingly.

It is sometimes true that the kids might have to survive without designer jeans or $100 sports shoes but, in reality, they will be all the better in the long run for these "sacrifices"— provided that mom and dad don't view them as suffering.

Most of us have fears about one thing or another; fears are not abnormal. But giving in to those fears leads to defeat and frustration. I believe that's why so many Christians go through life defeated and frustrated. Be assured that the vast majority of women who leave productive careers to return home have some fears. In fact, one of the things that impressed me most about the women who responded to our survey was the way they did what God called them to do—in *spite* of their greatest fears. In my Bible, that's called *faith*.

As Esther said, when her uncle Mordecai confronted her with God's plan, "Pray and fast for me for I will go; and if I perish, I perish" (Esther 4:16 paraphrased).

Don't allow fears, real or imagined, to rob you of your peace. That may sound a little contradictory, but it isn't. True peace comes only from doing God's will.

The greatest disadvantage of young people today is that they have too many advantages.

—*anonymous proverb*

121

*I will go before you and make the rough places smooth; . . . I will give you the treasures of darkness, and hidden wealth of secret places, in order that you may know that it is I, the Lord, the God of Israel, who calls you by your name.*

Isaiah 45:2–3

There *will* be times of struggle and sacrifices. But there also will be times of victory and God's supernatural provision, as hundreds of women who wrote to us testified. They also attest to the fact that victories are so sweet they overwhelm the times of struggle.

I would like to share three responses from stay-at-home moms that really spoke to my heart. I trust they will help solidify your commitment and decision.

Trudy tells of her "evolution" in becoming a full-time mom.

*"When my husband and I first married, over 20 years ago, I considered myself a Christian feminist. My future was clear in my mind: a career in teaching music, hours of daily piano practice, plenty of traveling and a rigorous work-out schedule. Since we never planned to have children, there was really no reason for my being at home much at all.*

*"My metamorphosis began with a sort of restlessness, one that intensified when I turned 30. I held a good position, enjoyed my students, loved my husband, had supportive friends and family, and yet something was missing. For the longest time I could not put my finger on what that elusive something was.*

*"A turning point came when my husband [and I] read* The Way Home *by Mary Pride. [She] exposes the dangers of feminism and shows how it has invaded Christian thinking. [My husband] and I came to believe that at least part of our lifestyle was contrary to scriptural teaching. In particular, we realized that God was calling us to make ourselves open to having children.*

*"Discontinuing birth control pills after nearly 15 years, I became pregnant in two weeks time!*

Spenser was born. . .I resigned my teaching position and worked at a part-time clerical job, one that provided insurance benefits for my family. (My husband was freelancing in art at the time.)

"I'd like to say my first year with a child was cozy and rewarding. It wasn't. For a woman used to unlimited freedom and little real responsibility, having a fussy baby was a nightmare. I only survived through the help of a supportive husband, plenty of prayer, and a conviction that [we] had been obedient to the Lord. I wasn't an ideal mother: to tell the truth, I could hardly wait to get out of the house and go to work every morning.

"Nineteen months later, we had another child. I couldn't believe it, but two were less trouble than one! [Sixteen months later another baby was born]. I took my six weeks maternity leave and found myself dreading the return to work. Still, I went back, as we needed the money and the insurance benefits.

"As soon as I walked through the door, my boss informed me that my part-time position had been eliminated, and I had the option of going full-time or leaving. I chose to leave. It was a difficult decision, but one of the best I ever made, one that led me home.

"It's now been five years since I gave up my job. I homeschool my three oldest children and write articles and books, when I can find the time. I have my own company. . .and I cannot express the joy I experience in working, living, and growing together with my family at home. I have found the missing something."

Grace's situation is more complicated but it demonstrates that God doesn't have one "pat" plan. We're all unique individuals and God

We count those blessed who endured. You have heard of the endurance of Job and have seen the outcome of the Lord's dealings, that the Lord is full of compassion and is merciful.

James 5:11

deals with us individually.

*"I married a wonderful man in 1986. I had a Bachelor's degree in Psychology and had worked as an intake counselor for a non-profit residential home for unwed mothers. When I married, we moved to near Dallas and I got a job as a Chapter Service Coordinator with the March of Dimes, making about $15,000 a year. Combined with my husband's income of $12,500, we were very comfortable. We lived in an apartment at the time, and our only monthly bills were utilities and a low car payment. I am sorry to say we lived pretty high on the hog, saving only about 3% of our income and using credit cards without a second thought.*

*"I got pregnant about 10 weeks after we were married and was thrilled. I worked until the seventh month, when a partial abruption of the placenta forced me on to complete bed rest for the remainder of the pregnancy. My maternity pay started then, and was long gone by the time I had delivered. My husband's pay had risen to about $15,000 by then, and we really felt called to have me stay home with our newborn son, so I resigned from my job.*

*"I stayed home with [our son] because I really believed that no one could possibly have his best interests at heart the way I and my husband did. . .I received lots of support for this decision from both sides of the family, my Bible study group, and nearly all of my friends. We were content to do without, and even to go into debt, in order for me to just plain BE THERE.*

*"When he was six months old, our finances were getting tight. We were floating checks and taking cash advances on our cards to make monthly payments on other cards. I did two things then. I signed up to be a Tupperware lady,*

earning about 30% of the total sales for home parties I did, and I found a part-time morning job as a day-care attendant in a health club. This job allowed me to take my son with me, and was an easy and pleasant way to earn $4.25 an hour, 4 hours a day. Not much, but it helped, and I did not have to leave [my son].

"When [he] was 8 months old, my paternal grandmother died, leaving me enough cash to pay off nearly all our credit cards and to get us into a small "starter" home, a "handyman's special", about 1200 sq. ft. Two weeks after we closed, using up every dime we had, I turned up pregnant again. Our second child was born. . . and four months later, our "fixer-upper" home had termites swarm, and we discovered the down side of home ownership. . .repairs.

"We borrowed [money] from our family, and decided to do the repairs slowly, doing all the work ourselves. What a nightmare!! Fully one third of our home was literally a pit for the next two and a half years. We had no kitchen all that time, since that's the room all the damages were in, and I cooked on a stove set up in the hall and did dishes in the bathroom sink for two plus years.

"During this period, I had a few weeks of panic about our finances, and convinced my reluctant husband that the ONLY option for us was for me to go back to work for a couple of years. Our credit card balances were climbing again, and the cost of fixing the house seemed insurmountable to me. I did not feel I could survive, living in such a mess of a house with two small children.

"I should have prayed about that decision, but I didn't. I relied instead on my own feelings, and on the world's advice. I thought getting the house fixed was the most important thing for us

A man with surplus can control circumstances, but a man without a surplus is controlled by them, and often he has no opportunity to exercise judgment.

—Harvey Firestone

*as a family and I could not see any farther than that.*

*My grace is sufficient for you, for power is perfected in weakness.*

2 Corinthians 12:9

"*I re-entered the corporate world. . . .I didn't count on was how desperately I would miss my kids, and how much I worried about them. I was not entirely comfortable with the day care arrangements, but I felt I had no choice.*

"*About four weeks into this new lifestyle . . . , I went to a baby shower for a friend. Someone approached me and innocently said, 'So, I hear you've gone back to work. How's it going?' To my great surprise and embarrassment, I promptly burst into tears, and said 'I hate it!'*

"*I knew then I had a problem. That night my husband and I prayed together about the problem for the first time. I kept working, hoping for a way out. And we kept praying. Two weeks later, my day care fell through. I could not find another home I was happy with and would not put them into a center. Three days of missed work later, it occurred to me (during prayer time. .of course) that I could not be the only woman in my town with the problem.*

"*So I solved. .or rather, God solved. .our problem by having me quit, and open up my own in-home day care. Through word of mouth I got three children in just one day, all three of whom stayed in my care for two years. God is SO good!! It was hard work and long hours but I earned $225.00 a week and I stayed home. I also really felt like I was helping the families of these three kids, by giving them an in-home day care that they could trust.*

"*Whenever I felt trapped at home, I would remember being back in the corporate world, sitting in my business clothes at a desk in an office, staring longingly at the picture of my two beautiful babies. And I learned to pray more, to call on God throughout the day. I had friends* come over to my house during the day as often as I could, and my husband made sure that on Saturdays I got out of the house alone for a couple of hours.

"I think nearly anyone who really wants to be at home can find a way to do so, even if it's only part time. I can always work later to pay off any debts. . .I can't have my 18 month old twins be at home with me later. This is such a short season in my life. . .they'll be grown before I know it. I may go back to work then, if we need the income. But for now, I'm staying home, with God's help."

*We desire that each one of you show the same diligence so as to realize the full assurance of hope until the end, that you may not be sluggish, but imitators of those who through faith and patience inherit the promises.*

Hebrews 6:11–12

Grace continues to work part time and constantly seeks the balance between being full-time mom and a financial helpmate.

I'll close this chapter on a positive note from Raven. Her testimony speaks of something we often tend to miss: that God provides even in the smallest areas—if we will allow Him to.

"After being a working mom for several years, I decided to stay at home when our second child was born. It wasn't easy, but I felt that my place was at home raising my children.

"We did not own a lot of things like some of the other people we knew; there was no money for luxuries, but with God's help we made it just fine. Many times when we had a need He would provide extra work for my husband, or help us find a bargain. It was as if when we couldn't afford something He would put it into our grasp at a price we could afford.

"When we met my husband was already practicing the discipline of tithing. I had heard of tithing, but had never met anyone who actually practiced it. I respected his commitment. There have been so many instances in our life together *that we have seen His provision over and over.*

*"For example, when we wanted to buy a farm (our first home), my husband was fresh out of the army, we had no savings and a brand new baby. The farm that we wanted to buy had been a dream of my husbands for years. It had a small house with 44 of the most beautiful acres of land that we had ever seen.*

*"When we called the lady who owned the land, we learned that the house had been vacant for some time, her parents were the previous owners and they had died without leaving a will. We believe that God gave us favor with her because it became important to her that we buy her farm. At that time there were some others interested in it also but she decided she wanted us to have it. She even took a second deed of trust in lieu of a down payment from us and it became ours for the price of seven thousand dollars.*

*"Another instance occurred when our daughter was a baby. It was her birthday and I went to the toy department to buy her a gift. I wanted a quality toy and in front of me were the Fisher Price toys. I narrowed it down to three. It was between a large red musical apple, a large, clear ball with hobby horses inside and a xylophone with a drum on the other end. I could only buy one so I asked the Lord to help me make the best decision. It occurred to me that if I bought the xylophone I would actually be getting two toys in one, so I chose that one.*

*"A few days later I went to some yard sales with my mother. I had a mental list of items that I wanted to find. On my list was a diaper bag, a toy guitar for our son and blocks for our little girl. Imagine my surprise when at one yard sale we visited there was that Fisher Price red apple and the clear ball that I had wanted so badly and*

*Faith is the assurance of things hoped for, the conviction of things not seen.*

Hebrews 11:1

*they were only fifty cents each! Oh yes, I also found a toy guitar and a bag of blocks and the diaper bag that I needed, all that same day. One of my sisters said that I was the only person she knew that could go to yard sales with a list and come back with everything I wanted.*

*"Many, many times we have seen things happen just like these in our life together. We are in our middle forties now, our son was married a few months ago and our daughter is a college bound high school senior. We own a business and I no longer need to shop at yard sales, but we love to share with young people how God was there for us and continues to be there for us to this day. We know from personal experience that 'He is faithful!.'"*

*The Lord is good, a stronghold in the day of trouble, and He knows those who take refuge in Him.*

Nahum 1:7

# Chapter Nine

# Confronting Disapproval

*"A friend loves at all times, and a brother is born for adversity" (Proverbs 17:17).*

**P**erhaps the number one caution I heard in attempting to write a how-to book for working mothers who want to stay home was, "Don't make value judgments of women who choose not to leave the work force." I heartily agree.

The ministry I head, Christian Financial Concepts, presently employs about 125 people, of whom 60 are women, and 19 of these women have children still at home. Therefore, it is clear that many of our staff have opted not to become stay-at-home moms. Of course, some of these are single mothers and have to work for the time being, but others have working husbands and choose to work.

As I said earlier, it would be supremely hypocritical to write a book condemning mothers who work outside the home while our ministry and many others continue to employ working mothers.

In truth, most organizations, Christian or otherwise, would be hard pressed today to operate without working wives, most of whom will eventually become mothers.

We have a variety of jobs available, many of which have flexible hours for working mothers. My own secretary is a mother of two who works flexible hours, which allows her to be available when her children are at home.

We also have had many employees who, after having children, decided to discontinue working. That's fine; I heartily supported their decisions.

It clearly must be the choice of every mother to work or not to work, as she and her husband feel led. I will readily confess that I hated to see some of those young women leave our ministry; they were superior workers. But when they bring their children into the office for a visit, it's easy to see the decision to stay at home was right for them. But, not every mother can quit her job, and several who work for us have no desire to do so.

*Holding fast the faithful word which is in accordance with the teaching, that he may be able both to exhort in sound doctrine and to refute those who contradict.*

Titus 1:9

All of this is to say that the decision to be a stay-at-home mom is one that is personal and individual. Women who choose to work often sense disapproval from the stay-at-home group, and those who choose to stay at home are frequently alienated from the ones who continue to work.

Most of the letters we received in our survey group were from working mothers who had quit to become full-time moms, and most were success stories—but not all, as we will see later.

I recall one Christian mother from one of our focus groups who admitted that she just didn't have the temperament to be around her children all day. She said she had tried staying home for several months and found her relationship with her children steadily deteriorating as she alternately screamed and then cried because she knew she shouldn't scream at them.

I empathized with her because I grew up in a home like that. I remember that my relationship with my mother was for me to disappear as quickly as I could and come home as late as possible, without incurring her wrath.

It took me several years as an adult to establish any meaningful relationship with my mother. I honestly believe we would have been better off if she had worked outside the home more than she did.

We certainly will not settle the issue of working mothers in this book and, as previously noted, I don't want to get bogged down in theological or emotional arguments on either side.

## Learning to Live with Criticism

Common sense says that when a woman makes the decision to quit a job and stay home it does lower the overall family income, making their lives appear to be more difficult (at least from the outside). This fact by itself will make some friends and family negative. Stay-at-home moms have to learn to live with that negativism.

On the other hand, working mothers often sense the disapproval of stay-at-home moms—especially within the Christian community. This can lead to great hurt, because very often the choice is not theirs. In the focus group,

There are two good rules which ought to be written on every heart—never to believe anything bad about anybody unless you positively know it to be true; never to tell even that unless you feel that it is absolutely necessary; and that God is listening while you tell it.

—*Henry Van Dyke*

*133*

comprised of working and nonworking mothers, I observed that emotions can run very high on both sides.

As I said earlier, the feminist movement that took hold in the sixties had great success in undermining the perceived worth of women who choose to stay at home. To some degree the rhetoric has eased as more women from the sixties have had children. Liberal theories about how others should live their lives and raise their children tend to change when feminists are confronted with the problem of their own children.

However, the feminist movement is not dead by any means. Clearly, there are more mothers opting to leave the workplace than ever before since this dual-income movement began in the late fifties, but there are still more mothers who work an outside job than those who don't.[1]

But it is important to realize that mothers who choose to work outside the home, even when the choice is theirs, experience virtually the same feeling of rejection and resentment from their friends and family for their decision to work as the stay-at-home moms do for their decisions to quit work.

## Self-Disapproval

The worst kind of disapproval that many stay-at-home moms face is self-disapproval: the feeling of lowered self-worth.

It is a fact that in our society a large part of our self-worth is tied to our vocations. The most commonly asked question of new acquaintances is, "What do you do?" For a woman who once could answer, "I manage an insurance agency," the response of, "I change diapers and fix meals," doesn't have the same ring to it.

*By His doing you are in Christ Jesus, who became to us wisdom from God, and righteousness and sanctification, and redemption.*
1 Corinthians 1:30

Some personalities are able to shake it off and say with honest enthusiasm, "I'm a home-maker and proud of it." Others struggle with their self-worth.

For some women, to change from an active career, in which people asked for and respected their opinions, to keeping kids and cleaning house, can be a traumatic adjustment.

Many of the mothers in our survey group handled the transition well, including doctors, lawyers, scientists, and top-level salespeople. But others, many of whom held less visible positions in industry, said they sat around their homes crying for lack of recognition and companionship.

Who we are and how we are equipped emotionally can affect the way we see ourselves—including stay-at-home moms. As I discussed earlier, we all have differing personalities that affect our feelings of self-worth too.

*The steadfast of mind Thou wilt keep in perfect peace, because he trusts in Thee.*

Isaiah 26:3

A High S mother (the Steady pattern) will generally have far less difficulty adjusting at home than a woman will who is a High I (Influencing pattern) or a High D (Dominant pattern).

I am a High D personality, as I mentioned earlier. As such, I get much of my self-worth from accomplishing projects that I can control, such as writing this book. The same obviously can be said of many women with similar personalities. There is no question that personality will influence how well anyone, man or woman, adjusts to home life.

I continually find that I am hooked on big projects. I like a constant challenge, and I need to express my creativity. If I were a stay-at-home mom, I would have to find outlets for that creativity, and even then I would quickly get bored unless I had lots of unique things to do on a regular basis. I suspect many stay-at-home moms with High D personality patterns can identify with this.

After reading the letter we got from Donna, I asked her to take our personality profile, which she did. Her profile was so similar to mine it could have been a photocopy. In making the adjustment to becoming a stay-at-home mom, she had been dealing with her symptoms (depression, anxiety) instead of the real problem: her need to feel productive.

Rather than reprinting her rather long letter, I will summarize it for you.

Donna started working as a bank teller when she graduated from high school. She had worked her way up to new accounts manager—a job she loved. It allowed her to help people, and her bank had even allowed her to teach a basic budgeting course one evening a week for customers who needed one. The course had become so successful that she started a second class—Spanish speaking—using a bilingual co-worker.

Then she was overjoyed to find that she was pregnant. She had always wanted children, and her husband begged her to stay home after the baby was born. After some doubts and lots of prayer, she resigned her job.

Donna started what she assumed would be a new adventure: motherhood. After the new wore off, she found herself home alone with a screaming, colicky child and almost no adult contact outside of church on Sunday and late evenings with her similarly exhausted husband.

Donna said she couldn't have felt more isolated in a prisoner of war camp. She cried—a lot! Sometimes all day.

Then a discerning stay-at-home mom from

her church began to call and drop by. She got Donna involved with a mothers-day-out group, an elderly care group, and a Wednesday morning Bible study—complete with volunteer child care.

Donna went from a very probable drop-out stay-at-home mom to an active, interested full-time mom. She couldn't deny her personality. She just had to be able to utilize it outside the workplace.

## Secular Theology

In doing research for this book I came across a lot of discussions about stay-at-home mothers in various secular newspapers and magazine articles. Most of them implied the homeward-bound movement either was exaggerated or was limited to the "radical right" Christian groups. Neither is accurate.

I believe this type of rhetoric is designed to drive a wedge between Christians and non-Christians and deter many mothers from making the transition, for fear of being labeled a "religious fanatic." Personally I think that's an honorable label.

What Christian stay-at-home moms have to avoid is thinking of working mothers as unrepentant sinners.

Is there a middle ground on which a working mother and a nonworking mother can respect each other's right to stay at home or on the job, as they believe God leads them? That's really hard to say right now.

However you feel, the truth is that working a full-time job should not be classified as a sin; nor should stay-at-home moms be viewed as drop-outs.

The focus groups that were a part of the research on this book were interesting micro-

*And the peace of God, which surpasses all comprehension, shall guard your hearts and your minds in Christ Jesus.*

Philippians 4:7

cosms of our society—or at least a view of our society with the veneer of politeness stripped away. These groups were made up of women with similar interests and backgrounds but, since they didn't know each other previously, there were not the normal reservations between friends to try to avoid hurting one another's feelings.

Once the formalities were over, and the conversations worked their way around to the real topic for discussion, Should Mothers Work or Stay at Home?, the gloves came off.

In one group the discussions eroded to the level of a shouting match as working mothers accused stay-at-home moms of being narrow-minded, brainwashed, and even lazy.

On the other side, some of the full-time mothers insinuated that working mothers were abandoning their children for the sake of their careers, dumping their latchkey kids on the full-time moms in their neighborhoods, and being more attached to things than their families. Sound familiar? It does to many women on both sides of this issue.

Usually, in the everyday world, the feelings aren't expressed so openly or with outright hostility. For a mother in an office environment who has decided to quit and stay at home, the barbs often are toned down to comments like, "I can't believe you would give up a good job just to babysit kids." Or, "You mean you're going to waste all your education?" Or, "It's too bad since you have what it takes to make it in the real world." Or simply, "That's okay for you; you can afford it."

*Let us not become boastful, challenging one another, envying one another.*

Galatians 5:26

These kinds of jabs not only are unnecessary and hurtful, they often undermine the confidence of a woman who is already questioning her decision.

*138*

The key ingredient for any potential stay-at-home mom in this environment is obedience. If God told you to do it, do it! What anyone else thinks (other than your husband) is irrelevant.

Unfortunately, all too often the barbs also come from friends and family outside the work place. Many of the surveyed stay-at-home moms said that even family members would insinuate that they were not pulling their own weight (in the marriage).

Several stay-at-home moms shared that friends and family accused them of being selfish for wanting to stay home and even said they were lazy. One distraught young mother of two said that her mother-in-law called almost daily for the first month, accusing her of putting her family in the poorhouse, and telling her it was time to grow up!

Jerri wrote about some of her frustrations with co-workers when she decided to quit a company where there were several other working mothers who elected to stay on the job.

*Humble yourselves in the presence of the Lord, and He will exalt you.*

*James 4:10*

*"From the beginning of our marriage, we had decided I would resign with the birth of our first child, but when the three months of my maternity leave was over, it seemed to make more sense that I return to work in order to earn the [promotion, with a 25% increase in salary].*

*"At that point I returned to work for four months. I truly can see how God used those four months in my life to help me appreciate the gift of being able to stay home full time with my son. I was overworked, over-stressed, and full of guilt. I was not a good employee, mother, wife, housekeeper. I felt incredible amounts of stress about my child being in someone else's care and not with me, about being absent from work too*

much to care for a sick child, and never having the energy to give quality time to my child or my husband.

"The spiritual warfare was so great with co-worker after co-worker telling me they couldn't believe I would give up a good salary, a corner office, good benefits, great annual stock options, a four million dollar budget to wipe mouths and change dirty diapers. The 'world' was working very hard to deceive me into thinking that I was giving up everything to become a second class citizen. And, I might have believed it, but God in His faithfulness was working too.

"Even today when I have lunch with my old working buddies, I always hear 'when are you coming back to work?' I always tell them not anytime soon, but. . .I never forget anyone's birthday, [now I take] advantage of going to the homeless mission with my Acteens, growing in God's Word through my Bible study, or just having a lazy day at the house with my son. How many full-time working mothers can say the same? So when people ask me why I quit working, I tell them I didn't quit, I just got a fantastic promotion."

## Pressure from the Other Side

Michelle wrote about her experience with pressure from her Christian community. All too often Christians seek to play the Holy Spirit's role in the lives of other people.

*We shall all stand before the judgment seat of God. . . .So then each one of us shall give account of himself to God. Therefore let us not judge one another anymore, but rather determine this—not to put an obstacle or a stumbling block in a brother's way.*

Romans 14:10–13

"After 16 years my husband and I had our first child. I made the big step to quit working outside the home to be a full-time mom. I made the decision not by seeking God's will in prayer, but because I felt it was best for our child. I also felt incredible pressure from the Christian culture that this was the only acceptable thing for a

140

*Christian mother to do. . . . The world doesn't bother me. They are not my peer group. But the Christian community is and their pressure can hurt.*

*"After a few months at home I began to have problems with depression. I just wandered around that house at times feeling so isolated and bored. I put too much pressure on my husband. I couldn't wait for him to come home. If he was late, I was resentful. It was tough on the marriage.*

*"When our child was 18 months old I decided to go to work 12 hours per week. We have 2 children now and for 4 years we've had a sitter who comes to our home. We profit from this arrangement in several ways.*

*"We enjoy the income. I net over $10,000 per year. [With my husband's income] we have enough to have a 3 bedroom home which would be much more difficult to afford on the one income.*

*"Getting out into the working world saves my sanity at times. Some women do fine and thrive being full-time mothers. But others suffocate.*

*"Work part-time has kept my career from going stale. Many careers, especially nursing, cannot be put on hold for 10 years.*

*"I'm a firm believer that kids need mom. I am so grateful to God that I have not had to park my kids in a day care center 5 days a week. My heart aches for the children whose only contact with Mom and Dad is at the end of the work day when everyone is tired and grumpy. I do not think our children have been harmed by our routine. The Lord has kept them safe with their sitter when I'm away.*

*"We belong to a church with many affluent members. Occasionally someone will start talking about how terrible it is for mothers to work*

*outside the home. Or, women who don't stay home are just greedy for money and similar comments.*

*"We need to encourage women and their husbands to **seek God's will for all decisions**. What works for one family may not for another. We can't all be the Proverbs 31 women.*

*"God has different paths for all of us to walk. It's not as cut and dried as the Christian community makes it out to be."*

## This Is My Commandment . . . That You Love One Another

I have to admit that I am biased toward mothers who have decided to become stay-at-home moms. Our society is tough on kids and they need all the help they can get; and a full-time mom is one of them. However, I would never attempt to put a guilt trip on a mother who does not feel God's leading to stay home. Personally, I don't believe anyone in the church has the right to decide this issue for anyone else.

It's okay to point out the advantages of being home and the disadvantages of working with dependent children. But we also must allow for God's sovereignty in our dealings with one another. Until the church is willing to provide for working single parents the same opportunity it expects from working mothers in a two-parent environment, we are being very hypocritical.

I once heard a pastor with great personal convictions about mothers staying at home ask that all working mothers in his church either quit their jobs or quit the church. But when asked how working single mothers would do this, he had no answer.

The point is, if we want more working

*"My thoughts are not your thoughts, neither are your ways My ways," declares the Lord. "For as the heavens are higher than the earth, so are My ways higher than your ways, and My thoughts than your thoughts."*

Isaiah 55:8–9

mothers to become full-time moms, we need to demonstrate the advantages of doing so. There are many working mothers who like to work and would not return home even if they could. But there are a great many more who say they like their jobs but, in reality, they know they don't have the option to quit.

If finances were the only consideration, any mother could quit her job and stay home. It might take a while and require selling a home, car, camper, boat, or other items. But there are often other significant factors that must be considered, such as a belligerent spouse, a major illness in the family, or emotional instability. So be careful not to judge others too quickly.

If you're a stay-at-home mom facing criticism, the best way to deal with the negative reactions of others is simply to prove them wrong. Trust the direction that God has given you, invest your time wisely at home, and believe that, without exception, God will do what He has promised.

*Truly I say to you, whoever says to this mountain, "Be taken up and cast into the sea," and does not doubt in his heart, but believes that what he says is going to happen, it shall be granted him. Therefore I say to you, all things for which you pray and ask, believe that you have received them, and they shall be granted you.*

Mark 11:23–24

---

1. "Demographics," *The Wall Street Journal*, 9/1/94.

# Chapter Ten

# Are You Wasting Your Education?

*"How blessed is the [one] who finds wisdom, and the [one] who gains understanding"*
*(Proverbs 3:13).*

O ut of the hundreds of stay-at-home moms we surveyed, 55 percent were college graduates and 11.2 percent had masters degrees or a higher educational level. In total, 99 percent were at least high school graduates—many with additional specialized training.

So contrary to what many in the secular media, and the feminist movement in particular, would have us to believe, full-time mothers are not uneducated drop-outs who have no other choice than to be house "slaves."

At one time several years ago, I might have questioned whether parents were wasting their money educating daughters, many of

The primary purpose of education is not to teach you to earn your bread, but to make every mouthful sweeter.

*—James R. Angell*

whom eventually would opt to become home-makers. I no longer ponder this question. Without getting into a discussion about the deficiencies of many college courses (which easily could be a book itself), I have long since concluded that if we are to assume a college education is useful, it is especially useful to full-time moms.

The whole idea that being a stay-at-home mom is a waste of an education is an absurd notion. If what a woman learns in school is not applicable to raising the next generation, then the school is at fault—not the mom.

To allow this deception to continue, that somehow raising children is a waste of an education, is not only wrong, it can be very harmful, because it places false guilt on many women.

More than one woman wrote to share her heartache over being pressured to place her career above her family so that a "valuable" education wouldn't be wasted. Unfortunately some women lost their marriages in the process. Just as not all women are content to be full-time mothers, not all men are satisfied to have part-time wives.

An education can be a useful tool, or it can be a stumbling block.

## Future Use

In addition to helping raise and educate children, an extended education can be very useful to a woman after the children have left home. The empty-nest syndrome is very real to many women who, after investing 20 or more years in their children, need to redirect their lives. Education is often the key that unlocks the door to opportunity.

That is not to say there aren't many excep-

By nature all [people] are alike, but by education become different.

*—unknown*

tions in which both men and women have risen to the highest ranks in their chosen fields, based on proven abilities, irrespective of their education.

President Harry Truman is a classic example of this. After graduating from high school he went to work in construction for the railroad before serving in the military. It was only after a failure in the business world years later (it took him 15 years to pay off his debts) that he went into politics. In spite of his lack of formal education, his farm background, war record, and personality made him a viable political candidate. But, all things being equal, an education does help.

After reading through the hundreds of letters from stay-at-home moms who left professional careers, I gleaned something that was never actually stated. Those with more education usually had more self-confidence.

The fact that these women had "made it" in the workplace instilled a confidence that they could make it anywhere. I suspect that some of that confidence took root in college when they found they could compete and succeed against the best students society had to offer. Confidence in one area is usually carried over into other areas of life.

I know that was true with me. I loafed my way through most of my pre-college years. There were some very good students in my school but, as in most schools, the majority were more or less average, so I could pass without really having to exert a lot of effort. Therefore, I reserved my energy for sports.

In college the competition stiffened, and considerably more effort was required to get by. I went into the service prior to college and was paying my own way. So, getting by was

Learning is like rowing upstream; not to advance is to drop back.

*unknown*

147

not good enough then. Faced with a challenge, I buckled down, applied myself, and discovered that I had a knack for learning. It built my confidence considerably.

That confidence spilled over into every area of my life. A lot of what I learned in college turned out to be pretty useless in real life, but the learning process certainly was not.

Self-confidence can be just as helpful in the home as it is in the business world. When controlled properly, confidence is a tremendous help.

In some ways, having a skill, abilities, or education is like having money in the bank (so to speak). You know that if the totally unexpected happens you always have them to fall back on. That is not to say that skill, ability, or education should ever be a substitute for trusting God.

As Proverbs 11:28 says, *"He who trusts in his riches will fall, but the righteous will flourish like the green leaf."* The same can be said of skills, abilities, and education. But again, all things being equal, it is better to have money in the bank than to be in debt.

## *Answering the Critics*

*Examine everything carefully; hold fast to that which is good.*

1 Thessalonians 5:21

I don't want to mislead any current or future stay-at-home moms by suggesting that if a husband dies or gets sick they can always reenter the work force where they left off. That may or may not be true. My purpose is to assure you that if you have decided to become a stay-at-home mom you are not wasting your education. Every asset you bring into your home is ordained by God and useful in your primary role as educator.

I'd like to share excerpts from several testimonies of mothers who have applied their gifts, abilities, and education in their roles as full-time moms. I trust they will bless you as they have me.

*"I left the work place eight years ago, shortly before my first daughter was born. At that time I had a challenging job in agricultural research . . . . I have a Ph.D. However, I felt the Lord tugging at my heart to do something that would last for longer than a lifetime.*

*"We have three wonderful daughters now. It is a joy to see them grow physically, mentally, and spiritually. We have home schooled our children . . . [and it has been] one of the greatest challenges of my life. . . . I work harder now than I ever did outside the home; but the rewards are greater."*

---

*"I graduated with an M.S. in Public Policy Analysis following a B.A. in Economics. . . . I was never one of those women, even as a child, who was crazy about children. I'm still not, except my own. And even now, motherhood comes as a struggle.*

*"Even though we weren't sure we wanted children early in our marriage (we were married for seven years before our first was born), we always agreed that I would stay home with them, as had our mothers with us. We believe that raising children is a responsibility God specifically gives to parents and should not be delegated to others unless absolutely necessary.*

*"I have never regretted leaving the workplace, though when things got very stressful after [my third child's] birth, I was tempted to look back. Because my calling is so clear, I find fulfillment in knowing that I am doing just what God*

*wants me to do, no matter how mundane, frustrating and tiring it gets. God [has] reminded me that I am making disciples as I help my children to know God and [as I] model repentance, submission and obedience to them.*

---

The hallmark of courage in our age of conformity is the capacity to stand on one's convictions—not obstinately or defiantly (these are gestures of defensiveness, not courage), not as a gesture of retaliation, but simply because these are what one believes.

—*Rollo May*

*"When my husband and I were married he was very insistent that we would plan our finances so that I could stay home when we had kids.*

*"I had graduated valedictorian of my high school class, graduated summa cum laude with a major in computer science and a minor in mathematics and was working on my masters degree. I had been with [my employer] for seven years and worked my way from a $16,000 a year job to $40,000 and was an officer in the company. I was very ambitious and success driven. At the time I could not picture myself staying home as a full time mom. But I agreed to plan our finances. . .just in case I might have a change of heart.*

*"My position was eliminated. . . . I decided to take my severance package and stay home. I continued to work as an independent consultant over the next two years on a part time basis. Satan knew that pride and success were my weak areas and used every opportunity to tempt me.*

*"I have been freed from my success-driven and prideful behavior. Having me home has had unforseen benefits. Our lives are a lot more stress-free. We have learned to scale back our lifestyle. We don't 'have to have' the latest and greatest of anything. My children are thrilled to get a 'new' toy or clothes from a friend or garage sale. They are learning the value of money and*

*hard work. I look back at our two income lifestyle and wonder how we wasted so much money."*

———

*"I went to college for 6 years to get a B.A. in Elementary Education and an M.A. in Education with the Acoustically Handicapped. I worked in the public school system and loved teaching in one of the highest paying counties for teachers in the United States.*

*"My husband made less than I did with no benefits. So our decision to live on one income was based on a conviction. Are there any moral principles or biblical guidelines for us to follow in the decision to work as a mother of small children or stay home with them and nurture them myself?*

*"Our conviction is based on Titus 2:4–5 (NAS). 'That they may encourage the young women to love their husbands, to love their children, to be sensible, pure, workers at home, kind, being subject to their own husbands, that the word of God may not be dishonored.'*

*"God has given me a responsibility as a mother under my husband's direction and leading to train up my children in His way by teaching them from the home. This means I must be home with my children to impart disciplines to them.*

*"I love being home although I have struggled at times, especially on first leaving the workplace, with [self] worth in vacuuming and doing dishes. My criteria of a worthwhile job was the pay. To be home with no income left me feeling worthless at times. I have since learned what being a homeworker entails. It is not just cleaning and cooking but building an environment that is hospitable for outsiders, warm for my*

*Thou dost scrutinize my path and my lying down, and art intimately acquainted with all my ways. Even before there is a word on my tongue, behold O Lord, Thou dost know it all.*

Psalm 139:3–4

husband, and enjoyable yet teachable for my children.

"Does God care if I work outside the home or stay home with my children to nurture, train and discipline them? Yes He does!"

———

"Some people probably thought I was a little crazy—leaving a job that I had trained many years for. I heard a lot of 'you won't be using your degree' or 'you are wasting your education'. I don't feel an experience in education is ever wasted.

"[When you] receive a Ph.D. in a particular field of study; what drives you to seek that degree is a quest for knowledge. . .and can be passed on to your children. What I did in the work place will last for a few years. The work I do at home for our children will last for generations and into eternity if it's done for Christ.

## Chapter Eleven

# Bartering: The Alternative to Paying Cash

*"Poor is he who works with a negligent hand, but the hand of the diligent makes rich"* (Proverbs 10:4).

I t has often been said that there is no free lunch, and that's probably true; but there are ways to make lunches cheaper. One of those ways is through bartering.

Several years ago I wrote a book entitled *How to Prosper in the Underground Economy*. It dealt primarily with how to arrange legal barter exchanges that are to the advantage of both parties. I still believe that bartering is one of the best kept secrets in our economy.

Simply put, a barter is when two or more people exchange goods or services without any money changing hands. Almost everyone has bartered at one time or the other. It is a simple procedure and the nice thing about it is that both parties win. That may or may not be true when making a cash transaction.

You can basically barter anything: time, skills, products. All you have to do is find someone who has something you want and trade them something they want. Let me give an example.

Mary Beth is a mother of two pre-school-age children and is a stay-at-home mom. Obviously from time to time her children have need of medical services, but Mary Beth and her husband are able to afford only a major medical plan, which doesn't pay for office visits. At $40 to $60 a visit, Mary Beth can't afford to take her children regularly and, in the past, has limited visits to crisis incidents only.

Mary Beth met Carole at one of her church's stay-at-home moms' support groups. Carole is a licensed pediatrician who has given up her practice to stay home with her daughter.

Carole would like to work part-time to retire her school loans of nearly $60,000, but she has had two bad experiences with sitters before leaving her medical practice.

Once Mary Beth and Carole got to know each other they realized that both had needs the other could fill, if the right trade could be arranged. Mary Beth agreed to babysit Carole's daughter in her home two days a week in exchange for her pediatric services.

Both women said it was the best of both worlds. Carole's daughter is six months younger than Mary Beth's oldest and they love playing together. By the time Carole's debt is repaid (about two years), she will be ready to start her new career venture: home-based pediatric care—something we haven't seen since doctors made house calls back in the thirties.

*He who trusts in the Lord, lovingkindness shall surround him.*
Psalm 32:10

## Church-Wide Bartering

Bartering can be as simple as a mutual agreement to trade between two people, but it doesn't necessarily have to be. Miriam wrote about the church-wide barter system she had helped to start.

For several years Miriam had been bartering for the things her family needed whenever possible. Everyone in her church knew that if they had something to trade Miriam was the one to call. She just had a knack for swapping what one person had for what another needed.

Miriam had developed a small business around her bartering abilities that helped meet her family's needs. Often a church member would call and tell her they needed something—for instance, a lawn mower. Miriam would call around until she found another church member with a lawn mower to trade, at which point she would put the two together and each would pay her a small fee.

However, many times the person who needed an item had nothing the other person really wanted. Of course the buyer could always purchase the item for cash, but in many ways that defeated what Miriam was doing. After all, any good used merchandise store could do that.

Then Miriam got an idea: "What is money but a means of exchange? You can't eat money," she reasoned. "It's only worth what others are willing to trade for it." Suppose she established another way of trading goods? She could actually create her own money, which is exactly what she did.

She established a system of credits: one church member could trade something like a lawn mower, babysitting services, dental care, or car repair, and they would receive a credit to

Some people regard private enterprise as a predatory tiger to be shot. Others look on it as a cow they can milk. Not enough people see it as a healthy horse, pulling a sturdy wagon.
—*Winston Churchill*

their account for the value (established by trial and error) of their item. They could redeem the credits for anything Miriam had on file. Miriam had effectively established a barter currency, good for trade within the "system."

Eventually she established a means of evaluating the worth of virtually anything traded, and her customers trusted her judgment. Miriam was operating a micro-economy: her own cashless economy.

You may not want to start a barter system as extensive as Miriam's, but you certainly can barter for some items your family needs. Probably the most common barter exchanges among individuals are services.

For instance, if you have a talent for teaching piano, tutoring, housekeeping, or babysitting, these usually can be bartered since they are so universally needed. Often it is simply a matter of printing a notice and posting it on the church bulletin board (with proper permissions of course).

The bartering of services was one of the most common savings tips offered by the mothers who responded to our survey. One entrepreneurial mom had bartered prepared hot meals for all of her family's dental and medical care. She swapped her prepared meals, delivered to the doctors' homes, for professional services.

The doctors covered the cost of the ingredients; she cooked the meals and delivered them to their homes on selected evenings. By preparing several meals at one time she kept her time and expenses to a minimum. All she had to do to sell her idea was to look for doctors with working wives. She actually turned down five out of six respondents.

## Tax Implications

Unfortunately, just as every cloud has a silver lining, every silver lining also has a cloud. In this case, the cloud is the IRS. As silly as it may seem, the IRS treats even these exchanges as taxable transactions.

The reasoning is that the exchanges of goods or services have value and, therefore, the government should get its "fair share." Of course the IRS agents won't help you cook the meals or watch the kids, but the government still wants a cut of each trade.

The estimated value of any goods or services you receive must be included as a part of your gross income on your tax form. That value will be added to your total income and taxed accordingly. Can you deduct the cost of any services you provided? Not without a lot of complicated bookkeeping that most homemakers do not maintain. In reality, unless you barter on a fairly large scale it isn't worth the hassle.

Bartering is a good deal, even after the IRS takes its bite. If you're paying for medical or dental care you normally do so with after-tax dollars (with some exceptions). This means, if you pay $40 for a visit to the doctor's office, assuming you are in a 25 percent (average) tax bracket, that visit costs you about $55 in earned income. But if you barter for the service and claim the $40 fee as income, you pay only $10 in additional taxes. Thus you still saved $30 in the exchange.

*What is a man profited if he gains the whole world, and loses or forfeits himself?*

Luke 9:25

## Professional Barter Exchanges

Some $880 million worth of goods and services changed hands through barter exchanges in the U.S. and Canada last year. A barter cus-

> Much ingenuity with a little money is vastly more profitable and amusing than much money without ingenuity.
>
> —*Arnold Bennett*

tomer pays the same fees as a cash customer but pays in "trade dollars," which the seller can bank with the exchange and later "spend" on just about anything imaginable. The exchange acts as a broker and bookkeeper.[1]

On a national and international scale, bartering exchanges do what Miriam is doing on a smaller scale in her church: They provide a common exchange currency and make non-cash trades possible. For more information about bartering agencies, write to the address in Appendix 2.

In general, these bartering agencies are not beneficial to small trade barterers. If you just want to swap services with a neighbor, in most instances you are better off arranging the barter yourself on a small scale at the local level.

Professional exchanges usually charge an enrollment fee, from $60 to several hundred dollars a year, as well as a transaction fee. Very often consumers who use barter exchanges discover that once they submit their goods and services for barter company credits, there is little or nothing offered by the exchange that they want.

Also, if the barter exchange company goes out of business, the credits are lost forever. So if you ever decide to use a barter exchange company, be sure it's well established and reasonably certain to be around when you want to redeem your credits.

## The Illegal Underground Economy

One word of caution is in order: Do not participate in the illegal underground economy. Although many people don't consciously set out to cheat on their taxes, it ultimately ends up that way. Establish your standards based on

> In today's complex and fast-moving world, what we need even more than foresight or hindsight is insight.
>
> —*Unknown*

what God's Word says—not on what is acceptable in the eyes of society.

The illegal underground economy is operating all around us. It is all too easy to get caught up in it when money is tight. The following are a few common examples.

### 1. Hiring undocumented workers.

Several of the cabinet-level appointments made by President Bill Clinton were withdrawn because the people had hired illegal (undocumented) workers and employed them without paying the proper taxes. You certainly can get cheaper domestic help that way, but in doing so you break the law. It's not really worth it financially and, most certainly, not spiritually.

### 2. Paying cash for discounted services.

One day several years ago a man showed up at our home asking if we needed some dead trees removed, which we did. He offered to do the work for far less than any previous estimate we had received, provided we agreed to pay him in cash. The obvious conclusion was that if he didn't have to declare the income he would discount the work. We refused and he left.

> It is being twice right not to yield to one who is in the wrong.
>
> —*unknown*

This kind of transaction is not abnormal today. A lot of business is done in cash so that the taxes can be avoided. But to participate knowingly is the same as committing the crime yourself. If you know someone is cheating and you assist, you are an accessory.

As Isaiah says, *"But your iniquities have made a separation between you and your God, and your sins have hidden His face from you, so that He does not hear"* (Isaiah 59:2). Nothing is worth blocking God's direction in your life.

### 3. Operating a business without paying taxes.

Most Christians would consider themselves honest, and yet many violate the tax laws regularly. One of the most common examples for stay-at-home moms is operating a small business, such as a babysitting service or home product sales, but not declaring the income for tax purposes.

There is no question that our current tax laws punish married couples and, particularly, stay-at-home moms. For working mothers to have to pay upwards of 40 percent of their earnings in taxes is unconscionable. Moms who babysit at home have to cope with screaming kids to earn precious little income and then forfeit up to 40 percent of it to some bureaucrat in Washington, who promptly flushes it down the drain called "entitlements."

But the answer is not to cheat. It is to get involved and change the system (not to mention the politicians).

Use the underground economy to your advantage—but only the legal underground economy.

*Because of this you also pay taxes. . . . Render to all what is due them: tax to whom tax is due; custom to whom custom; fear to whom fear; honor to whom honor.*

Romans 13:6–7

---

1. *Kiplinger's Personal Finance Magazine,* October 1993, p 34.

# Chapter Twelve

# Budgeting Your Time

*"There is an appointed time for everything. And there is a time for every event under heaven"* *(Ecclesiastes 3:1).*

T he principles and techniques employed in time management are deceptively simple.

## 1. Budget your time.

Many people think they're organized and use their time efficiently, but in reality most of us work according to external pressures, with the most demanding things getting done first. It's called the tyranny of the urgent. Most mothers, both those working in an outside job and those working at home, know the feeling well. A screaming child will attract the most attention—and quickly. Unfortunately, as the child learns this principle too, he or she

Time wasted is existence, [time] used is life.

*—unknown*

Money lost can be replaced but time lost is gone forever.

*—unknown*

begins to exercise control.

Many of the stay-at-home moms responding to our survey identified with the questions on time management in their homes. The most common comment was something like, "It seems like I never get everything done now. I don't know how I was able to work and keep a home, but I did."

Most of us can remember a time when we made very little money but we always seemed to get by. Then as the income grew, spending grew to match it and, with double or triple the income, it still seems that there's barely enough to do more than just get by.

The same principle applies to time. When a mother is working, there is precious little "free" time, so she has to budget that time well or face a crisis every single day (as, unfortunately, some do).

Then when she stops working an outside job, that mother assumes she will have all the time she needs to do her housework and child care and still have some "spare" time. After all, she's gaining the 10 hours or so each day she had been spending on the job. But all too often this "spare" time is absorbed, just as the increased income is absorbed.

Beverly shared that when she quit her job she was sure that she'd have time to spare.

*"I had not been an especially disciplined person. Because my job demanded that I show up on time, I had forced myself to become more structured. As I was getting the children ready for school in the mornings, I struggled with guilt over serving them cold cereals and guilt over losing my temper too often. My husband would enter the kitchen just as I was exiting. More often than not, I was shouting at one of*

*the children, who was dragging around. I was
sure they were conspiring to make me late.*

*"After several frustrating years we decided
that I should stay home and raise our children
in a more sane environment. My husband's new
job provided just enough surplus to allow me to
do so. I naturally assumed that all of my frustrations would disappear and I would become this
super mom who had time for the kids, time to
prepare all these meals, and time to do volunteer
work as well, but it just wasn't so.*

*"I found myself constantly running behind in
housework; the kids still rushed off to school
half dressed; the laundry often piled up because I
didn't have time to fold it; and, worst of all, I
still had little or no time for myself. I realized
that not long before I had done all this and
worked as well, but I couldn't remember how."*

Personal disorder
not only wastes money
and precious time; it is
also an emotional bar-
rier to success.
—*Mary and Michael Martin*
(Home Filing Made Easy!)

Beverly's change started when she and her
husband attended a seminar at their church on
the advantages of homeschooling.

*"You have to be kidding," she told her hus-
band. "Home school three kids? I can barely
keep the house straight when they're gone. I
don't have the time—or the patience."*

Beverly's husband was wise enough to drop
the subject and leave it to the Lord.

The more Beverly thought about why she
had come home and what she had heard at the
homeschooling conference, the more she knew
it was God's plan for her family, but she was
even more frustrated by her failed attempts to
organize her days. In desperation she called an
older woman in her church who had helped
lead the homeschooling conference.

*"I want to homeschool, but I just don't know*

*He who abides in Me,
and I in him, he bears
much fruit; for apart
from Me you can do
nothing.*

John 15:5

*if I can do it. I barely get my work done now, with the children in school. I just don't have any discipline."*

I know the "rest of the story," as Paul Harvey might say.

I met Beverly at a conference, where I was teaching on financial management and she was teaching on time management. The same person who had not been able to get her housework done was now teaching other women how to organize their personal schedules. Her methods proved so successful that several companies hired her to help organize their staffs.

Beverly shared that the principles this older woman had taught her changed her entire life. She had struggled most of her adult life with a nagging feeling of disorder. Even her best efforts usually did little more than get her by. What she suffered from was what I call "chronic disorder syndrome." She had allowed little habits to become ingrained in her life until they became routine. We all have them to some degree.

It may be staying in bed that extra ten minutes after the alarm goes off. In itself this is a benign habit, unless your morning schedule is thrown into disarray and panic because you needed that ten minutes. Or it may be allowing your car's fuel level to reach empty before filling the tank because you can't "afford" the time—that is, until you run out of gas one busy day.

As one mother told us, it can be as simple as putting off washing clothes, knowing that there is still one clean towel left—only to discover when stepping out of the shower that the kids used it to dry the dog—before replacing it on the shelf.

Disorganization isn't one big thing. It's an

Why kill time when one can employ it?

—*unknown*

accumulation of little bad habits all strung together.

In *Home Filing Made Easy!* Mary and Michael Martin say that disorganization is a major enemy of personal success. "This seems to be true across all segments of our population regardless of the levels of formal education or income."[1]

Beverly was neither lazy nor lacking in intelligence; she was disorganized. I have found the very same thing in many of the people I have counseled financially over the years. Often those who appear to be slothful and undisciplined are merely disorganized and ignorant (lacking knowledge). If they are willing to learn, they often become some of the best money managers around and, almost always, become the best teachers.

Coach Vince Lombardi of the Green Bay Packers (professional football team) used to say that the most gifted athletes rarely made good coaches. They were so good naturally that success came too easily for them. They had a difficult time relating to the average players. The same principle applies to the disorganized people who learn how to discipline themselves: They can relate to others with the same problems.

At that conference I listened as Beverly told some universal truths about time budgeting that can help anyone in any career field— including stay-at-home moms. I have personally used many of them myself and continue to do so today. I have a close friend who became a wealthy man by teaching these principles to business people.

In truth, people can generally make time for what they choose to do; it is not really the time but the will that is lacking.

—*Sir John Lubbock*

## 2. Write it down.

As I said earlier, I am primarily a visual person: If I can see it written down, I usually will remember it because I think I have a good memory, but I tend to rely on it too much—to my own detriment. So every day I begin my day by writing down the things I need to accomplish, in order of importance. Then I work on the important items first.

There is a very good book entitled *Tyranny of the Urgent* by Charles Hummel (InterVarsity Press 1976) that still holds many truths about our time-crazy society. I recommend it for anyone seeking to order time.

When you prioritize your time, be honest about it. There are only so many things you can realistically accomplish in one day. Concentrate on the important ones, while still allowing some "down time."

I do much of my writing at my office in the midst of a very busy schedule. I used to get frustrated at all the interruptions that would keep me from writing. Then I discovered two revelations: one, interruptions are a fact of life for any busy person, and if you get frustrated about them you will be frustrated most of your life. Second, if I scheduled a specific number of pages I needed to write to meet a deadline, I would be more likely to accomplish my goal. In other words, I avoid the tendency to procrastinate and then "cram."

### 3. Learn to say no!

I have also discovered that much, if not most, of my unrealistic schedule was of my own doing. I hate to say no to people, especially when there are so many good things to do. Some of this tendency is probably ego: I like to be asked to do things. Some of it is naïveté: thinking that I could teach full time, travel full time, write full time, and run an organiza-

*God is not a God of confusion but of peace, as in all the churches of the saints.*

1 Corinthians 14:33

tion—all at the same time.

Instead, what I found was, the busier I am, the more behind I get; the more behind I get, the more frustrated I get; and the more frustrated I get, the less productive I become.

*Be careful how you walk, not as unwise. . . but as wise, making the most of your time. . .so then do not be foolish, but understand what the will of the Lord is.*

Ephesians 5:15–17

Therefore, I have learned to say "No." And you know what? The world just goes on turning anyway. I have long since discovered that I am not God's plan—just a part of it.

## 4. Schedule some "down time."

I find personally that without some daily devotion time I tend to run down spiritually.

If you want to be a successful stay-at-home mom, it is critical that you schedule some down time too. My oldest son Allen and his wife Lauree have six children. She home-schools the children and still has her sanity. How? She schedules their nap times every day and an early bedtime that allows her some time of her own. A one- to two-hour nap in the afternoons is not only good for the kids, it's absolutely essential for the mental health of stay-at-home moms. Also, a seven o'clock bedtime ensures adequate time in the evenings to read and interact as a couple, which is essential to your marriage.

The key to achieving this quiet time is consistency. If you will establish the schedule and stick to it, no matter what, the kids will eventually believe you mean it. That's one lesson all mothers can learn from day care workers: They mean it, and the kids know they mean it.

## 5. Relax.

Being relaxed is not the same as scheduling a quiet time or down time. It means you must learn to live with some things that tend to "bug" you. Excessive/compulsive personalities

167

(High C or Conscientious) tend to drive themselves and others around them to distraction.

If you're going to stay home, with children in the house, things will tend to get messy. Obviously you should require the children to pick up after themselves, but what a young child may think is clean may not meet a mother's inspection. There will be plenty of time to teach them the fine points of cleaning, but learn to ease up a little for your sake and theirs.

My wife and I love to have our grandchildren over (for a day or so). And can they make messes quickly! We have virtually all ages from infants to nearly teens, so we try to set our pick-up standards based on what they can do. We require more from the older children but try to be practical with all of them.

We keep a lot of play things for our grandchildren, and instead of storing them in drawers or boxes we simply keep them in several large baskets in the play areas. All we require is that they pick the toys up and put back them in the baskets before they leave, which even the youngest can do. Having baskets of toys exposed around the house is a real compromise for us perfectionists, but it's worth it for our overall peace of mind.

## 6. Control the idiot box.

One of my pet peeves is mothers who use the television as a babysitter for their children. I'm sorry if you happen to be one, but the net result is a nearly brain-dead generation of kids growing up on the garbage dished out by the most liberal segment of our society: the media.

There are some good things on TV, but you have to pick and choose carefully for your kids and for yourself as well. You can waste endless hours uselessly in front of a television set if

*Bring [your children] up in the discipline and instruction of the Lord.*
Ephesians 6:4

Discipline doesn't break a child's spirit half as often as the lack of it breaks a parent's heart.
—*anonymous proverb*

you are not careful.

If you haven't done so, I encourage you to discover Christian radio. The music usually is uplifting, the programs are beneficial, and you can work while you listen.

In this generation the same principle of wasted time can apply to computer games for kids. Some computer games are great learning tools for children, but others are mind-numbing fantasies that will dull your kids' intellectual abilities. Limit your children's time in front of any video screen—television or computer.

## 7. Organize your personal files.

Often, when I sit at my desk at home with a glazed look in my eyes, it is because I either can't find something very important, or I know I should be doing something but can't remember what it is.

If you also wonder where you put important papers or what to do with the bills when they arrive, you need some organization. One of the best purchases any family can make to help get organized is a file cabinet. If you shop enough garage sales you will eventually find a good used file cabinet for very little money.

Almost every discount store now stocks the office supplies you will also need. You'll need some file folders and filing envelopes. Then it's just a matter of separating your important files into the appropriate categories. Make it a habit to promptly file anything that you *think* you might need later: insurance premiums, tax records, credit card bills, receipts. It is far better to have too many files than to have too few.

I have a plastic file pocket in the front of our budget notebook. All unpaid bills go into that pocket as soon as they arrive. Once a bill is

First radio, then television, have assaulted and overturned the privacy of the home, the real American privacy, which permitted the development of a higher and more independent life within democratic society. Parents can no longer control the atmosphere of the home and have lost even the will to do so. With great subtlety and energy, television enters not only the room, but also the tastes of old and young alike, appealing to the immediately pleasant and subverting whatever does not conform to it.

—*Allen Bloom*
(The Closing of the American Mind)

paid, my copy goes into a folder in my file cabinet. Each utility company, each car, each piece of equipment (refrigerator, stove, washer) has its own file. This has helped to ease my frustration level significantly when I need to locate our records.

## Keep a Good Balance

As important as good organization is, don't go overboard. If you budget your time, build in some slack as well. I have a good friend who is a very busy professional. He said he used to get frustrated when emergencies would arise that threw his schedule off. Then he realized that these emergencies were happening on a regular basis, so he told his receptionist to pencil in at least one emergency per day on his schedule. If perchance he didn't have an emergency one morning, he had an extra twenty minutes or so to relax.

I am a real believer in writing things down so that you can see them. Go to your Christian bookstore, ask for *Home Filing Made Easy!*, or look at the array of daily organizers there; then choose the item that best suits your needs.

*Your ears will hear a word behind you, "This is the way, walk in it," whenever you turn to the right or to the left.*

Isaiah 30:21

---

1. *Home Filing Made Easy!*, Mary E. Martin and J. Michael Martin. Chicago: Dearborn Financial Publishing Inc.

# Chapter Thirteen

# How to Handle Unexpected Expenses

*"Be anxious for nothing, but in everything by prayer and supplication with thanksgiving let your requests be made known to God"* (Philippians 4:10).

A majority of all the stay-at-home moms who responded to our survey listed "ununforeseen financial disasters" as one of their main concerns. That's certainly understandable because it is one of the problems most single-income families face.

Many working women feel that their jobs are a buffer against calamity, and in some ways they are.

The additional income, even if it is being spent, can be included when calculating the family's loan potential. In other words, the second income allows the family to borrow more in a time of crisis. Unfortunately, the additional loans make them more dependent on two incomes. It really doesn't make a lot of sense when you look at it that way.

If a mother's long-term goal is to stay home with her children, she needs to adhere to very stringent guidelines for borrowing to buy anything. The budget guidelines provided in Chapter 14 will help to do that.

Remember this well: Once you borrow to pay a bill, even for an "emergency," more often than not you have committed to a debt you cannot repay. This is especially true if you use credit cards to buffer these emergencies. Open-ended loans, like credit cards, are structured by the lenders to never be paid off. Think of it! If you had your money on loan at 14 to 21 percent, would you want the principal back? Hardly so. You would want just what the card companies want: interest payments only.

## There Are Very Few Real Emergencies

In the vast majority of families, there are very few real financial emergencies. The lack of adequate planning can create some emergencies but, in reality, most of these can be avoided by good planning, provided the available funds are rationed on a month-by-month basis.

*How precious is Thy lovingkindness, O God! And the children of men take refuge in the shadow of Thy wings.*
Psalm 36:7

The decisions you and your family make when you leave the workplace often can make or break your finances later. For instance, if you are living in a home that consumes 40 percent of your net income while both of you are employed, and the decision is made to remain in that home when you leave the workplace, the net cost may rise to 60 percent. Unless your husband's income is in excess of a $60,000 a year, there is virtually no way your budget can balance.

It might initially appear that the budget is

okay because you can make the house payment every month. But just as a nail in a tire doesn't always result in an immediate flat, eventually enough air escapes that the tire sags; then it will go flat, and so will your budget.

The same principle applies to cars, boats, vacations, and any other budget categories. Unless the right financial decisions are made before the income is reduced, financial emergencies will always happen.

The truth is, cars regularly break down, young couples usually have more babies, kids fall out of trees and break their arms, and your utility bill will usually be higher when you're home full time. These and many more irregular events should be built into your budget. If not, then some radical actions are needed.

If your budget is so tight that it is virtually impossible to put aside any surplus to take care of these expenses, then adopt at least one fundamental idea: You will not borrow to pay for them. You must believe that God already has provided what you need and has put it in the hands of someone else.

That's why all Christians, but especially stay-at-home moms, need to be involved with support groups. Often these are the people God uses to meet the "impossible" needs. As Solomon said, *"I have not seen the righteous forsaken, or his descendants begging bread"* (Psalm 37:25).

I absolutely believe that all churches need to be organized and trained in how to meet the needs of their congregations. But others can't help you if they don't know what your needs are, so you have to be willing to share those needs.

Allow me to use a personal example. Not long ago a friend of our ministry donated a car

*The Lord will open for you His good storehouse, the heavens, to give rain to your land in its season and to bless all the work of your hand; and you shall lend to many nations, but you shall not borrow.*

Deuteronomy 28:12

to CFC for us to give away. He even donated the funds to have the car thoroughly serviced. We spread the word to the local churches that we were looking for a needy family that didn't have a good, dependable vehicle. As we all know, there are many such families in every community, but in two months we did not receive one response. Why? Because some Christian in need didn't share that need.

From past counseling experiences, I know that in a community of 100,000, as ours is, there are hundreds of needy families, including single parents and stay-at-home moms. But all too often churches are not involved in actively meeting these needs, so the needy often keep them to themselves.

Several weeks later I met a man who told me that he and his family were without a car during that time and had borrowed beyond their budget to purchase one. I didn't have the heart to tell him that his car went to someone else—but we didn't know about his need.

## *Borrowing Is Not the Problem*

A reasonable amount of credit can be managed by most families, but it must be diligently controlled. For instance, a home mortgage, which is a debt, is not necessarily bad. If you and your family can buy a home at or near the cost of renting one, it makes more sense to buy. You can never pay off a rented home. At least with a mortgage you have the opportunity of eventually owning the home.

Just because you have a 30-year mortgage, that does not mean you have to pay on it for 30 years. If you prepay the principal, even a small amount each month, you can significantly lessen the number of years you must pay and save a tremendous amount of interest as well.

*The rich rules over the poor, and the borrower becomes the lender's slave.*

Proverbs 22:7

In fact I encourage the vast majority of our counselees to concentrate on paying off their homes even before they put money into a retirement account. There are some exceptions, however, and for more detail I refer you to another book, *Debt-Free Living* (Moody Press).

Just remember that there is no good logic for using consumer credit. I encourage you and your spouse to make a vow to use credit cards only according to the following rules.

1. Never buy anything with a credit card that you don't have money in the bank to pay for.

2. Pay off your credit card debt every month.

3. Vow that the first month you can't pay your credit card balance you will destroy the cards and never use them again.

Follow these simple guidelines and credit cards will no longer be a problem.

## Where to Go for Help

Leaving the job force and staying home can seem pretty lonely and frightening if you have no support group, so I again recommend that you join one as soon as possible. If there is no support group in your area, I encourage you to help start one. In Appendix 2 you will find organizations listed that can help you to find or to start a group of your own.

If you have a financial crisis of some kind, there are two primary sources of help available in your community: friends and family. There is actually a third: the government. I encourage you not to use the third unless the first two cannot or will not help.

Using government aid is not unbiblical, it is just highly inefficient and costly. I received many letters from stay-at-home moms whose families were accepting some form of government assistance. More often than not, it was in the form of food stamps, Aid for Dependent Children, and most commonly, Medicaid.

It is a sad indictment of Christianity that hardworking Christian families are forced to turn to the government for help that should be provided by other Christians. With virtually no exceptions, any group of local churches can provide for the reasonable needs of their members. It is simply a matter of caring enough to organize. It is small wonder the secular humanists laugh at us. They hear what we say, but they also see what we do.

Until we find a fix for the sky-high medical expenses many families face, there is little hope for adequate health care for lower income families. It is the law that if a hospital accepts government funding (and virtually all do) they cannot, I repeat, cannot, refuse to treat you or your family in an emergency— with or without health insurance.

If the subsequent bill you receive is too high for you to pay (and it will be), then pay what you can. All the hospitals or doctors can do is report your unpaid portion as a slow-paying account. That will be reflected on your credit report, but remember, you can only do what you can do. God does not hold us responsible for what we can't do—only for what we can but don't. If you commit to repaying the entire debt, you have done all you can.

## Health Care Centers

In most communities across the country there are community-run health clinics that

Experience should teach us to be more on our guard to protect our liberties when the government's purposes are beneficent. . . . The greatest dangers to liberty lurk in insidious encroachment by men of zeal, well meaning but without understanding.

—*Louis D. Brandeis*

*It is better to take refuge in the Lord than to trust in man.*

Psalm 118:8

will provide basic care, including childhood disease immunity shots.

In many communities there are also private clinics run on a charity basis. In our community we have four such clinics: two are tax supported and two are privately run. These can substantially reduce your preventative health care costs. If you use one of the private services you can always volunteer time to help them in return.

## Don't Panic, Pray

I was traveling in my car recently and tuned to a Christian radio station playing a song with the lyric, "God said it and I believe it." That should be the standard by which we all live our lives. Unfortunately, all too often we allow doubts and fears to get in our way.

*He will call upon Me, and I will answer him; I will be with him in trouble; I will rescue him, and honor him.*

Psalm 91:15

There is no problem too big for God to solve, if we believe. That doesn't mean that God will keep every problem away from us, nor does it mean He must miraculously solve every crisis, although I have seen Him do so many times.

Sometimes the problems are for our growth. Other times they are for discipline. Other times we simply don't know why things happen to us. But through it all God is still there comforting us. I have learned that although God never promised to remove every difficulty, He has promised that we can have peace in the midst of them.

Usually it is not the actual problems that defeat us; it is the fear that defeats us.

As the apostle Paul says in Philippians 4:11, *"I have learned to be content in whatever circumstances I am."* So don't let your fears keep you from doing what God has called you to do: be a full-time mom.

177

I'd like to give you portions of some testimonies from women who made the transition from the workplace to home in spite of their fears. They all share a common thread: The sacrifices are worth it.

*I never felt I "fit" into the typical work place. I was always on the "outside" of the office group. Whenever I was in between jobs, I felt very comfortable being at home even without kids. My husband had made it very clear before we got married, that I would not work when we had children. I was overjoyed!*

*"I have found when I have Christian radio, my Bible and chances to pray, I am much more focused on God. I was never able to keep that focus when I worked.*

*"Our family consists of three children (5 yr, 2 yr, 3 mo) and both parents. My husband works full time. He only makes $12,000. We may not have "everything", but we are comfortable and happy! Our children are very well adjusted and know God. You can't get that in day care!*

———

*"After I became an RN, it never occurred to me not to work. Even though my mother and her mother were both homemakers, no one every encouraged me to be one. It always seemed understood that I would be trained to work.*

*"My first child was born 5 years later, and it absolutely killed me to take him to a sitter every day. Still, it never occurred to me that I could stay home and raise him. Five more years passed, and my little girl was born. I continued working, trying to be a "super mom."*

*"We were barely making it on both our incomes . . . my husband never seriously consid-*

He who dwells in the shelter of the Most High will abide in the shadow of the Almighty.

Psalm 91:1

*ered that we could live without my income [but we] both believed that I needed to become a home maker. . . . I gave a month's notice and resigned from my position. I was very surprised at many reactions, but nevertheless I knew I was doing the right thing.*

*"My husband will have no income for the 1st 3 weeks of January, and I have no idea how the bills will be paid. . . . Truly I know [God] will [provide]. Believe me, seeing the smile on my second graders face when I pick her up at school is infinitely more rewarding than [anything in my job]."*

Elaine writes that after her marriage she left her career of nearly 7 years to begin her vocation as a wife by taking a couple of months off. She had planned to work until their first child came. However, circumstances prevented her from returning to work, and because of some health problems, their traveling, and her husband's unemployment, they depleted their savings. Even after her husband began a new job they had difficulty making ends meet. She wrote the following.

*"Returning to work was not a viable option for me. The student loans, medical bills, and an old and frequently in need of repair car would be enough reason to look for a second income. We decided, however, that the financial benefits would never surpass the multitude of other benefits to our son, our marriage, our home and family life that my staying home brought. . . . Garage sales and Thrift shops are our shopping malls, and we found it very possible to do cloth diapers at the laundromat.*

*"We rent an apartment, own one car (7 years old with over 123,000 miles), and don't own a*

TV (by choice). We also began tithing. Evenings and weekends are cherished family times that aren't cluttered with the household tasks that can be done during the week days. I marvel at the miracle of new life and development of our son, and I am blessed with witnessing moment by moment changes.

"Our life is very simple—taking walks, learning the names of wild flowers, reading to each other comprise our entertainment. But with simplicity and prayer comes peace and joy, intangibles we are not willing to live without."

———

*Let us not lose heart in doing good, for in due time we shall reap if we do not grow weary.*

Galatians 6:9

Sydney wrote about her experience.

"In 1985 we had 36 debts (including 4 school loans, car loans, furniture loans, etc.). We made a written commitment not to add any more debt to this list. We cut up our credit cards and began a process of becoming debt free. It was at the end of these 3 plus years that I became pregnant with our first child.

"We had always said that I would stay home to "mother" our children. [This] came just in time. The contract for my job ended on my due date, if you can believe that! I worked up until that day and delivered our son 12 days later. (We now have 3 sons.)

"The wonderful thing is how the Lord has provided for our family. We never once questioned my decision to be a full-time mom. We believe that is what scripture teaches and it's what we believe is best for our children. But, we also knew it would require a change in our lifestyle, as our income would be reduced almost in half.

*And the Lord will make you abound in prosperity, in the offspring of your body and in the offspring of your beast and in the produce of your ground, in the land which the Lord swore to your fathers to give you.*

Deuteronomy 28:11

"We stopped trading cars; we started buying

more of our clothes second-hand and we enter-
tained our family in simpler ways. We tithed,
but we weren't able to do more at that time
[and] thought that was just the way it would
always be. But, we had much to learn about our
God.

"Within the next 2 years my husband received
raises almost double the amount that is the
norm in his company. We were given a washing
machine free when ours broke down. We were
given cash for a much needed vacation. To this
day, a family from our hometown sends us
boxes of clothes for our children.

"We purchased 4 acres in the country (debt
free!). Then the Lord provided an interest free
mortgage from a Christian brother. . . .Our total
giving is now double (on one income) what it
was when we both worked.

"None of what has happened was even
dreamed of a few years ago. What we have seen
our Lord do in our lives is beyond expression.
We have witnessed with our eyes and hearts the
love and power and provision of our heavenly
Father.

"Our greatest difficulty, debt, was used to
open our hearts to God's word in finances and
subsequently to His word in all areas of our
lives."

> If God gives a bless-
> ing, He usually gives it
> in such proportions
> that we don't have
> room to receive it all.
>
> —*Charles Spurgeon*

# Chapter Fourteen

# A Workable Budget

*"Instruct those who are rich in this present world not to be conceited or to fix their hope on the uncertainty of riches. . . . Instruct them to do good, to be rich in good works, to be generous and ready to share, storing up for themselves the treasure of* **a good foundation for the future"** *(1 Timothy 6:17–19 emphasis added).*

I often teach on family budgeting, and I know that in order to develop a workable budget you need a good plan, as well as the proper materials. If we were sitting down to counsel together I would provide a copy of our *Financial Planning Organizer* (FPO), which has all the necessary forms, dividers, and tabs, and also a binder to keep them in. Since we aren't face to face, the best I can do is to encourage you to get a copy and use it to plan and maintain your household budget.

Since you probably don't have one of the Organizers handy, I'll try to share enough information to get you started on a workable budget without it.

The concept of budgeting is really very simple: *You need to be certain that what you spend month in and month out doesn't exceed your income month in and month out.*

You could well say, "That's so simple it's stupid." But, in reality, about half of all families, including Christian families, fail to do this. Most think that by keeping their checkbooks reasonably in balance they have a budget. They do not!

To be honest, most people don't even keep their checkbooks balanced every month. When asked if they balance their checking accounts every month, I have had many people respond, "Well, I didn't bounce any checks last month." That also is not good enough!

## What Is a Budget?

A budget is more than a monthly accounting of what has been spent. Actually it's more than a monthly estimate of expenses, such as home mortgage, food, car payments, and the like. A budget is a plan for everything your family will spend in one year, including all nonmonthly expenditures.

Thus your budget must include irregular expenditures like car repairs, medical bills, annual vacations, clothing—even fluctuating utility costs. If a budget doesn't include all of these things, you easily can find yourself facing unexpected "emergencies" that may force you back into the workplace.

## Steps in Budgeting

There are some simple basic steps in budgeting that will make the process much easier to understand.

The river of God is flowing; it is ready to supply your needs. What else can you want?

—*Charles Spurgeon*

184

**1. Listing Income and Expenses.** Form 1 in Appendix 1 is a one-page summary for income and expenses. If after listing your total annual income and expenses you still have money left over, all you will need to do is go directly to step 5 and start on the account forms. ·

But, if your expenses exceed your income, as the following example shows, some adjustments are going to be necessary.

# MONTHLY INCOME & EXPENSES

| | | |
|---|---|---|
| **GROSS INCOME PER MONTH** | | **$2,083** |
| Salary | 2,083 | |
| Interest | | |
| Dividends | | |
| Other | | |

**LESS:**

| | | |
|---|---|---|
| **1. Tithe** | | 125 |
| **2. Tax** (Est.-Incl. Fed., State,FICA) | | 500 |
| **NET SPENDABLE INCOME** | | 1,458 |
| **3. Housing** | | 589 |
| Mortgage (rent) | 423 | |
| Insurance | | |
| Taxes | | |
| Electricity | 70 | |
| Gas | 20 | |
| Water | 16 | |
| Sanitation | | |
| Telephone | 40 | |
| Maintenance | 20 | |
| Other | | |
| **4. Food** | | 230 |
| **5. Automobile(s)** | | 285 |
| Payments | 140 | |
| Gas & Oil | 40 | |
| Insurances | 60 | |
| License/Taxes | 5 | |
| Maint./Repair /Replace | 40 | |
| **6. Insurance** | | 39 |
| Life | 14 | |
| Medical | 25 | |
| Other | | |
| **7. Debts** | | 90 |
| Credit Card | 90 | |
| Loans & Notes | | |
| Other | | |

| | | |
|---|---|---|
| **8. Entertainment & Recreation** | | 100 |
| Eating Out | 35 | |
| Babysitters | | |
| Activities/Trips | 20 | |
| Vacation | 10 | |
| Other | 35 | |
| **9. Clothing** | | 50 |
| **10. Savings** | | 0 |
| **11. Medical Exp.** | | 20 |
| Doctor | 20 | |
| Dentist | | |
| Drugs | | |
| Other | | |
| **12. Miscellaneous** | | 145 |
| Toiletry, cos. | 19 | |
| Beauty, barber | 15 | |
| Laundry, cl. | 15 | |
| Allow., lunches | 16 | |
| Subscriptions | 20 | |
| Gifts (incl. Christmas) | 25 | |
| Cash | 35 | |
| Other | | |
| **13. School/Child care** | | 0 |
| Tuition | | |
| Materials | | |
| Transportation | | |
| Day Care | | |
| **14. Investments** | | 0 |
| **TOTAL EXPENSES** | | 1,548 |

**INCOME VS. EXPENSES**

| | |
|---|---|
| Net Spendable Income | 1,458 |
| Less Expenses | 1,548 |
| | - 90 |

**15. Unallocated Surplus Income[1]**

[1]This category is used when surplus income is received. This would be kept in the checking account to be used within a few weeks; otherwise, it should be transferred to an allocated category.

**Figure 14.1**

**2. Using a Guideline Budget.** Usually in developing a budget it is helpful to be able to compare your family's spending to another family's spending—someone in your income range. Form 2 in Appendix 1 is provided for this purpose. The data is given as a percentage of Net Spendable Income (NSI); that is, income after taxes and tithes (giving) have been deducted. I use Net Spendable Income because it removes the variable of taxes and giving, which are unique to each family's situation.

The guideline covers income ranges from $15,000 to $65,000 per year because these incomes fit 98 percent of all the families we surveyed. You will notice that in many categories the percentage of Net Spendable Income allocated will not vary significantly by income level; but remember, the actual amount of money to be spent does vary, because the guideline is a percentage of total net income.

The thing you need to keep in mind is that these percentages are merely guidelines; they are not absolutes! The amount spent on any one category can vary family by family. Often the amount will vary by area of the country. For instance, on average, housing costs will be higher for a family living in California than for one living in Georgia.

But what cannot vary is the total amount spent. In other words, your total expenses cannot exceed your Net Spendable Income, or you're going to be in trouble.

When any one category consumes a disproportionate amount, the other categories are going to suffer. If your budget is to work, every category must have some reasonable allocation. An extra 10 percent spent on housing means some other category is going to get slighted.

*Not that I speak from want; for I have learned to be content in whatever circumstances I am. I know how to get along with humble means, and I also know how to live in prosperity; in any and every circumstance I have learned the secret of being filled and going hungry, both of having abundance and suffering need.*

Philippians 4:11–12

If you are still trying to lug along your own resources, stop striving. God doesn't expect you to generate your own energy. Learn to be a user of his ever-ready blessings.

—*Charles Stanley*

I have counseled with many people who thought they could make their budget work by simply eliminating any provision for variables like clothing, entertainment, vacations—even medical bills. Now they might never get sick or take a vacation, but I know they spent something on clothing because I never counseled with a naked couple. Every category must have some allocation, or your budget won't work long-term.

Many of the women who responded to our survey will testify that it is possible to beat the percentages in any one category if you are willing to sacrifice. But, in balance, it is far better to be realistic and allocate some money to each category. Otherwise, the tendency is to spend "blindly" each month.

For instance, if you know there is very little money for vacations, it gives your family something specific to pray about. If God provides the needed funds, it's okay to take a vacation to Disney World; but, if He doesn't, you'll know you need to stay closer to home.

To use Form 3 in Appendix 1, list each area of the family's spending and make the comparisons to the guideline budget. See the following example. Remember, no budget will work unless both spouses are committed to it.

# BUDGET PERCENTAGE GUIDELINES

**Salary for guideline= $25,000 / year**

| | | | | | |
|---|---|---|---|---|---|
| Gross Income Per Month | | $2083 | | | |
| 1. Tithe | (10% of Gross) | ( 2083 ) | = | $ | 208 |
| 2. Taxes | (15.5% of Gross) | ( 2083 ) | = | $ | 322 |
| | | | | | |
| Net Spendable Income | | 1553 | | | |
| 3. Housing | (38% of Net) | ( 1553 ) | = | $ | 589 |
| 4. Food | (12% of Net) | ( 1553 ) | = | $ | 186 |
| 5. Auto | (15% of Net) | ( 1553 ) | = | $ | 232 |
| 6. Insurance | (5% of Net) | ( 1553 ) | = | $ | 78 |
| 7. Debts | (5% of Net) | ( 1553 ) | = | $ | 78 |
| 8. Entertainment & Rec. | (5% of Net) | ( 1553 ) | = | $ | 78 |
| 9. Clothing | (5% of Net) | ( 1553 ) | = | $ | 78 |
| 10. Savings | (5% of Net) | ( 1553 ) | = | $ | 78 |
| 11. Medical | (5% of Net) | ( 1553 ) | = | $ | 78 |
| 12. Miscellaneous | (5% of Net) | ( 1553 ) | = | $ | 78 |
| 13. School/Child Care | (8% of Net)[1] | ( ___ ) | = | $ | |
| 14. Investments | (0% of Net)[2] | ( ___ ) | = | $ | |
| | | | | | |
| Total (cannot exceed Net Spendable Income) | | | | $ | 1553 |
| | | | | | |
| 15. Unallocated Surplus Income[3] | | ( N/A ) | = | $ | |

[1]Note: This percentage has not been factored into the total percentages shown for net income.

[2]Note: Considering the given obligations at this income level, there is no surplus for investing long term.

[3]Note: This category is not part of the budget system but can be used to record and show disbursements of unallocated surplus income.

**Figure 14.2**

Husbands are the biggest spenders in almost every family and absolutely must be a part of any successful financial plan. Under impulse a woman may buy too much food and too many clothes; but, under the same impulse a man may buy a boat, car, motor home, or even an airplane. So please don't attempt a one-person budget. It just won't work.

**3. Preparing for Variable Expenses.** You will need to be sure that all variable monthly expenses have been accounted for. Form 4 in Appendix 1 lists some of the more common variable expenses for most families: eating out, vacations, car repairs, annual insurance payments, medical expenses (including deductibles and co-payments), and clothing. Most of these expenses will not occur every month, but they will occur at some point during the year, and you should prepare for them.

The monthly amount allocated must be reflected in your budget and funded whenever possible. This becomes your surplus account for these contingencies. Probably the single biggest mistake most families make in budgeting is not anticipating and funding variable expenses.

**4. Making Adjustments.** If you find your monthly expenses exceed your monthly income, obviously some adjustments must be made. If the percentages are too far out of line and the deficits are excessive, it may mean drastic adjustments, such as selling a home or a car. I trust that is not the case in your budget and all you need are some minor adjustments and better record keeping. But whatever the case, it's better to know the facts and face them honestly.

No matter what the situation, God can provide. Many of the women who wrote to us testified of God's often miraculous provision. But many more testified of their own discipline and obedience in controlling their budgets.

God is faithful, but He is not some genie in a bottle who can be called out every time we have a need. We are to be good stewards of what we have.

**5. Keeping a Budget.** The actual process of maintaining a budget is very simple. It can be complicated, but only if you make it so. However, let me say again: No budget will work unless both husband and wife are committed to the process.

But I want to issue a caution here to single parents: Unlike two-parent families, in which one offsets the extremes of the other (God rarely puts two similar people together), single parents often lack this accountability.

If you are a single parent, you need to get with another woman in your church who has demonstrated financial discipline and make yourself accountable.

This budgeting system has been used by tens of thousands of families and has proved its worth. It's certainly not the only budget system available, but I do believe it is the simplest and, therefore, the best.

I teach the envelope system of budgeting. It's like keeping your money in envelopes—one for each category.

Each envelope is assigned to a category, such as housing, auto, clothes, or food. When the amounts in the envelopes are totaled, they are the sum of what is available to spend.

It is hoped that some envelopes will carry a surplus from month to month. These are the

*For whatever is born of God overcomes the world; and this is the victory that has overcome the world—our faith.*

1 John 5:4

variable categories we discussed, such as car repairs, annual insurance payments, vacations, and the like. If you spend the money in these envelopes for something other than what is intended, it's likely you'll end up with a crisis when the need arises.

Obviously most families don't want to keep their money in envelopes. It's much too risky and provides too much temptation. Instead, the budgeted funds are deposited into a checking account, and account sheets are substituted for the envelopes. But the principle is the same as with the envelopes: Each account sheet reflects how much is available to spend for each category. And the sum total of all the account sheets is what is in the checking account.

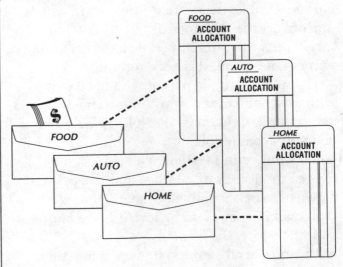

Figure 14.3

Some of your monthly funds, such as entertainment, gas, allowances, and the like, can actually be kept in envelopes, if you like. The cash system is very simple: If you go out to eat, you pay for the meal from the entertainment envelope; then you put the change back into the envelope. That way you always know how much you have left to spend between pay periods. The key to any budget is found in the next step: If you look in your entertainment envelope and it's empty, you stop spending in that category until you get paid again!

The following example demonstrates how to use the account sheets.

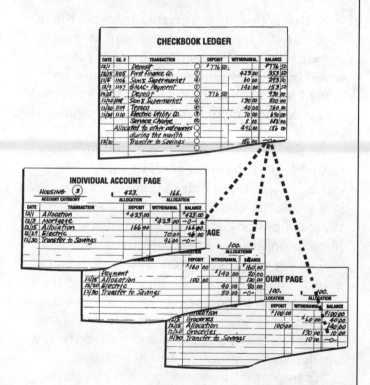

You will find a sample copy of Form 5 in Appendix 1. Due to the physical size of this book, you will need to enlarge the form on a photocopier if you're actually going to use it for budgeting.

Another alternative is to purchase a *Financial Planning Organizer*, with all the forms in it, at your local Christian bookstore. Or, if they don't carry it, call CFC at 1-800-722-1976 or write to our ministry at 601 Broad St SE, Gainesville GA 30501.

*The wisdom of this world is foolishness before God. . . . And again, The Lord knows the reasonings of the wise, that they are useless.*

1 Corinthians 3:19-20

**6. Budgeting on a Variable Income.** Since many stay-at-home moms generate at least some of the family's income through home-based businesses and many spouses are on some form of commissioned sales, it's important to know how to budget on an irregular income.

All too often spending is done on an as-available basis by those with variable incomes—meaning that the money is spent as it is available. That often leads to debt during the slack periods and the danger of a stay-at-home mom being forced back to work.

The key to budgeting on a variable income is twofold. First, always budget based on the lowest realistic income for the year, not the highest. Second, put the funds into a savings account as they are earned and pay yourself a regular salary, month in and month out.

It's important that you look at both your income and your spending as a yearly cycle, not monthly. Otherwise your family will live above its means in the high-income months and then be short of funds in the lower-income months. On Form 4 in Appendix 1, you can figure your variable expenses.

**7. Balancing Your Checking Account.** The last area to cover in this chapter is balancing your checking account. No budget will work without knowing exactly how much you are spending; and you cannot know that unless you balance your checking account to the penny every month, with no exceptions.

Form 6 in Appendix 1 demonstrates how to quickly and simply balance any checking account. There are some basic rules for checking accounts that also should help you to keep the account balanced each month.

### a. Use checks that have a duplicate attached.

This will provide an exact duplicate of every check written. These are available at most banks and also can be ordered by direct mail from several different companies for a small cost.

### b. Avoid the use of automated teller machines (ATMs).

Very often those who use ATMs for cash withdrawals fail to keep a proper accounting of these transactions. If you have budgeted properly, emergency cash withdrawals will be eliminated.

### c. Avoid the use of automatic overdraft protection.

These conveniences promote poor bookkeeping habits and result in additional fees, as well as debt accumulation.

### d. Maintain a minimum balance to qualify for no-fee checking privileges.

The amount of fees you will save with a minimum balance normally is greater than the interest the same amount of savings would earn in most banks.

**e. Have only one bookkeeper.**

It is almost impossible to maintain good records with two or more people writing checks out of the same account. Again, if you are budgeting properly, there will be no reason for emergency checks to be carried by the non-record-keeping spouse.

I also recommend that you do not have two checking accounts. Having his-and-hers accounts are often a symptom of having a mine-and-yours attitude. Both spouses should be involved in the budgeting process, but only one should write the checks and balance the account.

Obviously I have not covered all the details of developing and living on a budget. There are too many issues to cover in one chapter. But if you will apply what has been presented and use the forms suggested, you will be able to establish and maintain a basic budget.

*Know that wisdom is thus for your soul; if you find it, then there will be a future and your hope will not be cut off.*

Proverbs 14:14

A budget is not magic. It won't pay the bills. It won't stretch the amount of money you have. But, what it will do is help you think about what you can spend—and where. And it will provide accurate reports on whether or not you are still on track every month.

It probably will take nine to twelve months for your budget to work properly. Unless you already have a sizeable surplus with which to fund all the budget categories, accumulating a surplus will take some time.

As sure as you start your budget and fund your car repair category by $50, you'll have a $200 car repair bill. But don't get discouraged. Rob the other categories if you have to; then start again. It will work!

*Chapter Fifteen*

# Keys to Success in a Home Business

*"By wisdom a house is built, and by under-
standing it is established; and by knowledge the
rooms are filled with all precious and pleasant
riches" (Proverbs 24:3-4).*

Some 25 million Americans now operate a full-time or part-
time business from home, according to Link Resources, a
New York research firm.[1]

Without question, one of the major business trends in America
is people working from their homes. We see major corporations
now allowing employees to work one or more days a week at
home and most have seen an overall net increase in productivity.

With the technological advances in computerized telephone
interfaces, it is possible to link home and office computers to
exchange notes and letters and interconnect the office and home
telephone systems so that a business caller dials an employee's

To recognize opportunity is sometimes the difference between success and failure.

—*unknown*

*Gird your minds for action, keep sober in spirit, fix your hope completely on the grace to be brought to you at the revelation of Jesus Christ.*

1 Peter 1:13

home as easily as an office extension.

This trend is sure to expand, and by sometime in the twenty-first century I believe at least one-half of all existing office jobs will be home-based.

Just as the transfer of traditional office work has benefitted companies and their employees, it also has spawned whole new opportunities for full-time moms.

Companies are finding great benefits in hiring contract personnel who operate out of their homes and offer their services to several companies, rather than just one. The benefit to the businesses is lower per-hour overhead (no insurance costs, retirement benefits, and the like). The benefits to the self-employed are flexible work hours and little work-related overhead, such as transportation, office attire, and regular child care costs.

Totally removed from the traditional business environment, other home-based businesses have developed over the last several decades whose economic impact is beginning to rival the retail stores. Direct- or home-sales companies now offer virtually every kind of product imaginable.

Millions of people buy billions of dollars of products, ranging from vitamins to automobiles, through home-based suppliers: the so-called direct marketers. Most of these suppliers are part-time workers who need to supplement their incomes—a ready match for a stay-at-home mom.

This chapter is not meant to be a "how-to" guide to starting a home business. It is meant to introduce the idea and direct you to some of the better resources available (also see Appendix 5).

Donna Partow is one of the most knowledgeable people I know in this area, so we asked Focus on the Family for permission to use information from one of her books.[2]

———

You do not need a Harvard Business School degree or an MBA to prosper as an entrepreneur. As a mother, you have accumulated far more skills and abilities than you give yourself credit for. You must rid yourself of the notion that a successful business must be something terribly complex and difficult. Some of the most prosperous businesses are the most simple. And besides, success, like anything else, is in the eye of the beholder.

For you, success may be contributing a few extra dollars to the family budget—or it may be building a full-fledged career. Set your own goals, and when you achieve them, consider yourself a success. But whether you want to establish a Fortune 500 company or just earn an extra fifty dollars a week, there are a few key ingredients that will help you reach your goals. We'll examine nine elements that will enable you to build a successful business.

> The world is always ready to receive talent with open arms.
> —*Holmes*

## 1. Choose a Business You Really Enjoy

Time and time again, home businesses fail because the proprietor selected an endeavor for all the wrong reasons: The woman down the street is starting a typing service and I can, too. Never mind that you hate to type, there's money to be made and you intend to make it. That, my friend, is a formula for disaster.

Choose a business you can pour your heart into, something you can believe in and feel good about. Consider your talents, interests and background, and strive to match these to

> Before you can score you must first have a goal.
> —*unknown*

The ladder of success must be set upon something solid before you can start to climb.

—*unknown*

*Whatever you do in word or deed, do all in the name of the Lord Jesus, giving thanks through him to God the Father.*

Colossians 3:17

*Be diligent to present yourself approved to God as a workman who does not need to be ashamed, handling accurately the word of truth.*

2 Timothy 2:15

your new venture. You'll enjoy your business more and will be less prone to burn out.

## 2. Conduct Thorough Research Before You Begin

Almost all the successful women I interviewed have taken courses on some aspect of running a small business. They have also taken advantage of the free counseling and training services available to them through the Small Business Administration, local university extension services and similar nonprofit organizations.

Don't be a stranger to the library, either. Read up on your line of business and find out how other people in similar circumstances have succeeded. Also, be sure to learn what competition exists in your area. The more research you do before opening your doors for business, the longer those doors will stay open.

## 3. Be Persistent

Your business is not going to succeed overnight. However, if you believe your endeavor is worthwhile and you really want to work from home, all that remains is planning and persistence. In time, you will reap the harvest, but first you must plant the seeds! Don't be content with the current "crop" of clients or your business will soon dry up.

Be willing to invest the time and energy required to continually cultivate future business. Send out flyers to people who have never used your product or service before, and send thank you notes to those who have. Maintain a list of previous customers and mail them a newsletter or updated product list from time to time, just to keep your name fresh in their minds.

Persistence plays a particularly important role in getting started. You may run into obstacles and resistance, and you may be tempted to give up. Knocking on doors and drumming up business day after day can be emotionally and physically tiring. The difference between those who fail and those who succeed often comes down to knocking on one more door.

## 4. Discipline Yourself

There's no doubt that self-discipline is critical for success. To some it comes naturally, while others have to work at it. Of course, the degree of self-discipline required varies according to circumstances. A mother of five who works forty hours a week requires more self-discipline than an empty-nester working twenty hours.

If this is an area you struggle with, don't let that hold you back. Go straight out and buy Anne Ortlund's *Disciplines of the Beautiful Woman*. Self-discipline, more than any other characteristic included here, can be learned. Establish accountability with your spouse, partner or friend, and determine deadlines and checkpoints for progress.

## 5. Work Like a Professional

Your image is an extremely important part of your business. Although it's hard to define precisely what is meant by "professional," there are a number of factors that can work together to ensure you make a favorable impression on your associates and clients.

- *Your appearance.* It's nice that home-based businesswomen don't have to spend a fortune on clothing and grooming supplies. What you wear while working around the house is no one's business but your own. In fact, you can skip the morning makeup

*The Lord your God will bless you in all your produce and in all the work of your hands, so that you shall be altogether joyful.*
Deuteronomy 16:15

Faith, mighty faith, the promise sees, and looks to that alone; laughs at impossibilities, and cries it shall be done.
—*John Wesley (Hymns)*

*The mind of man plans his way, but the Lord directs his steps.*
Proverbs 16:9

To get through the hardest journey we need take only one step at a time, but we must keep on stepping.
—*unknown*

madness altogether if you wish. On the other hand, if you want to set an atmosphere to promote work, you may find that wearing a professional-looking outfit is more inspiring than your old bathrobe and fuzzy slippers. On those occasions when you do come in contact with the public, be sure to present the image appropriate to your industry and clientele.

- *Your office.* If clients or vendors come to your home, your office should be neat, professional and clearly distinguished from the rest of the house. If your office can be reached only by passing through the rest of the house, be sure it's clean and orderly before potential clients see it. As much as possible, try to be available during normal business hours.

- *Phone manners.* Much of your business will probably be conducted over the phone, so make sure you or another responsible adult answers the phone in a professional manner. If your children often use your residence line, it is wise to install a separate business phone unless you can prohibit them from answering the family phone (good luck!). An answering machine is also a wise investment, enabling you to receive calls when you are away from home. Even if you are home but madness is reigning, it's better to let the machine take the call. You can respond once the household is under control again.

### 6. Build a Solid Support System

Over and over again, the women interviewed for this book said one of the keys to their success was a supportive husband, family

*Hope does not disappoint, because the love of God has been poured out within our hearts through the Holy Spirit who was given to us.*

Romans 5:5

Success comes from having the proper aim as well as the right ammunition.

—*unknown*

and friends. Unfortunately, this is something you have little control over—but you can exert some influence. Long before you put up the "Open for Business" sign, work to win the enthusiastic support of your family and friends. Sell them on your ideas and assure them you are serious about your endeavor.

Once things are underway, you can head off potential conflicts by clarifying expectations. Prior to going into business, you may have taken your child's forgotten book to school or dropped off a report at your husband's office. Make it clear that you remain willing to help in a crisis, but by and large your family shouldn't expect you to do all the things you once did as a full-time housewife. (Balance this with grace and mercy, of course!)

If you are moving from full-time outside employment to a home-based business, make sure your family understands that you're still working—just in a different place. In other words, if you worked at a downtown office from nine to five, would your daughter expect you to drop everything to bring lunch money to school? Of course not. Be very careful here or you can end up with the worst of both worlds: the pressures of a working mother and none of the slack usually afforded.

Friends also may have expectations you will no longer be able to fulfill. Perhaps you used to make five dozen brownies from scratch for PTA meetings. Let them know they'll have to settle for store-bought cookies or find another refreshment volunteer. Maybe a special friend is in the habit of dropping in unannounced during the day. She needs to know you're unavailable for socializing during work hours. All of this should be done with tact, of course, so feelings aren't hurt and friendships aren't damaged.

*Be kind to one another, tender-hearted, forgiving each other, just as God in Christ also has forgiven you.*

Ephesians 4:32

Only those who have the patience to do simple things perfectly ever acquire the skill to do difficult things easily.

—*unknown*

*Search me, O God, and know my heart; try me and know my anxious thoughts; and see if there be any hurtful way in me, and lead me in the everlasting way.*

Psalm 139:23-24

On the positive side, you can enlist the aid of your friends. One of my best friends, Beth Riley, serves as my proofreader. This project has drawn us closer and has built mutual respect. Alberta Benster, founder of Accessories by Alberta, which makes children's hair and clothing accessories, has provided jobs for fifteen of her neighbors and friends.

### 7. Cultivate Self-Confidence

When you exude confidence in your skills and services, your customers and clients will be reassured as well. Likewise, if you're unsure about what you have to offer, others are likely to detect this and have the same misgivings.

*Success is a ladder that cannot be climbed with your hands in your pockets.*

*—unknown*

One way to gain confidence is to do your homework and be fully prepared. Be precise and knowledgeable about every aspect of your business. Know your products, customers and competition. You can't afford to wing it. Have your spouse or a friend ask you tough questions about your venture. Also, completing the form  and answering the questions at the end of this chapter will help instill confidence, forcing you to think through all the details of launching your business.

You certainly don't need to apologize for being a home-based businesswoman. What you're doing is extremely important. Think of yourself as an exciting trend setter, paving the way for future generations of mothers.

*The foundation for a better tomorrow must be laid today.*

*—unknown*

### 8. Learn to Deal Effectively With Others

Your business will inevitably bring you into contact with many new people, including customers, subcontractors and vendors. Your ability to deal effectively with them will directly affect your success.

Each morning, you should pray over the

day's events, the people you are scheduled to meet and the unexpected interruptions that will occur. Ask God to give you wisdom and grace as you deal with each one.

### 9. Be Flexible

Days will come when your son or daughter has a 104 degree temperature. Or perhaps it's sunny and eighty degrees and simply too beautiful not to go to the park. As long as you do not behave irresponsibly (e.g., missing a deadline), you can scrap the daily schedule every now and then. You're the boss, so give yourself a day off once in a while.

Flexibility, however, is also necessary to meet the challenges of combining career and family. You may have to postpone a meeting to take your child to the hospital, or you may be forced to bail out of a family outing to meet a pressing deadline. It's all part of being a home-based entrepreneur!

## *Do You Have What It Takes?*

Not every home business is a smashing success. In fact, some are doomed to failure before they begin. The following evaluation tool will help determine if you're prepared to launch your business.

*I love the Lord because He hears my voice and my supplications. Because He has inclined His ear to me, therefore I shall call upon Him as long as I live.*

Psalm 116:1-2

Success comes in cans; failure in can'ts.
—*unknown*

## Home-Based Business Success
## Evaluation Tool

Rate yourself on a scale of one to ten, with ten being the highest.

| Quality | Rating |
|---|---|
| You are persistent when the going gets tough | _____ |
| You are self-disciplined (no boss is watching you) | _____ |
| You are professional (you are your business) | _____ |
| You are imaginative (able to go from idea to product) | _____ |
| You are courageous and willing to take calculated risks | _____ |
| You are patient (it takes time to lay a solid foundation) | _____ |
| You are a planner (able to plan ahead) | _____ |
| You are self-confident (to carry out your plans) | _____ |
| You are resilient (able to bounce back from disappointments) | _____ |
| You have selected a business you enjoy | _____ |
| You have thoroughly researched your endeavor | _____ |
| You have developed a support system to encourage you | _____ |
| You have acquired faith to cope with financial insecurity | _____ |
| You have a sense of humor | _____ |
| Total | _____ |

**Rating Scale**

| | |
|---|---|
| 101+ | What are you waiting for? Go for it! |
| 76-100 | Consider yourself most likely to succeed. |
| 51-75 | Likely to succeed. |
| 26-50 | Give it your best shot. |
| 0-50 | It's probably not for you. |

## What Business Is Right for You?

By far the most important decision you have to make is what type of business to launch. Remember, this is a very personal matter, and what's right for someone else isn't necessarily right for you. Don't make the mistake of leaping into an arena that may be totally unsuitable for you just because opportunities exist.

Donna Kessel, founder of Lynne Designs, Inc., started three home-based businesses before finding one she enjoyed. All three failed, because she went into them for the wrong reasons. "I made decisions based on what was convenient and what I had the equipment to do," she says. "I saw other women making money and figured I could do it the same way."

Today, Donna runs a successful mail-order business manufacturing and selling baby bracelets. She has one employee (who works out of her own home) and earns a very respectable salary working just twenty-five hours per week. Donna strongly urges other women to choose a business they really enjoy: "Do something you've always wanted to do, something you can put your heart into. Don't choose something just to make money."

That's about the best advice anyone can give you. So set aside some time to complete the Skills and Interests Inventory at the end of this chapter. Since being objective about yourself may be difficult, ask your spouse or a friend to complete the Third-Party Analysis Worksheet. By comparing the two evaluations, you will get a good idea of your strengths.

## Developing a Business Plan

You've probably heard the saying "Failing to plan is planning to fail." Nowhere is this more true than business. Once you have determined

*Those who wait for the Lord will gain new strength; they will mount up with wings like eagles, they will run and not get tired, they will walk and not become weary.*

Isaiah 40:31

The great question is not whether you have failed, but whether you are content with failure.

—*unknown*

Keep trying. It's only from the valley that the mountain seems high.

—*unknown*

what business is right for you, the next step is writing a business plan. Don't make the mistake of relying on intuition or vague, unwritten objectives. Get your plan in writing.

An important part of being taken seriously is taking yourself and your business seriously. So be sure to take the extra time to produce a plan that is thorough, accurate and neat. If you plan to remain a one-woman operation forever, it need not be more than a couple of pages. Nevertheless, it's a vital document that indicates to you and all interested parties (financial institutions insurance agencies, etc.) where you plan to go and how you intend to get there.

Before you set about devising your business plan, take a few minutes to answer the following ten questions. They will help guide you through the planning process.

1. What do you enjoy doing with your free time? If you enjoy horseback riding, why not become an instructor?

2. Are any of your hobbies or talents marketable? If you're good enough to play piano at church, surely you would be able to offer at least beginner-level lessons. Do you like to cross-stitch? Why not sell some of your projects.

3. Are you imaginative and inventive? How about writing greeting cards? Or are you more detail-oriented and enjoy repetition? In that case, you could serve as a book keeper for a local doctor.

4. Do you possess any technical skills? Maybe you worked as a systems analyst before the children were born; why not start a computer consulting business?

5. What do other people say you're good at? What do you think you're good at? If everyone raves about your cooking, consider starting a catering business. Offer cooking lessons in your own kitchen. Have you come up with dessert recipes you know are terrific? Why not bake them and offer them exclusively through a local, upscale restaurant? Maybe you've got a million-dollar recipe on your hands. You'll never know unless you try.

> The world does not pay for what a person knows. But it pays for what a person does with what [that person] knows.
>
> —*Laurence Lee*

6. What type of support will be available to you? If you will be working on your own, a modest business venture with minimal investment is best. Perhaps you could do housecleaning two mornings a week. If, on the other hand, you've got a supportive husband and two teenage kids looking to earn extra money, perhaps you can launch an office-services company and get the whole family involved.

> The trouble with opportunity is that it always comes disguised as hard work.
>
> —*unknown*

7. How much time are you able to devote to your home-based business? A mother with two preschoolers has a lot less free time available than a woman with an empty nest. The first may want to plan children's parties on an occasional basis, whereas the empty-nester will want steadier work, such as a mail-order business.

8. How much money do you need to earn? If the family budget is coming up four hundred dollars short per month, five haircuts a week (twenty dollars each) will cover it. But if you've made major financial commitments based on two incomes and a baby has just arrived, you had better aim higher.

> *The laborer is worthy of his wages.*
>
> Luke 10:7

Remember that all successful business stands on the foundation of morality.

—*Henry Ward Beecher*

*What does the Lord your God require from you, but to fear the Lord your God, to walk in all His ways and love Him, and to serve the Lord your God with all your heart and with all your soul.*

Deuteronomy 10:12

9. What are some problems you've solved as a mother? What are some gadgets you've come up with that make life easier? Chances are, other mothers are facing similar dilemmas. Think of the person who came up with the "Baby on Board" sign a few years back. How many times did you think to yourself, *I wish people realized I'm driving slowly because the baby is in the car.* A recent craze was glare screens for car windows. Hasn't every mother tried her own techniques for keeping the sun out of her baby's eyes? Someone has to invent these gadgets. Why not you? If you've got an innovative solution to a common problem, why not develop it into a marketable product?

10. Finally, list all the activities you usually do in an ordinary week (grocery shopping, cooking, etc.). Then analyze each area to determine what skills are involved (writing, planning, communication, etc.). What personal qualities (flexibility, self-motivation) enable you to accomplish these tasks successfully? Now, how can you channel those skills and personal qualities into a business venture?

## Skills and Interests Inventory

1. List five things you enjoy doing with your free time.

_____

_____

_____

_____

_____

2. List any hobbies or talents you have that may be marketable.

_____

_____

_____

3. What type of temperament do you have: creative or analytical? meticulous or carefree? determined or easily discouraged?

_____

_____

_____

4. List any technical or unique skills you possess.

_____

_____

_____

5. List five things other people say you're good at.

_____

_____

_____

_____

_____

6.  List five things you think you're good at.

_____

_____

_____

_____

_____

7.  What type of support will be available to you?

_____

_____

_____

_____

8.  How much money do you want or need to earn?

    Per week _____ Per month _____ Per year _____

9.  What are some problems you've solved as a mother? Have you designed some gadgets to make life easier?

_____

_____

_____

_____

_____

_____

_____

_____

_____

_____

10. List all the activities you usually do in an ordinary week in the "Task" column, and indicate the skills involved in the "Skills" column.

**Task**                                    **Skills Involved**

_____          _____

_____          _____

_____          _____

_____          _____

_____          _____

_____          _____

_____          _____

_____          _____

_____          _____

_____          _____

11. Based on this information, list ten possible home-based businesses that might be suitable for you.

_____

_____

_____

_____

_____

_____

_____

_____

## Third-Party Analysis

Complete the following exercise, evaluating the skills and interests of your friend or spouse. The information will be most helpful if you are as honest as possible.

1. List five things she seems to enjoy doing with her free time.

_____

_____

_____

_____

_____

2. List any hobbies or talents she has that may be marketable.

_____

_____

_____

_____

3. What type of temperament does she have: creative or analytical? meticulous or carefree? determined or easily discouraged?

_____

_____

_____

_____

4. List any technical or unique skills she possesses.

_____

_____

_____

_____

5. List five things other people say she is good at.

_____

_____

_____

_____

_____

6. How supportive of a business venture will her friends and family be?

_____

_____

_____

_____

_____

7. How much time do you think she could devote to a home-based business?

   Per day _____ Per week _____

8. Based on the above, list five possible home-based businesses that might be suitable.

_____

_____

_____

_____

_____

1. *Fortune* magazine, May 29, 1995.
2. *Homemade Business*, by Donna Partow. Copyright © 1992, Donna Partow. Used by permission of Focus on the Family.

# Chapter Sixteen

# Homeschooling

*"To receive instruction in wise behavior, righteousness, justice and equity; to give prudence to the naive, to the youth knowledge and discretion" (Proverbs 1:3–4).*

"Homeschooling restores the home as the center of life and faith, for the child and for his [or her] parents."[1]

Twenty-five years ago, when I first heard of the homeschooling movement, I thought it had to be some kind of a weird cult. How could untrained parents think they could teach their children the educational skills they would need to compete in our technological society?

But no one asked for my opinion (fortunately), and the movement continued to grow. According to the Home School Legal Defense Association, in 1994 there were between 750,000 and 1.2 million children being homeschooled in America alone.

Why has the homeschooling movement literally exploded? Because of the steady deterioration of our public schools and the soaring costs of private schools. Parents are desperate to insulate their children from the permissive attitudes taught in public schools, declining achievement scores, and the total denial of basic religious values at any level in public education.

The educational results of homeschooling speak for themselves. Homeschooled children consistently outperform those who are educated by "professionals."

Beyond the education level, homeschooled children also have been very successful in real life. They now work in every industry, at all levels, and compete very successfully.

Even more importantly, homeschooled children bring their acquired moral and social values into their own families, thus solidifying the moral foundation that our society so desperately needs today. It has been my observation that you will rarely see a homeschooled child using drugs, spouting foul language, or beating up other kids. Apparently discipline and accountability still work if applied properly.

Realistically, homeschooling is not for every parent (or child), but it is an option available to stay-at-home moms. You do not have to be an education "expert" to homeschool. The materials, daily plan, and periodic level evaluations are offered by several excellent resource companies. But the ingredients for success as a homeschooler are determination, patience, love, and consistency.

One of our staff writers, Chuck Thompson, wrote the rest of this chapter, based on a volume of data provided by Connie Brezina, a homeschooler of five and wife of ex-football

The whole art of teaching is only the art of awakening the natural curiosity of young minds for the purpose of satisfying it afterward.

—*Anatole France*

great, Greg Brezina. Greg and Connie now have a ministry to families called Christian Families Today, Inc. in Fayetteville, Georgia.

————

As little as 20 years ago, homeschooling was basically a new idea with a limited following. Like other events of the seventies, teaching children at home represented a break from tradition, and many Americans probably saw homeschooling as just another radical departure from the way things used to be.

But as problems in American education became more severe, and liberal philosophies became more pervasive in the nation's schools, many Christians began to recognize homeschooling as a viable alternative to the public school classroom.

In a paper prepared for the U.S. Department of Education, *Estimating the Home Schooled Population*, researcher Patricia Lines determined that the number of homeschooled children in 1978 was only 12,500.

Homeschooling parents of 15 years ago were truly modern-day pioneers. The variety of teaching materials, conferences, and publications available to them was limited and, to some extent, they were on their own in uncharted territory.

Today, the situation has greatly improved. In *The Home School Market Guide* (Bluestocking Press), author Jane Williams says that homeschooling parents now have access to 148 catalogs, 135 conferences, 146 newsletters, 22 magazines, and 47 stores.

*They act as my accusers; but I am in prayer.*

Psalm 109:4

## *Advantages to Homeschooling*

Many full-time moms may not feel confident about their ability to homeschool their children. But Connie Brezina says the abundance of homeschool teaching materials is just one of many reasons that parents should not be afraid to educate their children at home.

Connie and her husband Greg began homeschooling their four sons 11 years ago while Greg was still an all-pro linebacker with the Atlanta Falcons. Connie listed other advantages of homeschooling for the full-time mom as follows.

### Socialization

Education experts have worried that homeschooled children may be missing important socialization because they are not in age-segregated classrooms with their peers, but studies reveal the opposite is true.

Last year, the *Home School Researcher* journal (Vol. 10, No. 3, 1994) featured an article by Richard Medlin that said homeschooled children as a group have good social skills and a positive self-concept.

Medlin, with the department of psychology at Stetson University, says studies comparing the self-concept of homeschooled children to that of children in conventional schools "have found either no difference between the two groups, or a better self-concept among home schooled students."

### Reduced Peer Pressure

Self-image is one of the most important concerns of young people and, to a large extent, their self-image is determined by how well their classroom peers accept them. If

*Pray on my behalf, that utterance may be given to me in the opening of my mouth.*

Ephesians 6:19

"everybody's doing it," they will be tempted to go along too.

From drugs to alcohol, from premarital sex to dangerous driving, peer pressure has coerced many young people into doing things that otherwise might have seemed harmful and unreasonable.

*He who walks with wise men will be wise, but the companion of fools will suffer harm.*
Proverbs 13:20

Parents can't walk into a school and eliminate the bad influences from their children's classroom.

But Connie Brezina says homeschooling parents can exercise more control over who their children associate with, which is critical in light of Scripture: *"Foolishness is bound up in the heart of a child"* (Proverbs 22:15).

A child's foolishness, or lack of maturity, can be dangerous under the influence of the wrong friends, as many parents have discovered.

## Time

Homeschooling parents may devote more time to correcting a child's weaknesses and encouraging his or her strengths. There's a greater opportunity for family bonding. Thus, homeschooled children may have more respect for what their parents say.

Also, there's an opportunity for dads to be involved in the teaching and for both parents to captivate the primary teaching times listed in God's Word.

*And these words, which I am commanding you today, shall be on your heart; and you shall teach them diligently to your sons and shall talk of them when you sit in your house and when you walk by the way and when you lie down and when you rise up."*
Deuteronomy 6:6–7

## Disadvantages to Homeschooling

Although there are many advantages to homeschooling, parents who want to teach their children at home should be prepared to make some sacrifices and commitments.

### Reduced Time for Outside Activities

Homeschooling parents may have to give up

or cut back on activities outside the home, such as bowling, fishing, golf, or other social events.

## Lack of Accountability

The success or failure of homeschooling depends on parents' willingness to do their jobs, and only parents who are seriously committed to teaching their children at home should do so.

After all, homeschooling parents don't have someone beside them every day holding their hands and encouraging them to take the next step. But they can find motivation through local homeschool associations and by building friendships with fellow homeschoolers. If they need further motivation, they can use a correspondence program with teacher interaction and assignment deadlines.

## Sports

Homeschooled children who want to participate in sports may find limited opportunities to do so; some parents have filled this gap with community activities. However, a number of states have opened the door for homeschoolers to participate in high school sports.

## College

Mrs. Brezina says some colleges don't recognize homeschool diplomas, but many are beginning to recognize them because they see the positive results of homeschooling.

One of the greatest college success stories involving homeschoolers is the Colfax family of California. Three of their children received scholarships to Harvard University.

*I have chosen him, in order that he may command his children and his household after him to keep the way of the Lord by doing righteousness and justice.*

Genesis 18:19

Knowledge always desires increase, it is like fire, which must first be kindled by some external agent, but which will afterwards propagate itself.

—*Samuel Johnson*

# *Homeschooling Research*

## Academic Achievement

In his article for *Home School Researcher*, Richard Medlin noted that homeschooled children are "not educationally disadvantaged" and that their achievement scores are, in fact, "above average."

He pointed to a 1992 study by the National Center for Home Education, which looked at the achievement scores for more than 10,000 homeschooled children from kindergarten through the 12th grade.

The average percentile rank of these children ranged from a low of 65 to a high of 82, depending on their grade level. This compares to a national average percentile rank of 50, Medlin said.

Another major study of academic achievement among homeschoolers was conducted in 1990 by Dr. Brian Ray, publisher of the *Home School Researcher* and president of the National Home Education Research Institute.

Dr. Ray mailed his study to 2,163 families who held membership in the Home School Legal Defense Association. More than 1,500 families (representing about 4,600 children) responded.

Results of the study were described by Dr. Ray in a report titled "A Nationwide Study of Home Education." On average, children in the study scored at or above the eightieth percentile in reading, listening, language, math, science, social studies, basic battery (typically reading, language, and math), and complete battery (all topics included in the overall testing of the student). Again, this compares to a national average percentile rank of 50.

The dictionary is the only place where success comes before work.

—unknown

223

### Characteristics of Homeschoolers

In 1992 Dr. Ray released another home-schooling report titled "Marching to the Beat of Their Own Drum!", which was prepared for the Home School Legal Defense Association.

Combining the results of several studies, Ray listed the "principal characteristics" of homeschooling families. Some of those characteristics are as follows.

*O taste and see that the Lord is good; how blessed is the man who takes refuge in Him!*

Psalm 34:8

- Both parents are actively involved in homeschooling, with the mother/home-maker doing most of the teaching.

- More than 75 percent regularly attend religious services.

- About 55 percent of homeschooling families are in the $25,000 to $50,000 annual income range.

- Children spend three to four hours in "school," and the rest of their time in individual learning.

- The learning program is highly individualized.

- About 65 percent of the students are 5 to 11 years old.

- The "average" parent has graduated from college or at least attended college.

- The average homeschool family contains three children.

### Parents' Education Level Versus Children's Achievement

"Am I educated enough to do teach my children?" No doubt, many parents have asked that question, and some have probably shied away from homeschooling because they believed their education level wasn't "good enough." But in his report, "Marching to the Beat of Their Own Drum!," Dr. Ray notes that a number of studies have shown no relationship between parents' education level and their children's academic performance.

Ray pointed to studies by Dr. Jennie Rakestraw in Alabama and Dr. Joan Havens in Texas, as well as studies that he conducted nationwide and in Oklahoma.

The Alabama, Texas, and Oklahoma studies "found no relationship between parents' educational attainment and the academic achievement scores of their home-educated children," Dr. Ray said.

Weak to moderate relationships between parents' education and children's performance were discovered in Dr. Ray's nationwide study and in a study he did in North Dakota. Similar results were found by researcher Jon Wartes in Washington state.

"Even with these correlations, which do not necessarily indicate casual relationship, the home educated still tended to score above average on achievement tests," Dr. Ray concluded.

## Homeschooling Costs

In his study of 1,500 homeschooling families, Dr. Ray discovered an average expenditure of $488 per student per year, which is small compared to the per-pupil expenditure of public education.

"The statistical abstract of the United States reports the 1993 expenditure per pupil enrolled in public elementary and secondary schools was $5,171," says Jane Williams in *The Home School Market Guide*. "In comparison, $500 per year per home school student might seem a paltry sum. However, if you look at the per-

*You are from God, little children, and have overcome them; because greater is He who is in you than he who is in the world.*

1 John 4:4

centage of that $5,171 that is actually spent on classroom textbooks per child, the statistics take an interesting turn.

"Cleo M. Lorette reported in a 1987 *Curriculum Product News* article . . . that a district may spend only 2.5 percent of the average cost-per-pupil allowance for textbooks. In many districts the percentage is less than one percent. This means that only $130 of the $5,171 would be spent at the optimistic 2.5 percent level and only $52 at the 1 percent level."

As noted earlier in this chapter, homeschool curriculums tend to be very individualized. Thus, expenditures by one homeschooler may vary greatly compared to those of another.

For example, one homeschooler may rely more heavily on the public library than another. One may buy an entire curriculum that includes all subjects, while another buys separate teaching materials for individual subjects. One may do all the teaching, while another uses courses on videotape. And one may buy few materials, while another buys encyclopedias, a computer, charts, maps, and other helpful items.

*He will not allow your foot to slip; he who keeps you will not slumber.*

Psalm 121:3

All of these decisions will affect costs, but according to Connie Brezina, homeschoolers can save money on the following items.

• School clothing.

• Travel to and from school.

• Tuition. This comes into play if the child would otherwise be in a private school.

• Books. Homeschoolers can buy books at used book sales or from people they know. And they may trade books with friends or pass books down from one child to another.

## Legal Requirements for Homeschooling

The legal requirements placed upon home-schoolers vary from state to state, and parents should become familiar with their particular state's laws.

One source of this information is the local school superintendent's office. The Home School Legal Defense Association also has information on state homeschooling requirements. (See the end of this chapter for further information.) Families pay $100 annually for membership in the HSLDA, which operates in both the U.S. and Canada and provides legal representation for homeschoolers.

Unfortunately, homeschooling has faced its share of legal challenges, but since the HSLDA was founded in 1983, many of these challenges have been removed.

"The most clear-cut victory of the past 10 years is that the legality of home education is recognized in every state of the union," said a 1993 HSLDA report. "In fact, 'parental choice in education' has become such a prevalent theme in our society that U.S. Education Department official Michelle Easton in 1992 cited home schooling as 'the ultimate expression of parental choice' in American families."

Membership in the HSLDA now stands at more than 45,000 families and, according to the organization, the vast majority of the legal threats facing its members are successfully resolved outside of court. If a family does end up in court, the organization provides them with free legal representation.

HSLDA members receive a subscription to *The Home School Court Report* magazine, which is published six times per year and features legal news and other matters of concern to homeschoolers.

We must develop a fair appreciation for the real strengths and limitations of government effort on behalf of children. Government, obviously, cannot fill a child's emotional needs. Nor can it fill his spiritual and moral needs. Government is not a father or mother. Government has never raised a child, and it never will.

—*William J. Bennett*
*(1990, Notre Dame)*

*The Lord's lovingkind-nesses indeed never cease, for His compas-sions never fail. They are new every morning; great is Thy faithfulness.*

Lamentations 3:22–23

I have been driven many times to my knees, by the over-whelming conviction that I had nowhere else to go. My own wisdom, and that of all about me seemed insufficient for that day.

—*Abraham Lincoln*

## *Is Homeschooling For You?*

If you've been a parent for several years, you've probably encountered and overcome a lot of challenges in your children's upbringing. Still, educating your children at home may be a challenge you wouldn't dare to face.

Some parents aren't sure they could handle being with their children all day; but, they may be more suited for the task than they realize.

"I think it's probably those very parents who think their kids would drive them crazy who ought to do it the most," said homeschooling expert Mary Pride on CFC's "Money Matters" radio program. "They haven't dealt with a lot of issues in their children's lives, and they're just letting them get worse and worse by shov-ing it under the rug and sending them away from home as much as possible to summer camp and after-school activities. Homeschool-ing provides, if nothing else, an intensive envi-ronment in which you can get to know your children well."

Mrs. Pride was expecting her ninth child when she appeared on "Money Matters." She said her greatest source of chaos during the day does not come from her children but from trying to run a home business along with a homeschool. She receives help from her older children, who are trained to teach and lead.

Connie Brezina, who homeschooled four boys, had concerns about teaching her chil-dren at home until she visited a family that was homeschooling six children.

Mrs. Brezina says the main step parents must take before homeschooling is to ask God about His will for their children's education. Outside of that, they should talk to other homeschooling parents and, if the wife is going to homeschool, she should be certain that she has her husband's support.

"You're going to need his support on those days when you wonder, 'Why did I ever begin to do this?'" Mrs. Brezina says. "There will be days like that."

Other husbands may not be against homeschooling but, at the same time, they're not willing to help. Under these circumstances, Mrs. Brezina says a very determined wife with small children may succeed at homeschooling. But as the children grow older, they're going to need the involvement of a father in the teaching relationship, she adds.

For wives who feel led to homeschool but their husbands are nonsupportive, Mrs. Brezina suggests prayer. "Many husbands' hearts have changed simply by the prayers of their wives," she says. "The husband has gotten just as excited, if not more excited, than the wife about homeschooling." Some husbands have changed their minds after attending a homeschooling conference.

Parents who have decided to homeschool should be certain that they're willing to abide by the laws of their state, Mrs. Brezina says. They also should ask themselves if they have the discipline and willingness to sacrifice what the job will require.

Mrs. Brezina notes that when parents begin homeschooling, they should remember God's provision and seek His help on the bad days. She has been greatly encouraged by 2 Timothy 1:7, *"For God has not given us a spirit of timidity, but of power and love and discipline."* In addition, she says Ephesians 3:20 reminds her that God is able to do *"exceeding abundantly beyond all that we ask or think."*

Education commences at the mother's knee, and every word spoken within the hearsay of little children tends toward the formation of character.

*—Hosea Ballou*

229

## Getting Started

Under ideal circumstances, parents who want to homeschool will make that decision before their children reach school age. They will read and learn as much as possible about homeschooling before their children's education begins.

But not all parents have this luxury. Their children already are in school and they have just realized they need to begin homeschooling. For them, the best course of action is to do as much research as time will permit.

Connie Brezina also recommends talking to other homeschooling parents with children the same age, to get their opinion about the particular curriculum they are using.

"You can get a wealth of information from mothers and fathers who have already tried some of these curriculums," she says, noting that parents may obtain information on various curricula at curriculum fairs. State homeschool organizations can provide dates of curriculum fairs.

Review publications also can help you with your curriculum choices. These include *The Big Book of Home Learning* and *Pride's Guide to Educational Software*, by Mary Pride, and the *Christian Home Educator's Curriculum Manual*, by Cathy Duffy.

Mrs. Brezina suggests picking up various catalogs at curriculum fairs and studying them at home. She warns against buying too much too fast, however. "Most new homeschoolers think they need more material than they actually can cover."

Some curricula are very structured and provide lesson plans for every day. They tell you which words to write on the blackboard and which words to study. "If you try to follow

Let our children grow tall, and some taller than others if they have it in them to do so.
—*Margaret Thatcher* (1975)

Training is everything. The peach was once a bitter almond; cauliflower is nothing but cabbage with a college education.
—*Mark Twain*

everything you'll never get it done," Mrs. Brezina says.

"You have to pick and choose what's appropriate for your child. For example, when children know their vocabulary words, it's not necessary for them to write those words every day."

At the other end of the scale are flexible curricula that require creativity and decision making on the part of the parents.

After selecting a curriculum, Mrs. Brezina advises parents to (1) buy a lesson plan book, which will establish a plan for what their child will be covering in the upcoming school year, and (2) obtain a scope and sequence, which will detail how much material should be covered in a particular year. These may be obtained from some curriculum dealers or from the local school superintendent's office.

## Conclusion

Mary Pride once noted that the decision to homeschool involves both spiritual conviction and academic conviction. Thus, for many parents, homeschooling is an opportunity to not only give their children a good education but pass down the biblical moral standards on which our nation was founded.

As I've shown in this chapter, homeschooling involves challenges and decisions. It demands sacrifices and offers rewards. But the major factor in your decision to homeschool should be God's leading. After all, if homeschooling is His will for your children, His provision is sufficient to meet the challenges you will face.

*Thanks be to God, who always leads us in His triumph in Christ, and manifests through us the sweet aroma of the knowledge of Him in every place. For we are a fragrance of Christ to God.*

2 Corinthians 2:14–15

*Age should speak, and increased years should teach wisdom.*

Job 32:7

1. *Schooling Choices: An Examination of Private, Public, & Home Education*, Gregg Harris (Editor, H. Wayne House), Portland, OR: Multnomah 1988.

## Addresses

- National Home Education Research Institute. This non-profit organization was founded by Dr. Brian Ray, associate professor of science and education at Western Baptist College in Salem, Oregon. NHERI publishes the scholarly journal *Home School Researcher* and *The Home Education Research Report*, which are written in nontechnical language. NHERI's catalog offers research reports, fact sheets, books, a video, and audio cassettes. Write to: National Home Education Research Institute, Western Baptist College, 5000 Deer Park Dr SE, Salem, OR 97301.

- Home School Legal Defense Association, PO Box 159, Paeonian Springs, VA 22129.

- Christian Families Today. This ministry, founded by Greg and Connie Brezina, publishes a monthly newsletter and presents seminars on parenting and homeschooling. Write to Christian Families Today, 200 Providence Rd, Fayetteville, GA 30214-2844.

## Correspondence Courses

The American School (8th - 12th grades)
850 E 58th St
Chicago IL 60637
312-947-3300

Division of Continuing Studies (gives H.S. diploma)
Dept of Independent Study
University of Nebraska
269 Nebraska Center for Continuing Education
Lincoln NE 68583-0900

These courses vary in cost from approximately $600 to $800 per year.

## Catalogs

A Beka Book—1-800-874-2352

Bob Jones University Press—1-800-845-5731

## Resources—Check your local library.

*Better Late Than Early*—Dr. Raymond Moore
(don't start homeschooling too early)

*Christian Home Education Curriculum Manual*—Cathy Duffy
(how-to for elementary level)

*Christian Home Education Curriculum Manual*—Cathy Duffy
(how-to for junior/senior high school level)

*Christian Homeschool, The*—Greg Harris

*Every Day in Every Way*—Cynthia Hallay/Faraday Burditt
(Fearon Teachers' Aids)

*For the Children's Sake*—Susan Schaeffer McCauley
(philosophy of education)

*Home Grown Kids*—Dr. Raymond Moore
(examples of kids)

*Home Spun Schools*—Dr. Raymond Moore
(examples of homeschooling families)

*Home Style Teaching*—Dr. Raymond Moore
(how to begin)

*Homeschool Burnout*—Dr. Raymond Moore
(encouragement)

*Homeschooling Father, The*—Michael Farris

*Homeschooling for Excellence*—Kolfax

*Never Too Early*—Doreen Claggett

*Right Choice, The*—Chris Klicka
(pros and cons of homeschooling)

*What the Bible Says About Child Training*—Richard Fugate
(basic biblical principles in parenting)

*You Can Teach Your Child Successfully*—Ruth Bee Chick
(how-tos)

## State Home School Organizations

**Alabama** • Christian Home Education Fellowship, Box 563, Alabaster 35007 (205) 664-2232

**Alaska** • Alaska Private & Home Education Association, Box 141764, Anchorage 99514 (907) 696-0641

**Arizona** • Arizona Families for Home Education, Box 4661, Scottsdale 85261 (602) 941-3938

**Arkansas** • Arkansas Christian Home Education Association, Box 4025, N Little Rock 72190 (501) 758-9099

**California** • Christian Home Education Association, Box 2009, Norwalk 90651 (800) 564-2432

**Colorado** • Christian Home Education, 1015 S Gaylord #226, Denver 80209 (303) 388-1888

**Connecticut** • The Education Association of Christian Homeschoolers, 25 Field Stone Run, Farmington 06032 (800) 205-7844

**Delaware** • Delaware Home Education Association, Box 1003, Dover 19903, (302) 653-6878

**Florida** • Florida at Home, 4644 Adamson St, Orlando 32804 (407) 740-8877

**Georgia** • Georgia Home Education Association, 245 Buckeye Ln, Fayetteville 30214 (404) 461-3657

**Hawaii** • Christian Homeschoolers, 91-824 Oama St, Ewa Beach 96706 (808) 689-6398

**Idaho** • Idaho Home Educators, Box 1324, Meridian 83680 (208) 323-0230

**Illinois** • Illinois Christian Home Educators, Box 261, Zion 60099 (708) 670-7150

**Indiana** • Association of Home Educators, 1000 N Madison Ave #S-2, Greenwood 46142, (317) 865-3013 X7000

**Iowa** • Network of Christian Home Educators, Box 158, Dexter 50070 (800) 723-0438, out-of-state (505) 830-1614

**Kansas** • Christian Home Education Confederation, Box 3564, Shawnee Mission 66203

**Kentucky** • Christian Home Educators, 691 Howardstown Rd, Hodgenville 42748 (501) 358-9270

**Louisiana** • Christian Home Educators Fellowship, Box 74292, Baton Rouge 70874 (504) 769-5541

**Maine** • Homeschoolers of ME, HC 62 Box 24, Hope 04847 (207) 763-4251

**Maryland** • Association of Christian Home Educators, Box 3964, Frederick 21705 (301) 663-3999

**Massachusetts** • Homeschool Organization of Parent Educators, 15 Ohio St, Wilmington 01887 (508) 658-8970

**Michigan** • Information Network for Christian Homes, 4934 Cannonsburg Rd, Belmont 49306 (616) 874-5656

**Minnesota** • Association of Christian Home Educators, Box 188, Anoka 55303 (612) 753-2370

**Mississippi** • Home Education Association, 109 Reagan Ranch Rd, Laurel 39440 (601) 649-6432

**Missouri** • Association of Teaching Christian Homes, 307 E Ash St #146, Columbia 65201 (314) 443-8217

**Montana** • Coalition of Home Education, Box 43, Galatin Gateway 59730 (406) 587-6163

**Nebraska** • Christian Home Educators Association, Box 57041, Lincoln 68505 (402) 423-4297

**Nevada** • Home Education and Righteous Training, Box 42264, Las Vegas 89116 (702) 593-4927

**New Hampshire** • Christian Home Education, Box 961, Manchester 03105 (603) 569-2343

**New Jersey** • Education Network of Christian Home Schoolers, 65 Middlesex Rd, Matawan 07747 (908) 583-7128

**New Mexico** • Christian Home Educators, 5749 Paradise Blvd NW, Albuquerque 87114 (505) 897-1772

**New York** • Loving Education at Home, Box 332, Syracuse 13205 (315) 468-2225

**North Carolina** • Home Education, 419 N Boyian Ave, Raleigh 27603 (919) 834-6243

**North Dakota** • Home School Association, 4007 N State St, Bismarck 58501 (701) 223-4080

**Ohio** • Christian Home Education, Box 262, Columbus 43216 (800) 274-2436

**Oklahoma** • Christian Home Education Fellowship, Box 471363, Tulsa 74147 (918) 583-7323

**Oregon** • Christian Home Education Association Network, 2515 NE 37th, Portland 97212 (503) 288-1285

**Pennsylvania** • Christian Home School Association, Box 3603, York 17402 (717) 661-2428

**Rhode Island** • Guild of Home Teachers, Box 11, Hope 02831 (401) 821-1546

**South Carolina** • Home Educators Association, Box 612, Lexington 29071 (803) 951-8960

**South Dakota** • Home Educators Are Real Teachers, Box 528, Black Hawk 57718 (605) 348-2816

**Tennessee** • Home Education Association, 3677 Richbriar Ct, Nashville 37211 (615) 834-3529

**Texas** • Home-Oriented Private Education, Box 59876, Dallas 75229 (214) 358-2221

**Utah** • Christian Homeschoolers, Box 3942, Salt Lake City 84110 (801) 394-4156

**Vermont** • Christian Home Educators of Vermont, 2 Webster Ave, Barre 05641 (802) 476-8821

**Virginia** • Home Education Association, Box 1810, Front Royal 22630 (703) 635-9322

**Washington** • Association of Teaching Christian Homes, N 2904 Dora Rd, Spokane 99212 (509) 922-4811

**West Virginia** • Christian Home Education, Box 8770, S Charleston 25303 (304) 776-4664

**Wisconsin** • Christian Home Education Association, 2307 Carmel Ave, Racine 53405 (715) 637-5127

**Wyoming** • Homeschoolers of Wyoming, Box 926, Evansville 82636 (307) 237-4383

# Chapter Seventeen

# Some Comments from Kids

*"You shall therefore impress these words of mine on your heart and on your soul . . . and you shall teach them to your sons, talking of them when you sit in your house and when you walk along the road and when you lie down and when you rise up"*
*(Deuteronomy 11:18–19).*

O utside of each other, a couple's greatest blessing in this world is their children. But too often, these blessings are ignored because of the focus of the pressures of everyday life.

To provide the material things they think their kids "need," all too often parents overwork themselves, which results in unnecessary stress, conflict with each other, and emotional neglect of the very ones they are trying to provide for.

We have discussed the economic value of a wife and mother but, in reality, perhaps no one but a stay-at-home child can really appreciate the value of a stay-at-home mom. Too often the recipient of these sacrifices doesn't understand how valuable a full-time mom is. But those who spend any portion of their young lives in day care appreciate how valuable mom is. Only a mother can love like a mother.

This chapter contains comments from two groups: grown children whose mothers stayed home to raise them and young children still living at home with full-time moms.

At the end of this chapter is a testimony from a young woman who looks back on what she sees as the benefits of having her mom at home. This testimony is particularly touching for me because I have watched Elisa mature from a child to a teen and now to an adult. She works in our organization, where her father has ministered for nearly a decade. She is a great example of what parents would like their children to become.

### Tom, age 27

When Mr. Burkett asked me to comment on my mother, I had mixed emotions. My mother was herself an abused child and always had difficulty showing us love. I know she did love us but just had a hard time relating to others.

She worked most of my childhood, which at the time was okay by me because she yelled a lot.

I was a poor student in high school, which caused my parents a lot of grief, especially since all of my teachers told them I had the ability but wouldn't concentrate.

In the eighth grade I had been diagnosed with dyslexia and was sent to a "special education" school. This turned out to be a place for disruptive kids and I went from bad to worse. One of my mother's friends told her about homeschooling and how good it was for kids with learning disabilities.

Mom quit her job and started homeschooling me. Our vacations stopped, eating out stopped, and the car always seemed to be broken down, but my grades went up.

I could never play sports in school because I was always academically ineligible, but mom put me in the city soccer program. I graduated from high school (at home) with nearly an A average and scored 1200 on the SAT. That earned me a scholarship to a great college.

I now have my master's degree and will shortly have my PhD. I owe it all to a mother with the courage to overcome her own fears and become a stay-at-home mom.

### Mandy, age 10

I like having my mommy at home. She's homeschooling me, and I like reading. She plays games with me and we go places together. I like to hold my little brother, and mommy lets me take care of him. Sometimes she cooks a special treat called "mommy's surprise." It's great.

### Marci, age 17

My mom and dad are the greatest. My mom worked for a while when daddy didn't make much money, but she quit to be home with us and he makes a lot now.

I didn't really like being homeschooled because I wanted to be with my friends, so my mom and dad let me go to public school when I was 15.

I did some really dumb things that year and got pregnant. My parents supported me and I had my baby last year. Mom was there beside me all the time and now is helping me to finish high school at home.

I hope to go on to college one day and then

*Observe the commandment of your father, and do not forsake the teaching of your mother; bind them continually on your heart.*

Proverbs 6:20

A book that is shut is but a block.

—*unknown*

*Deny ungodliness and worldly desires. . .live sensibly, righteously and godly in the present age.*

Titus 2:12

get married. I know I will stay home with my kids and help them avoid making the mistakes I made.

### *Toby, age 11*

If mom was at work, we'd have to go to school [Toby and his two brothers are home-schooled]. We'd have to go to a baby sitter or something. If we got hurt, mom wouldn't be there. She'd have to break away from work a lot.

I've learned a lot about God from mom. In public school, it probably would be the opposite. Your mom is someone that you can trust. If we have problems, she'll come and talk to us a lot.

### *Joanie, age 33*

*It is the living who give thanks to Thee, as I do today; a father tells his sons about Thy faithfulness.*

Isaiah 38:19

Mom quit work six months before I was born. It was comforting to know that she would be there after school and I didn't have to come home to an empty house. She always had cookies or some other snack ready for us when we got home. It means a lot to have mom at home, and you don't realize it until you have children of your own. If I had problems, she was there to talk with me, and she was always there to help me with my homework.

### *Tiffany, age 15*

Having mom at home makes the family seem closer. Being at home allows a mom to develop a good relationship with her children. If she doesn't develop a good relationship with them while they're young, how will she be able to develop a good relationship with them when they grow older? This relationship is impor-tant, especially for a girl.

## Alice, age 22

My mother worked until I was about nine. Then, when she had my brother, she decided to quit her job and stay home.

I remember the first year or so as great fun. She would meet me at the bus stop and always had fresh baked cookies or something else ready when I got home.

My mother is vivacious and outgoing and is always a lot of fun to be around, so I looked forward to coming home every day and I loved summers with her.

But as time went by, she got more and more involved with church activities, the women's club, the book society, and so on. She was chairperson of nearly every committee in our community. From the time I was about 12, I rarely saw her, except at night. I became the stand-in mother and was expected to take care of my brother. After school, cleaning the kitchen, fixing dinner, washing the clothes, and a variety of other housewifely chores were mine, while she "helped" the community.

I grew very resentful because I lost out on a lot of my youth. Until I became a Christian, two years ago, I rarely talked with my mother. When she wanted to be friends with her adult daughter, I had totally shut her out of my life.

We are now friends, but I don't have great memories of my stay-at-home mother.

## Tyler, age 14

My mom has been home most of my life. She worked when I was very little, but that was a long time ago. She takes us places we need to go, for sports or other activities, so we don't have to carpool with someone else. Because mom is always home, I've always got someone to talk to.

Those who apply themselves too closely to little things become incapable of great things.

*—unknown*

*You were formerly darkness, but now you are light in the Lord; walk as children of light (for the fruit of the light consists in all goodness and righteousness and truth), trying to learn what is pleasing to the Lord.*

Ephesians 5:8–10

### Dana, age 14

My mother has never worked. My father has always made enough money to take care of us. She likes to sleep late so we always work together to fix our own breakfast and get ourselves ready for school.

I remember my early years without a lot of fond memories. My dad would get angry when he came home and dinner wasn't ready or the house was a mess. As I got older, mother would make me do all the work while she watched her soap operas. We fussed a lot because I didn't think she was taking good care of my brother.

She's trying to be a better mom now, but I don't think she knows how. Our grandmother did everything for her when she was growing up and she says mom never learned to be a responsible adult. That may be but I wish we hadn't had to pay for it.

### Brittany, age 8

Mommy and I do math and reading, but I really like science. It's fun. Sometimes we play a money game. It's about math, and you have to add things up. We play Monopoly too. When I get hurt, mommy bandages me up, but I don't usually get hurt. My favorite thing for mommy to cook is lasagna.

### Jimmy, age 5

I like having mommie home. She sleeps with me and we play dinosaurs, animals, and stuff. If I get hurt she puts a Bandaid on me and takes good care of me.

### Craig, age 26

My mother was a stay-at-home from the time I was born. She was there to take care of

*How blessed is everyone who fears the Lord, who walks in His ways. Your wife shall be like a fruitful vine, within your house, your children like olive plants around your table.*

Psalm 128:1,3

my older sister and me, and I have pleasant memories of my childhood.

My parents were divorced when I was six years old and mom took my sister and me to live in another town.

I went to school just one block from where we were living, and I can remember that when I would come out of the school I could look and see her standing on our front porch, and I really liked that. I guess seeing her there made me feel more secure.

Later, we moved to another town, but she found a job she could do at home, so she was able to take us to school, pick us up, attend the parent-teacher meetings, the school activities, and be room mother, as well as being a den mother when I was in Webelos and my sister was in Brownies.

We were in junior high before Mom got a job that took her away from home so, for the first time, she wasn't there when my sister and I got home from school, but by then we were old enough to stay alone for a little while. It gave us a chance to do our homework, and sometimes we even had dinner ready when she got home from work.

*They shall be My people, and I will be their God; and I will give them one heart and one way, that they may fear Me always, for their own good, and for the good of their children after them.*

Jeremiah 32:38–39

I know that it is much better for a mother to be at home with her children, if it is at all possible, and that is what my wife and I plan for our children.

## *Elisa, age 19*

If you're considering whether to be a stay-at-home mom or a working mom, first ask yourself what the definition of a "mom" is.

Being the daughter of a mom who stayed home throughout my childhood, my definition would not be someone I hardly saw and scarcely knew, who showed me her love by giv-

*My cup overflows. Surely goodness and lovingkindness will follow me all the days of my life, and I will dwell in the house of the Lord forever.*

Psalm 23:5–6

ing me a better lifestyle or more possessions.

I can remember my mother by the memories of working side by side in the garden, her helping me with homework, teaching me things I would someday need to know [Elisa was homeschooled], and being there when I needed her.

Even though I took it for granted then, I look back now and see her selfless devotion. She gave up material goals and career opportunities to be there for me. She gave me her love in place of things, and she let me know I was more important than anything else.

I was special enough for her to give up all else to be a full-time mother, not just be my mother when she had an available time slot for me. I was her priority.

———

All parents need to ask themselves how they want to be remembered by their children. Ask yourself whether you want to reinforce your own children, instill in them your beliefs, and bring them up in the way they should go, or let someone else do it for you.

Obviously many mothers have found ways of doing this, even while working outside their homes. But, in large part, the majority of working mothers sacrifice some or all of their family goals in order to work.

It's a tough world for kids, and it's going to get a lot tougher. They will need all the support they can get to avoid the pitfalls Satan has skillfully laid for them.

I have tried from the beginning of this project to remain as unbiased as possible, but I am biased. I understand the negatives of some stay-at-home moms, and the positives of a second income, but weighed in the balance I believe the scale tips decidedly toward full-time moms. That pattern has been established and proved for thousands of years: the working mother is a new idea. Thus far the results look pretty discouraging.

My advice for those who are thinking about becoming stay-at-home moms: When you are sure, do it! When you are in doubt, do it!

Positive self-worth and godly character are very important to your children. Maybe they will get this outside the home, but are you willing to take the chance? Your children only have one childhood and you only get one chance.

*The lovingkindness of the Lord is from everlasting to everlasting on those who fear Him, and His righteousness to children's children, to those who keep His covenant, and who remember His precepts to do them.*

Psalm 103:17–18

# Chapter Eighteen

# Tips from Stay-at-Home Moms

*"Through presumption comes nothing but strife, but with those who receive counsel is wisdom" (Proverbs 13:10).*

One definition of presumption is to take something for granted. In the case of a working mom, a couple may take it for granted that if she simply quits her job, the transition from office to home will be a smooth one.

But, as mentioned so many times before, the decision to leave the workplace should never be a hasty decision. Like other major decisions, it should be made patiently, leaving time for things like praying, planning and, as the above Scripture says, seeking the counsel of others (other stay-at-home moms).

Just in case you don't know any stay-at-home moms well enough to seek their counsel, this chapter focuses on input from

What makes us discontented with our condition is the absurdly exaggerated idea we have of the happiness of others.

—*unknown*

mothers who left the workplace to devote more time to their families. When asked what advice they would give to other women planning to return home, each responded with a slightly different suggestion; but they all had a common thread: prayer and planning.

Their advice is an opportunity for you to learn without repeating mistakes. I trust you will be strengthened by their encouragement and will benefit from learning what has made their lives easier.

## Two Key Mistakes You Want to Avoid

### Failing to Seek God's Will

Above everyone else, Christians are accountable to God. God's Word says, *"Keep seeking the things above, where Christ is, seated at the right hand of God. Set your mind on things above, not on the things that are on the earth"* (Colossians 3:1–2).

Most Christians acknowledge that it's important to operate according to God's wisdom and His timetable. But when a mother is eager to be home with her children, this principle is easy to violate.

For Heather, leaving work was a mistake because it was done according to her timetable, not God's. "Make very sure it's both the will and timing of God," Heather advises women today. "I've left the workplace when it wasn't the will of God or the right time, and I've left when it was, and there's definitely a difference."

Once a couple has established that having mom at home is God's will, they should continue to consult Him on all the follow-up decisions, Heather says. She also urges couples to set goals to ensure that the transition from office to home goes smoothly. One of Heather's goals was to be gainfully employed at home.

Today, she operates a successful home business and still has plenty of time for her children during their formative years. "[The business] is doing awesomely!" she says. "We're depending on the Lord, He's building it for us, and it's going great."

### Failing to Get Your Husband's Approval

The vast majority of the women we surveyed said that having their husband's support was critical. Those who failed to gain this support said the resulting discontent in their marriages negated virtually all the benefits of being at home.

Staying at home will require some sacrifices, and if a husband is not willing to make those sacrifices, the resulting tension can undermine a marriage.

Because of her enthusiasm to be a stay-at-home mom, Simone assumed she had her husband's approval to quit her job and do babysitting to make up for the lost income from her job, but she was wrong.

She said, "I thought that my husband agreed, and he said that it was okay. But after I started a business in my home it didn't work out. At that time I was doing child care. He didn't like people coming and going 11 hours a day, whereas it didn't bother me."

As a result of her marital friction, Simone had to stop keeping children in her home. Today, she's back in the workplace—somewhat discouraged and underpaid.

*The land on which your foot has trodden shall be an inheritance to you and to your children forever, because you have followed the Lord my God fully.*

Joshua 14:9

Look for a thing until you find it and you'll not lose your labor.

—*unknown*

If you get up one time more than you fall you will make it through.

—*unknown*

*Encouragement from*
*Stay-at-Home Moms*

### Stay Focused on Why You Are Home

Since the beginning of time, mothers have played a key role in world events, both good and bad, through the influence they exercised on their children. Two examples of mothers' influence from the Bible are the wicked queen Athaliah and the godly mother Hannah.

Athaliah counseled her 22-year-old son, King Ahaziah, to "do wickedly" (2 Chronicles 22:3), and only one year after he took the throne, he was executed. In contrast, Hannah dedicated her son Samuel to the service of the Lord. Not surprisingly, he became a great prophet. Two books of the Bible are dedicated to his life's work.

Stay-at-home moms must never lose sight of the tremendous influence they can exercise in their children's lives, even though Satan will try to discourage and defeat them. In Monica's case, financial struggles have threatened to distract her from full-time mothering, but she hasn't lost sight of her primary goal: being the best mother possible.

"You have to stay focused on why you're at home and why you're the best person to take care of your children. There are financial struggles, but God is sufficient. He never leaves us. He's always provides.

"You cannot find anybody who can replace you or believes just like you do. You can look and look, but there will always be something that's just a little bit different."

### Don't Be Ashamed of Your Profession

Since being a stay-at-home mom is not regarded as a "high calling" in our society, a

*Be of sober spirit, be on the alert. Your adversary, the devil, prowls about like a roaring lion, seeking someone to devour. But resist him, firm in your faith, knowing that the same experiences of suffering are being accomplished by your brethren who are in the world.*

1 Peter 5:8–9

woman who is dedicated to this profession must keep her eyes on the Lord and not on the approval of her peers.

If peer approval were a prerequisite for witnessing for Christ, few converts would be won among our friends. Don't shrink from the service God has given you. *"Be ready in season and out of season . . . with great patience and instruction"* (2 Timothy 4:2). The apostle Paul tells us to be ready to give an account of what we believe. That includes answering some critical questions.

- Why don't you work for a living?

- How can you stand being with kids all day long?

- Why don't you get a real job?

If you decide to leave the workplace, don't be surprised when you are confronted with questions like these from former peers. As I said before, homemaking simply doesn't fit the feminist mold but, as mentioned at the beginning of this chapter, your primary authority is God, not your peers.

One mother, Sammie, had been very successful before leaving the workplace, but she felt that her true calling was in the home, where raising children and meeting household needs is a challenging, though not always admired, job.

As many stay-at-home moms will tell you, it's definitely work ( with a capital W), but try telling that to people who believe "work" only takes place in a business environment.

*"I think the worst thing I had to deal with was when I went places and people asked, 'What do you do?'"*

Sammie urges stay-at-home moms not to be

Keep away from people who try to belittle your ambitions. Small people always do that, but the really great make you feel that you too can become great.

—*Mark Twain*

Where duty is plain, delay is dangerous; where it is not, delay may be wise and safe.

—*unknown*

Deliberation is not delaying.

—*unknown*

ashamed of what they do.

*"I'm a housewife because, for a woman who has chosen to be married and have children, that is the most godly profession there could possibly be."*

Sammie went on to say that stay-at-home moms should do their work according to the principle established in God's Word: *"Whatever you do, do your work heartily, as for the Lord rather than for men; knowing that from the Lord you will receive the reward of the inheritance. It is the Lord Christ whom you serve"* (Colossians 3:23–24).

*"We should be proud of the fact that we keep the family together. We make it run smoothly. Everything I learned in business, management, and leadership I can apply here at home. It's always a test. It's not like I'm wasting my talents, because I still use them every day."*

> People show what they are by what they do with what they have.
>
> —*unknown*

## Helps to Make Your Life at Home Easier

### Treat Homemaking Like Any Other Job

Anyone in the workplace knows that job performance depends greatly on organization. Schedules, files, and calendars help to meet deadlines, get to meetings on time, and keep track of important papers.

Lana's office job required a great deal of organization, but when she left the workplace, she didn't realize that her organizational skills would be just as important at home. Today, she wishes someone had told her.

"You have to treat home like you do a job," she says. "You have to have a schedule. I need to be up at a certain time and have things done by a certain time in order for my husband's day to go better and the children's day to go better.

"Arrange your schedule so you can have a definite time, at least once a day, to just sit down and play a game with your kids or spend time reading or talking with them. If you don't schedule your day in a pretty sane order, time slips away from you. As a result, you end up with your kids demanding the same amount of attention from you as if you had gone out and worked."

Lana says many women actually become so consumed with household duties, like washing and ironing, that they neglect their children. Children, she adds, shouldn't have to tag along behind mom's heels while she does housework to get a little attention.

In addition, Lana advises stay-at-home moms to schedule time each day with God. For her, the best time is 5 a.m., 30 minutes before her husband gets up to prepare for work. That's early, agrees Lana, but *"It's worth it in the long run because my day goes better."*

*There is an appointed time for everything. And there is a time for every event under heaven. . . .He has made everything appropriate in its time.*

Ecclesiastes 3:1,11

*The Lord will be your confidence, and will keep your foot from being caught.*

Proverbs 3:26

### Cut Your Grocery Bill with a Home Garden

Food sometimes is listed as a basic item, along with clothing and shelter, but there's nothing basic about much of the food we eat. For a family who's trying to make it on one income, cutting food costs is essential to help bring expenses in line.

One obvious option to help control food costs is to avoid prepared foods like frozen dinners. They not only are very costly, they offer very little nutritional value outside of the artificial vitamins added to them.

Another logical option to control food costs, depending on where you live, is a home garden. One of our stay-at-home moms, Sarah, offers this counsel: *"I raise all of our vegetables. It's something you really have to be committed*

255

Only human beings ruin their happiness, destroying what IS by thinking of what might have been.

—*unknown*

*to, but it does save a lot of money."*

Sarah's family also benefits from local apple and peach orchards. *"After they pick the peaches, they let you go through and get what's left,"* she says, noting that even though most of the leftover peaches are small, they're still good quality. *"A lot of people have applesauce apples, and when they're done, we go pick their apples and make our own applesauce."*

One observation: You may live in an urban area and therefore think this option is not available to you. Not so. Even big cities have farmer's markets, where vegetables and fruit are available well below retail costs. Even backyard gardens can yield good results if maintained diligently. This is also a great project for young children.

Other cost-cutting practices suggested by Sarah include shopping at warehouse stores and using secondhand clothes. *"My sister has two sisters-in-law who have girls about a year older than my oldest,"* she says. *"We get all our clothes from them. I have three girls, and they just pass right down. If you take care of [good clothes] they'll last forever."*

### Cut Expenses

Parents should work together as efficiently as two book ends.

—*unknown*

For the typical American family trying to live on one income, there usually will be some clear choices between staying home and buying "things." It will almost always be necessary to give up some wants and desires in order to spend your days at home, and Lili and her husband were willing to make those sacrifices.

"We tried to cut every cost we could imagine. If there was a car we had a payment on, we tried to sell it, and we got down to bare basics.

"There were times when we had milk and potatoes, and that was about it, but we've built back up from there. It's well worth it. I've been at home for about two years now and I have everything I've ever wanted."

## Get Your Finances in Order

There is an adage that says, "If you don't borrow money, you can't get into debt, and if you don't borrow more money, you can't get deeper into debt."

The excessive use of credit has consequences, and where children are concerned, one consequence is a mother having to work.

I recently had a young mother call to ask what she and her husband could do about their debts. They owed $20,000 in school loans, $10,000 on their car, and $19,000 on credit cards. She had recently quit her job to stay at home and her husband had quit his to go back to college (to get a better job to pay off their debts).

Unfortunately, she had few options in their situation. They owed the money, and God wants Christians to keep their word (vow). My counsel to her: "Your husband needs to get a full-time job and attend college part-time. You need to work at least part-time or find something you can do out of your home, like babysitting."

She responded that her husband didn't like having other kids around. "Then tell him to get two jobs," I replied.

## Establish a Network of Friends

"If you ask around you can find other stay-at-home moms who can be a real encouragement to you," said one of the stay-at-home moms we heard from. Melanie noted that she has established friendships with other stay-at-home moms through her Sunday school class.

The person who doesn't know where his next dollar is coming from usually doesn't know where his last dollar went.

—*unknown*

The way to stop financial joy-riding is to arrest the chauffeur, not the automobile.

—*Woodrow Wilson*

To get money is difficult, to keep it more difficult but to spend it wisely most difficult of all.

—*unknown*

Just as working women develop relationships with other women at their jobs, so can full-time moms. There is nothing like talking to others who have already trod the path you're about to walk down. Their successes and failures can reduce your learning curve significantly.

Additionally, once you know other stay-at-home moms, you can plan things together, provide your children with good playmates, and trade for some time off.

"It's an encouragement to go through your struggles together and to learn what works and what doesn't work for others," Melanie said.

Another stay-at-home mom, Becka, notes that when a woman is surrounded by active toddlers all day, she can be lonely for adult company. "You need a network of Christian friends to support you in prayer and to just listen with an understanding ear," she says.

We have a dear friend whose wife told a funny story. It seems they were eating dinner with her husband's boss one evening. It was her first time out of the home in several weeks, after quitting her job to homeschool their three children. About halfway through the dinner she noticed their host, who was sitting to her right, had some food on his chin. In a reflex action, she reached up with her napkin and wiped it away. Her face turned a cherry red when she realized what she had done. She explained, "Too much time with kids. I need to get out more."

### Be Persistent

Along with establishing friendships, stay-at-home moms need to hang in there and not get discouraged, advises Ramona.

*"Make sure that's what God wants for you*

*Let the word of Christ richly dwell within you, with all wisdom teaching and admonishing one another. . .singing with thankfulness in your hearts to God.*

Colossians 3:16

*and stick to it with all your guns no matter what anybody says or how they try to persuade you,"* she says. *"Be persistent about your convictions, because even though it may be hard, in the long run it will be worth it because of the fruit you'll bear in your children.*

*"Young couples want to give things to their children and that's nice, but your children just want you. They want your time, they want you not to be so pressured and rushed."*

I can testify, as a father and husband, that our children (and now our grandchildren) are just as content with a cardboard box playhouse as they are with an $800 prefab fort in the backyard.

*"Your top priority has got to be your family and your children,"* Ramona continued. *"We've tried to encourage others to look at their priorities, say, 20 years down the road. What are they going to look back and say was most important?*

*"It really makes a difference to be at home and be the stability of your family, to be there for everybody when they feel like the world is caving in on them. The fruit of it, in the long run, is going to be well worth your sacrifice now."*

*Not that I have already obtained it, or have already become perfect, but I press on in order that I may lay hold of that for which also I was laid hold of by Christ Jesus.*

Philippians 3:12

*Godliness actually is a means of great gain, when accompanied by contentment. For we have brought nothing into the world, so we cannot take anything out of it either.*

1 Timothy 6:6–7

# Chapter Nineteen

# Reasons for Returning to Work

*"For everything created by God is good, and nothing is to be rejected, if it is received with gratitude; for it is sanctified by means of the word of God and prayer" (1 Timothy 4:4).*

Now that we've discussed the viewpoint and aspects of leaving the workplace to return home, let's look at the other end of the spectrum. Why would a stay-at-home mom go back to work? I may not have all the reasons, but I want to list some of them and share excerpts from some of the letters we received.

## We Weren't Prepared

As I said earlier, the hundreds of letters we received in response to my request for testimonies from women who had returned home to be with their children identified one central theme for those who had made the most successful transitions: preparation.

If a couple had decided at the earliest stages of their marriage that once children came into their lives the wife would return home on a more or less full-time basis, the move was much easier. Obviously it doesn't take a genius to figure out that if they had lived on one income from the day they were married and saved all of the wife's income there would be little difficulty in making the transition; but that is the "ideal." What about those who didn't do this? What kinds of problems do they (you) face?

More common than any other inhibiting factor is that most couples have made financial commitments that require two incomes on a month-in, month-out basis.

*Which one of you, when he wants to build a tower, does not first sit down and calculate the cost, to see if he has enough to complete it? Otherwise, when he has laid a foundation, and is not able to finish, all who observe it begin to ridicule him, saying, "This man began to build and was not able to finish."*

Luke 14:28-30

Unfortunately that's a fact of life, and outside of bankruptcy or default there is no quick fix for this situation. As I also mentioned previously, I've seen far too many women make hasty decisions to return home, based on guilt and remorse over having to leave a child after their maternity leave expires. They do so in spite of the fact that even their debt service cannot be maintained on just one income. All too often they find themselves worse off than before because they ultimately are forced to return to work—usually with even more pressure.

The strains on their marriages, the pressure from irate creditors, and often the conflicts with spouses are worse in many ways than the guilt they felt about parking their babies at day care centers, or at least that's the way it seems in the short run.

Expenses will be the same, bills still have to be paid, but, since income is less, problems become greater. So, over a period of time, debt accelerates and, ultimately, the wife is forced to return to work, defeated and discouraged.

If this has happened to you, I want to

encourage you not to feel defeated. You can use this as an opportunity to lay some groundwork for resigning your job and returning home next time, if that is still your wish.

Take a realistic view of your budget. Compare your spending against some kind of guideline. Figure all your expenses, what payments must be made, what the total income will be, and while still employed, decide what steps must be taken to enable you to live on one income.

Perhaps when you get the figures before you, you'll decide you're living in a home too expensive for one income. You may have to get a smaller home. Do you and your spouse have too many cars—or more expensive cars than you need? Are you doing things for your children that cost so much you will be prohibited from coming home to be with them? For instance, do you have them in private schools? In some communities, public schooling is still a viable option. Or perhaps you should consider homeschooling as an option.

I absolutely believe that when God convicts us to do something Satan will usually try to condemn us for it. And as sure as a mother makes the decision to stay at home, guilt will set in (not to mention a lot of abnormal expenses).

Linda, a mother suffering from guilt, wrote,

*"I felt that God wanted me to stay home and thought with my husband's pay and no bills, we'd be able to make ends meet. Well it hasn't worked out that way. I have been home four months and we have maxed out our VISA card paying for groceries and gas for the car. . . . I feel very guilty staying at home. My family is doing without things they want and need. They love*

> The fundamental qualities for good execution of a plan are, first, naturally, intelligence; then discernment and judgment, which enable one to recognize the best methods to attain it; then singleness of purpose; and, lastly, what is most essential of all, will—stubborn will.
>
> —*Ferdinand Foch*

> It is harder to be poor without complaining than to be rich without boasting.
>
> —*unknown*

The root of discontent is self-love; the more self is indulged the more it demands.

—*unknown*

*me being at home but we are all discontented
. . . .And people who know about our situation
wonder why I am not working. I have been
doing some volunteer work. . . .But if I can go
through the effort to volunteer shouldn't I go to
the same effort to go back to work?"*

The decision to stay home may well have been the right one; the decision to use credit cards to pay bills clearly was not.

## Bad Financial Decisions

Sometimes going back to work doesn't result from bad preparation. It's making many wrong decisions after marriage.

Another letter said, "When we got married my husband promised in our wedding vows to 'provide and care' for me. I thought that meant financially." She went on to relate how he continually made bad choices: bad investments, buying or starting companies that didn't succeed, continually borrowing money. The rent went unpaid. Loans went unpaid. Bills went unpaid. She continued,

*Many are the plans in a man's heart, but the counsel of the Lord, it will stand.*

Proverbs 19:21

*"People told me I should work full time. I
think that would feed the problem of my husbands not being responsible rather than be a
solution to our situation. . . . I do think it was
healthier for me (even though it wasn't my first
choice) to be working and earning money, rather
than staying at home watching more bills accumulate. I still question what my husband meant
when he promised to provide and care for me on
our wedding day."*

## I'm a Single Parent

Another reason mothers are forced to go back to work is because they are single parents. Single parents are in a totally separate category, as Courtney wrote,

*"I am a Christian single mother working full time and working on my GED. Because of the pressure of a full time job and raising my daughter. . .about 3 months ago I started [working] nights so I could be home during the day and raise my own daughter. Now I can't pay my bills. I've gone from making $7 a hour to $4.25 an hour. Things have not balanced out yet, in fact it's got worse. My bills have fallen behind and I don't know how I'm going to catch up."*

*Commit your works to the Lord, and your plans will be established.*

Proverbs 16:3

Another single parent wrote,

*"I was in college when I became pregnant. The world said have an abortion. . .I wasn't sure at that time if abortion was really a choice or not. I figured God would handle any situation. So I left school to stay home [on welfare] after my daughter was born. I returned to work when she was 1 year old because I felt welfare was there for temporary help only."*

Government is not a substitute for people, but simply the instrument through which they act. In the last analysis, our only freedom is the freedom to discipline ourselves.

—*Bernard Baruch*

I applaud this young woman's attitude toward government assistance. Welfare should never be considered permanent. It's a terrible witness against Christianity today that (Christian) single parents are forced to work or live in poverty.

## The Residual Effects of Divorce

Celeste wrote,

*"When I was 19 years old and my son was four months old, I started to work out of necessity. I was a single parent. My husband had left me."*

Marriages break up whether you are staying at home or if you are going to work every day. Some of the letters I received indicated that their marriages were breaking up. In that instance you have to consider that your whole life has changed.

It's my heart's desire that Christianity will begin functioning as God designed His church to do. If it would, we would adopt those women as widows. We wouldn't treat them as lepers. Unfortunately, that's not the case yet.

I can't promise you that if you go to your local church they will promise to supply your needs so you can stay home with your children. In reality, there aren't many churches who will.

The alternatives many divorced women (and single parents) turn to are bad ones. They turn to the government for support and, as a result, they are being forced down to the lowest tier of society, with no way out of it, because most government programs literally discourage thriftiness (savings) and ingenuity.

My counsel would be, even if you accept government aid (and some will have to until they find a job), make a commitment that it will be temporary, and vow that as soon as you can you'll forego all government aid.

That doesn't mean wait until an opportunity arises. It means go out and actively seek employment someplace, because as long as you are on government aid, you're going to be at the lowest level of society with no hope of ever getting out.

Another bad alternative available to single mothers is to jump into another bad relationship. This usually means getting involved with any available man. Quite often this results in an immoral lifestyle because most of these

Government is the people's business and every man, woman, and child becomes a shareholder with the first penny of tax paid.

—*Ronald Reagan*
*(New York, 1/14/82)*

men aren't "providers," they are "takers," so the women end up living with them, simply to have someone to "take care of" them and their children. What they've done then: They've picked up a worse problem than the one they just got out of (a bad marriage). All too often the bums they choose are worse than the ones who took off and left them single parents.

This is not a rare situation with single mothers. Many of the women who wrote said it directly, some said it indirectly: They were out scouting for a new provider and some admitted they were living with men. As a result, they were having to deal with the guilt of immorality, in addition to their other problems.

It's very common for women who have quit their jobs and gone home to feel desperate. Some have given up good jobs to be at home with their children, and unfortunately, divorce is about as common among Christian families as non-Christian.

An excerpt from Kelli's letter:

*"His professional talent was growing quickly as I was growing spiritually, but we were growing apart. Since our divorce, I have examined and reexamined what went wrong, to come up with no definitive answers. I am currently back at work full time, to meet my expenses. It seems so wrong; I give almost half of what I make to the babysitter. But most of all my heart breaks for my children. I want a normal family!"*

## My Children Are Grown

One logical reason many women go back to work is that their children are grown or at an age when they don't require their mother's presence at home all the time. Many of these women are ready to go back into the workplace.

*Be very careful what you do, for the Lord our God will have no part in unrighteousness, or partiality, or the taking of a bribe.*

2 Chronicles 19:7

*The word of God is living and active and sharper than any two-edged sword, and piercing as far as the division of soul and spirit, of both joints and marrow, and able to judge the thoughts and intentions of the heart.*

Hebrews 4:12

What they don't want to do is face the modern workplace with obsolete skills. For many women, home-based businesses are the best option. For others, skill training is essential.

## *I Never Meant It To Be Permanent*

Many women plan to go to work (or back to work) as their children mature. They never planned to stay home forever.

On the other hand, there are those whose families never require two incomes, but they want to be active and involved in their communities, so they volunteer their time—at the church, for charities, at the hospital. That's where much of our voluntary labor in this country comes from. This helps to keep their work skills current.

One mother wrote,

*"Since my boys are in school, I fill my time with worthwhile volunteer projects (scouts, kids' choir, adult choir, Sunday school teacher, office volunteer, president of the women's group and part-time projects that allow me to be home when the boys are)."*

Our churches and Christian and civic organizations could operate much more efficiently if more Christian women would adopt the attitude, "If I don't need to work for money, I'll just go work for ten hours a week doing something I enjoy as a volunteer."

Let me digress for a moment and say that, no matter what your reason for staying at home with your children, if you have worked, at some point in time you may want to return to the workplace, so you should keep your skills up-to-date. If you were a secretary, keep up your typing skills. Learn all you can about

computers and what methods are being utilized in offices today.

If you were a nurse, read applicable medical
journals and renew your license regularly. If
you are a teacher, keep your certificate current.
(That's a lot easier than having to go back to
school to renew it.) You don't know when you
might be required to work (because of your
husband's illness or death or a divorce) and the
chances of getting a good-paying job will be
increased greatly if your skills are current.

The woman who helped me with my reha-
bilitation after cancer surgery is a licensed
physical therapist and mother of three who
kept her certificate current by attending annual seminars and taking the required tests. As
you might imagine, her skills are in great
demand now in our aging society.

Perhaps you can find a way to do something
in your home to keep those skills current,
whether it's by doing part-time work or just
reading about the latest technology. If you visit
your local library, you'll find journals and
videos on nearly any field or industry.

If you wait until your children have reached
an age that you're free to go back to work and
you haven't kept your skills up-to-date, your
chances of getting a good job will be slim to
none.

Another option is to take technical courses
at a junior college or vocational/technical
school. More education will enhance your cre-
dentials and help fill the gap in your work
record if and when you decide to reenter the
work force.

It may seem that I'm only addressing
women with professional skills—writing,
teaching, math, nursing—but the same counsel
also applies to others.

> Knowledge once
> gained casts a faint
> light beyond its own
> immediate boundaries.
> There is no discovery
> so limited as not to
> illuminate something
> beyond itself.
>
> —*John Tyndall*

All real education is
the architecture of the
soul.
—*William Bennett*
*(1992 Rep. Nat'l*
*Convention)*

Staying home is usually not an either/or situation, although it may seem so with infant children. Anyone can study and learn when the kids are old enough to be somewhat responsible for themselves. Use this time as an opportunity to attain the skills and confidence in yourself that isn't always possible for those who are working full-time.

## Staying Home Is Not for Me

Not every woman is equipped to be a stay-at-home mom. Not everyone becomes an ideal mother just because she is staying at home instead of going to the workplace. There are different temperaments, different personality types. Believe it or not, some children are better off if their mothers are working.

This is particularly true if their mom is continually irritated or depressed by being home. The last things impressionable kids need is someone who constantly screams at them or lays around in a bathrobe watching television most of the day.

Some mothers wrote in to say that they were frustrated staying at home and too often took it out on the children. Even though they were physically at home, their hearts and minds were somewhere else.

As I discussed before, some personalities prefer being with other adults and hate the isolation of being at home all day. More than one mother said, "I knew that my kids would be better off if I worked and someone else watched them."

Bonnie wrote,

*"Anyone with toddlers knows that the routine they thrive on is not exactly mentally challenging for adults. . . . Now that the children are older I*

270

*am ready to get involved in some outside work . . . . It has taken several years of struggling with feelings of guilt over not being happy as a full-time stay-at-home mom. I realize there are women who would give anything to be able to stay at home and I feel guilty when I think of that; however, I also realize I need to keep mentally fresh."*

Another letter, from Sharon, said,

*"We wanted to be the ones to influence our child, love her and nurture her so that's why I chose to stay at home with her. Everything was fine except I seemed to have this strange innate need to work outside the home."*

She eventually found a job where she could work her own hours and take her daughter to work with her. Unfortunately many mothers who feel the same way don't have this advantage.

Like it or not, there are mothers who feel this way. Sometimes they have been pressured into quitting their jobs and staying home (by their husbands or by peers), but they don't like their new roles.

We heard from a very candid mother of two who gave us several reasons why she wanted to return to work when her eldest child was fourteen months old.

- *"All my life I've been around role figures who are hardworking people who find great satisfaction in a job well done.*

- *I am a better wife and mother when I have time away from home. I feel more energetic and self-assured.*

*As for me, I would seek God and I would place my cause before God; who does great and unsearchable things, wonders without number.*

Job 5:8–9

- *I only work 20 hours a week.*

- *We live in a rural area. Most of my friends work so when I was home I was very isolated.*

- *I have a position I know the Lord provided for me. It is the only position of its kind in our entire county and it is in my area of training, which is rare in this area.*

- *I know that when my children are grown I will want to continue working and feel that part-time work will help me to continue with various contacts, organizations, and a feeling of involvement. My skills won't get rusty.*

- *I feel that by relieving my husband of total financial responsibility as well as allowing for us to have a little extra money, he will not feel so much pressure.*

- *My children are in a wonderful day care in the same building where both my husband and I work and I can see them when I want to.*

- *My supervisors are very supportive and I have never felt that my job had to come first. I can change my schedule when I need to.*

- *I have excellent chances to witness and make new Christian friends. At home all I ever saw were Christian friends.*

- *I feel less [financial] pressure knowing that we are able to pay extra money on various debts and will pay them off much faster."*

I was impressed with the honesty in the letters we received. One mother wrote,

*"This life of full time homemaking was not the bed of roses I had always pictured it would be."*

Another mother said,

*"I am glad I am able to work 5-10 hours a week because it brings in a little extra money, and it gets me out of the house (with a 1–1/2 and 3 year old, this is a real plus!)."*

According to my personality, if I were a woman, I would fit into this category. I love kids, but I would go nuts if I were around only kids all day.

If you fit into this category, it's very important that you face the situation honestly. For those who are satisfied stay-at-home moms, if you know someone who chose to return to work, don't make her feel guilty because she doesn't fit your ideal mother image.

I daily see examples of successful working mothers at the ministry I lead, Christian Financial Concepts. We presently employ 19 mothers with children ages 6 months to 16 years (a few of those are only part-time). These women are a vital part of a Christian ministry, using their skills while still raising some great kids.

There are some Christian leaders who teach that mothers should be home with their children because God commands it, and yet they themselves are mothers, and they continue to hire women with children. I believe that's called hypocrisy.

## We Had No Insurance

As mentioned before, sometimes insurance is not available through the husband's employer, and individual policies often are prohibi-

*I pray that your love may abound still more and more in real knowledge and all discernment, that you may approve the things that are excellent.*

Philippians 1:9

tively expensive, particularly when pre-existing conditions exist. This situation can pressure a mother to return to work.

Several women wrote in despair about this. As one woman said,

*"Because of our financial distress, we don't have any health insurance at this time. My husband has said, 'You'll have to go back to work.'"*

Another example came from Anna's letter:

*"I am forced to work in order to keep my health coverage. I was diagnosed with a rare disease."*

Her husband was not insured where he worked.

## *Who Am I?*

Since I devoted a chapter to the struggle for significance, I won't elaborate on this point. One of the letters said it better than I could anyway:

*"I have lost a lot of self-esteem. I just don't have the confidence in myself any longer. . . Sometimes I have to put on makeup just to feel like I'm a real person. . . .When it comes to buying things I need, I can't seem to buy those things. . . .I don't contribute anything."*

## *When a Husband Dies*

*"The brakes failed and a bus hit our car. It was there I became a widow. My daughter had a day care situation she liked fairly well. But to lose one parent completely, losing another one to a full time job must have added to the trauma. When I'd come home I wasn't completely there.*

*He made Him who knew no sin to be sin on our behalf, that we might become the righteousness of God in Him.*

2 Corinthians 5:21

*Grandparents filled a huge need for family con- nections for her."*

There are so many stories to tell . . . all sad. If a husband has planned carefully and provid- ed for his family after his death, it can be a different story. Unfortunately, that is not the norm in our society, and many mothers are left to fend for themselves and their children.

If that is your situation, call on your church first. God has all the provision you need, but don't assume others know what your needs are.

*From Him and through Him and to Him are all things. To Him be the glory forever.*

Romans 11:36

## A Reversal of Roles

An unusual situation but nevertheless a real one is the one in which, for one reason or another, the husband stays at home and the wife works. We had several letters that told of this working for them, at least for a time. Margo wrote,

*"We had been planning for over a year [for me to quit work and stay at home] and saved most of my pay check for the last year. Although we felt we were prepared, it was still very tough cut- ting our income in half, but we made the very tough decision. [My husband had had to retire from military service, the only work he's known since college] so [he] went from being 'Sir' to 'Mr Mom'. After a lot of adjusting for both of us, me with a lot of tears and frustrations at not being able to stay home and [my husband] with the same for being home, we began to adapt to our new life style."*

This mother went on to write that after a period of time they were able to reverse their roles and everyone was happier, but it did serve their purposes for a while. However, God has ordained the man to be the provider for his family, and this system has worked very well for the last several thousand years.

It's not always possible to leave the work force and return home under ideal financial circumstances, but let me hasten to say, it can be done, as thousands of women can testify, but it does take some time and planning. What you may suffer financially in the short run will be more than offset by the long-term reward of knowing you have done your best to raise godly children who will themselves live happy lives.

If, in fact, you find it impossible or untenable to remain at home, remember that God only holds us responsible for what we can do—not for what we cannot do.

You need not fight in this battle; station yourselves, stand and see the salvation of the Lord on your behalf. . . .Do not fear or be dismayed; tomorrow go out to face them, for the Lord is with you.

*2 Chronicles 20:17*

# Appendices

BOOKS

NEWSLETTERS

## 1. Budget Forms

# MONTHLY INCOME & EXPENSES

**GROSS INCOME PER MONTH** _____
- Salary _____
- Interest _____
- Dividends _____
- Other _____

**LESS:**

**1. Tithe** _____

**2. Tax** (Est.-Incl. Fed., State,FICA) _____

**NET SPENDABLE INCOME** _____

**3. Housing** _____
- Mortgage (rent) _____
- Insurance _____
- Taxes _____
- Electricity _____
- Gas _____
- Water _____
- Sanitation _____
- Telephone _____
- Maintenance _____
- Other _____

**4. Food** _____

**5. Automobile(s)** _____
- Payments _____
- Gas & Oil _____
- Insurances _____
- License/Taxes _____
- Maint./Repair /Replace _____

**6. Insurance** _____
- Life _____
- Medical _____
- Other _____

**7. Debts** _____
- Credit Card _____
- Loans & Notes _____
- Other _____

**8. Entertainment & Recreation** _____
- Eating Out _____
- Baby Sitters _____
- Activities/Trips _____
- Vacation _____
- Other _____

**9. Clothing** _____

**10. Savings** _____

**11. Medical Exp.** _____
- Doctor _____
- Dentist _____
- Drugs _____
- Other _____

**12. Miscellaneous** _____
- Toiletry, cos. _____
- Beauty, barber _____
- Laundry, cl. _____
- Allow., lunches _____
- Subscriptions _____
- Gifts (incl. Christmas) _____
- Cash _____
- Other _____

**13. School/Child care** _____
- Tuition _____
- Materials _____
- Transportation _____
- Day Care _____

**14. Investments** _____

**TOTAL EXPENSES** _____

**INCOME VS. EXPENSES**
- **Net Spendable Income** _____
- **Less Explenses** _____

_____

**15. Unallocated Surplus Income[1]** _____

[1]This category is used when surplus income is received. This would be kept in the checking account to be used within a few weeks; otherwise, it should be transferred to an allocated category.

**FORM 1**

# PERCENTAGE GUIDE FOR FAMILY INCOME
## (Family of Four)

| Gross Income | 15,000 | 25,000 | 35,000 | 45,000 | 55,000 | 65,000 |
|---|---|---|---|---|---|---|
| 1. Tithe | 10% | 10% | 10% | 10% | 10% | 10% |
| 2. Taxes[1] | 2% | 15.5% | 19% | 21.5% | 23.5% | 27% |
| NET SPENDABLE | 13,200 | 18,625 | 24,850 | 30,825 | 36,575 | 40,950 |
| 3. Housing | 38% | 38% | 34% | 30% | 27% | 26% |
| 4. Food | 15% | 12% | 12% | 12% | 11% | 10% |
| 5. Auto | 15% | 15% | 12% | 12% | 12% | 11% |
| 6. Insurance | 5% | 5% | 5% | 5% | 5% | 5% |
| 7. Debts | 5% | 5% | 5% | 5% | 5% | 5% |
| 8. Entertainment / Recreation | 4% | 5% | 6% | 6% | 7% | 7% |
| 9. Clothing | 4% | 5% | 5% | 5% | 6% | 6% |
| 10. Savings | 5% | 5% | 5% | 5% | 5% | 5% |
| 11. Medical/ Dental | 5% | 5% | 4% | 4% | 4% | 4% |
| 12. Miscellaneous | 4% | 5% | 5% | 7% | 7% | 8% |
| 13. School/ Child Care[2] | 10% | 8% | 6% | 5% | 5% | 5% |
| 14. Investments[3] | —— | —— | 7% | 9% | 11% | 13% |
| 15. Unallocated Surplus Income[4] | —— | —— | —— | —— | —— | —— |

[1]Guideline percentages for this category include taxes for Social Security, federal tax, and a small estimated amount for state tax. At the $15,000 level of income, the Earned Income Credit drastically reduces the tax burden.

[2]This category is added as a guide only. If you have this expense, the percentage shown must be deducted from other budget categories.

[3]This category is used for long-term investment planning such as college education or retirement.

[4]This category is used when surplus income is received. This would be kept in the checking account to be used within a few weeks; otherwise it should be transferred to an allocated category.

**FORM 2**

# BUDGET ANALYSIS

**Per Year** _____  **Net Spendable Income Per Month** _____
**Per Month** _____

| MONTHLY PAYMENT CATEGORY | EXISTING BUDGET | MONTHLY GUIDELINE BUDGET | DIFFERENCE + OR - | NEW MONTHLY BUDGET |
|---|---|---|---|---|
| 1. Tithe | | | | |
| 2. Taxes | | | | |
| NET SPENDABLE INCOME (Per Month) | $_____ | $_____ | $_____ | $_____ |
| 3. Housing | | | | |
| 4. Food | | | | |
| 5. Automobile(s) | | | | |
| 6. Insurance | | | | |
| 7. Debts | | | | |
| 8. Entertainment / Recreation | | | | |
| 9. Clothing | | | | |
| 10. Savings | | | | |
| 11. Medical / Dental | | | | |
| 12. Miscellaneous | | | | |
| 13. School / Child Care | | | | |
| 14. Investments | | | | |
| TOTALS (Items 3–14) | $_____ | $_____ | | $_____ |
| 15. Unallocated Surplus Income | $_____ | $_____ | | $_____ |

**FORM 3**

# VARIABLE EXPENSE PLANNING

Plan for those expenses that are not paid on a regular monthly basis by estimating the yearly cost and determining the monthly amount needed to be set aside for that expense. A helpful formula is to allow the previous year's expense and add 5 percent.

|  | **Estimated Cost** | **Per Month** |
|---|---|---|
| 1. VACATION | $_____ | ÷ 12 = $_____ |
| 2. DENTIST | $_____ | ÷ 12 = $_____ |
| 3. DOCTOR | $_____ | ÷ 12 = $_____ |
| 4. AUTOMOBILE | $_____ | ÷ 12 = $_____ |
| 5. ANNUAL INSURANCE | $_____ | ÷ 12 = $_____ |
| (Life) | ($_____ | ÷ 12 = $_____) |
| (Health) | ($_____ | ÷ 12 = $_____) |
| (Auto) | ($_____ | ÷ 12 = $_____) |
| (Home) | ($_____ | + 12 = $_____) |
| 6. CLOTHING | $_____ | + 12 = $_____ |
| 7. INVESTMENTS | $_____ | ÷ 12 = $_____ |
| 8. OTHER | $_____ | ÷ 12 = $_____ |

**FORM 4**

281

# INDIVIDUAL ACCOUNT PAGE

| ACCOUNT CATEGORY | $ ALLOCATION | | $ ALLOCATION | |
|---|---|---|---|---|
| DATE | TRANSACTION | DEPOSIT | WITHDRAWAL | BALANCE |
| | | | | |
| | | | | |
| | | | | |
| | | | | |
| | | | | |
| | | | | |
| | | | | |
| | | | | |
| | | | | |
| | | | | |
| | | | | |
| | | | | |
| | | | | |
| | | | | |
| | | | | |
| | | | | |
| | | | | |
| | | | | |
| | | | | |
| | | | | |
| | | | | |
| | | | | |
| | | | | |
| | | | | |
| | | | | |
| | | | | |
| | | | | |
| | | | | |
| | | | | |
| | | | | |
| | | | | |
| | | | | |

**FORM 5**

# CHECKBOOK BALANCE PROCEDURE

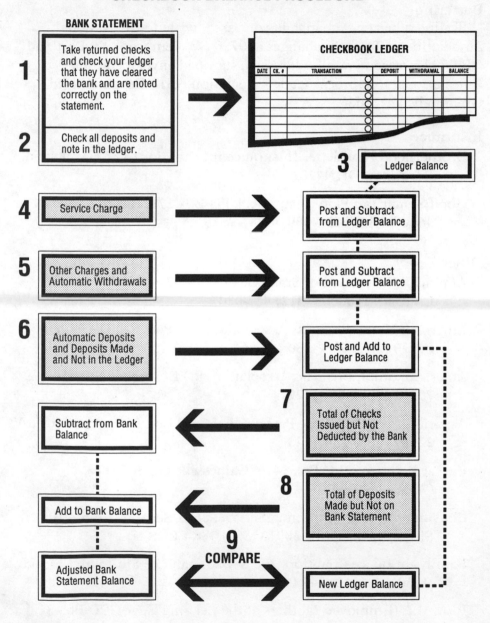

**FORM 6**

## 2. Organizations

**Bartering**

To find a barter exchange in your area, write to the National Association of Trade Exchanges at 9790 SW Tembrook St, Portland OR 97224, or send a self-addressed, stamped envelope to the International Reciprocal Trade Association, 9513 Beach Mill Rd, Great Falls VA 22066.

**Insurance**

Brotherhood Newsletter (Insurance information) 127 Hazelwood, Barberton OH 44203

Good Samaritan Plan (Insurance), PO Box 279, Beach Grove IN 46107 (317) 783-7080 or 787-9770

**Other**

American Federation of Small Business, 407 S Dearborn St, Chicago IL 60605 (312) 427-0207

American Home Business Association, 397 Post Rd, Darien CT 06820 (203) 655-4380

American Small Business Association, PO Box 612663, Dallas TX 75261 (800) 880-2722

Association of Part-Time Professionals, PO Box 3419, Alexandria VA 22302 (703) 734-7975

Career Pathways, PO Box 1476, Gainesville GA 30501 (770) 534-1000

Consumer Credit Counseling Service, 8611 Second Ave Ste 100, Silver Springs, MD 30910 (800) 388-CCCS

Family Resource Coalition, 200 S Michigan Ave Ste 1520, Chicago IL 60604, (312) 341-0900

FEMALE (Employed Mothers at the Leading Edge), PO Box 31, Elmhurst IL 60126

Growing Families International, 9257 Eton Ave, Chatsworth CA 91311 (818) 772-6264

Moms Club, 814 Moffat Cir, Simi Valley CA 93065 (805) 526-2725

MOPS International (Mothers of Preschoolers), 1311 S Clarkson St, Denver CO 80210 (303) 733-5353

Mothering Seminars, Inc., PO Box 712, Columbia MD 21045 (301) 381-5195

Mothers at Home, 8310-A Old Courthouse Rd, Vienna VA 22182 (703) 827-5903

Mother's Home Business Network, PO Box 423, East Meadow NY 11554-0423 (516) 997-7394

National Association for Family Day Care, 725 Fifteenth St NW Ste 505, Washington DC 20005 (800) 359-3817

National Association for the Self-Employed, PO Box 612067, DFW Airport, TX 75261 (800) 232-6273

National Association of Child Care Resources and Referral Agencies, 2116 Campus Dr SE, Rochester MN 55904 (507) 287-2020

National Federation of Independent Business, 150 W 20th Ave, San Mateo CA 94430

## 3. Personality Evaluation

Psalm 139:13-14 teaches that God designed you uniquely and that you were "woven" into your mother's womb. Weaving suggests that you have a particular pattern to your makeup that I will call temperament. Your temperament is a God-given predisposition to behave in predictable ways and, as such, is a major influence on your style of communicating.

Your communication skills can improve by understanding your temperament and the temperaments of others. Since marriage is the most intimate of all human relationships, it also provides the ideal setting in which to practice communication skills.

The following surveys will assist you and your spouse in discovering the strengths and weaknesses associated with your God-given temperaments.

The surveys reflect four primary dimensions of behavior: *Dominant, Influencing, Steady,* and *Conscientious.* This approach to describing human behavior is commonly called the DISC model of personality: D I S C is derived from the first letter of the four behavior dimensions above. Most people are a blend of two, and sometimes three, of these primary temperaments.

A number of other personality surveys use different names to gauge the same four dimensions of behavior. For instance, Gary Smalley and John Trent use the terms Lions (D), Otters (I), Golden Retrievers (S), and Beavers (C) in their books and presentations. Dr. Tim LaHaye and Florence Littauer have written books on temperament using the terms Choleric (D), Sanguine (I), Phlegmatic (S), and Melancholy (C).

The surveys contained in this book are designed to introduce you to the DISC concept of temperament. They are neither exhaustive tools, nor are they meant to diagnose mental illness. By following the guidelines below, you will maximize your use of this material.

## Guidelines for Using the Personality Style Surveys

a. The following two surveys are identical. The husband should take one and the wife take the other. Allow ten to twelve minutes each to complete the surveys. After you have completed your surveys, use the support materials to discuss your patterns of communication in marriage.

b. Since God has designed each of you uniquely, you may discover several differences in your personalities. That's no cause for alarm. As Larry has often said, "If two people exactly alike get married, there's no need for one of them." Being different doesn't mean something is wrong with your marriage or your spouse. Instead, your differences have the potential to enrich your marriage.

c. Accept and respect your spouse for the unique way God designed him or her. It's not your role in life to change your spouse's behavior. Only God is in the life-changing business.

d. By understanding your temperaments, you will be better equipped to understand one another, work more effectively as a team, and glorify God in your marriage.

(For more information or for further testing, please contact Career Pathways [a division of Christian Financial Concepts], PO Box 1476, Gainesville GA 30503 [770] 534-1000.)

**CAREER PATHWAYS**
PO Box 1476, Gainesville, GA 30503
(770) 534-1000

# HUSBAND'S PERSONALITY STYLE SURVEY

---

**DIRECTIONS:** Rate each line of words from left to right on a 4, 3, 2, 1 scale with <u>4 being most</u> like you and <u>1 being least</u> like you. *<u>Use each rating only once.</u>* Add the columns; then plot your graph below.

**Correct:** Example: A. __1__ Commanding __3__ Enthusiastic __4__ Cordial __2__ Detailed

**Incorrect:** Example: B. __4__ Commanding __3__ Enthusiastic __1__ Cordial __4__ Detailed
— *Incorrect: Use each rating only once as in Example A.* —

**FOCUS:** The focus for this survey is your typical behavior. Respond based on how you most naturally behave.

---

**CAUTION:** We all have ideas about how we would like to act in order to be more acceptable to others. However, that is not what we are looking for in this survey. Think of your core self, and answer based on your instinctive behavior, regardless of whether you consider it to be good or bad.

|     | **I** |     | **II** |     | **III** |     | **IV** |     |
|-----|-------|-----|--------|-----|---------|-----|--------|-----|
| A. | 1 | Commanding | 2 | Enthusiastic | 3 | Cordial | 4 | Detailed |
| B. | 1 | Decisive | 2 | Expressive | 3 | Caring | 4 | Particular |
| C. | 3 | Tough-Minded | 1 | Lively | 2 | Kind | 4 | Meticulous |
| D. | 3 | Independent | 2 | Fun-Loving | 1 | Peaceful | 4 | Follow Rules |
| E. | 1 | Daring | 2 | Outgoing | 4 | Understanding | 3 | High Standards |
| F. | 1 | Dominant | 3 | Promoter | 2 | Tolerant | 4 | Prepared |
| G. | 2 | Opportunistic | 1 | Loud | 3 | Adaptable | 4 | Precise |
| H. | 2 | Confident | 1 | Inspiring | 4 | Supportive | 3 | Logical |
| I. | 2 | Self-Reliant | 1 | People Person | 2 | Patient | 4 | Conscientious |
| J. | 1 | Bold | 2 | Talkative | 3 | Gentle | 4 | Analytical |
| K. | 2 | Adventurous | 1 | Popular | 4 | Even-Paced | 3 | Organized |
| L. | 2 | Take Charge | 1 | Uninhibited | 4 | Good Listener | 3 | Factual |
| M. | 1 | Assertive | 2 | Impulsive | 4 | Cooperative | 3 | Accurate |
| N. | 1 | Direct | 2 | Excitable | 3 | Gracious | 4 | Efficient |
| O. | 1 | Frank | 3 | Entertaining | 2 | Accommodating | 4 | Determined |
| P. | 1 | Forceful | 2 | Playful | 2 | Agreeable | 4 | Systematic |
| | **35** | **TOTAL** | **28** | **TOTAL** | **47** | **TOTAL** | **59** | **TOTAL** |

**Transfer these totals to the top of page CP-6**

24
8
9
/35

16
6
6/8

20
18
8
/47

44
15

CP-4

**CAREER PATHWAYS**
PO Box 1476, Gainesville, GA 30503
(770) 534-1000

# WIFE'S PERSONALITY STYLE SURVEY

**DIRECTIONS:** Rate each line of words from left to right on a 4, 3, 2, 1 scale with <u>4 being most</u> like you and <u>1 being least</u> like you. *<u>Use each rating only once.</u>* Add the columns; then plot your graph below.

**Correct:** Example: A. __1__ Commanding __3__ Enthusiastic __4__ Cordial __2__ Detailed

**Incorrect:** Example: B. __4__ Commanding __3__ Enthusiastic __1__ Cordial __4__ Detailed
—— *Incorrect: Use each rating only once as in Example A.* ——

**FOCUS:** The focus for this survey is your typical behavior. Respond based on how you most naturally behave.

**CAUTION: We all have ideas about how we would like to act in order to be more acceptable to others. However, that is not what we are looking for in this survey. Think of your core self, and answer based on your instinctive behavior, regardless of whether you consider it to be good or bad.**

| | I | | II | | III | | IV |
|---|---|---|---|---|---|---|---|
| A. | 1 Commanding | 2 | Enthusiastic | 3 | Cordial | 4 | Detailed |
| B. | 2 Decisive | 1 | Expressive | 4 | Caring | 3 | Particular |
| C. | 1 Tough-Minded | 2 | Lively | 4 | Kind | 3 | Meticulous |
| D. | 4 Independent | 2 | Fun-Loving | 1 | Peaceful | 3 | Follow Rules |
| E. | 1 Daring | 2 | Outgoing | 3 | Understanding | 4 | High Standards |
| F. | 3 Dominant | 1 | Promoter | 2 | Tolerant | 4 | Prepared |
| G. | 2 Opportunistic | 1 | Loud | 3 | Adaptable | 4 | Precise |
| H. | 2 Confident | 1 | Inspiring | 3 | Supportive | 4 | Logical |
| I. | 1 Self-Reliant | 3 | People Person | 2 | Patient | 4 | Conscientious |
| J. | 3 Bold | 1 | Talkative | 2 | Gentle | 4 | Analytical |
| K. | 3 Adventurous | 2 | Popular | 1 | Even-Paced | 4 | Organized |
| L. | 4 Take Charge | 1 | Uninhibited | 3 | Good Listener | 2 | Factual |
| M. | 4 Assertive | 1 | Impulsive | 3 | Cooperative | 2 | Accurate |
| N. | 4 Direct | 1 | Excitable | 2 | Gracious | 3 | Efficient |
| O. | 3 Frank | 1 | Entertaining | 2 | Accommodating | 4 | Determined |
| P. | 4 Forceful | 2 | Playful | 3 | Agreeable | 1 | Systematic |
| | **42** TOTAL | 25 | TOTAL | 41 | TOTAL | 53 | TOTAL |

**Transfer these totals to the top of page CP-6**

CP-5

| HUSBAND'S SURVEY TOTALS From page CP-4 | WIFE'S SURVEY TOTALS From page CP-5 |
|---|---|
| TOTAL: D 35 | TOTAL: D 42 |
| TOTAL: I 28 | TOTAL: I 25 |
| TOTAL: S 47 | TOTAL: S 41 |
| TOTAL: C 59 | TOTAL: C 53 |

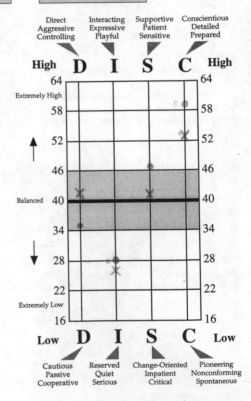

## Plot Your Profiles

a. Using the totals from above, plot your DISC dimensions on the graph to the right. The result will be your natural personality profiles.

b. Use a solid line for the husband's survey and a dashed line or colored pencil for the wife's survey. Refer to the example on page CP-9.

## Identify Your Natural Profile

Using your totals from the surveys, check the appropriate box below to indicate whether your D, I, S, and C points are High, Balanced, or Low. If a point is 46 or more, consider it high. If it is 35 through 45, consider it balanced. Points 34 or less are considered low.

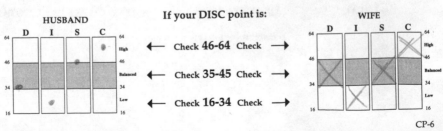

CP-6

290

# The Four Dimensions of DISC

## D

**DOMINANT:** People who have a high level of dominance (High D) are naturally motivated to be in charge of the home environment. They are usually assertive, direct, and strong willed. They are typically bold and not afraid to take strong action to get the desired results. They function best in a challenging environment.

Examples:

| | |
|---|---|
| Joshua | General George Patton |
| Sarah | Bill Cosby |
| Solomon | Barbara Walters |
| Paul | Sam Donaldson |

## I

**INFLUENCING:** People who are highly influencing (High I) are driven naturally to relate to others. Usually they are verbal, friendly, outgoing, and optimistic. They are typically enthusiastic motivators and will seek out others to help them accomplish results. They function best in a friendly environment.

Examples:

| | |
|---|---|
| Peter | President Ronald Reagan |
| Rebekah | Kathie Lee Gifford |
| Abigail | John Madden |
| Barnabas | Joan Rivers |

## C

**CONSCIENTIOUS:** People who have a high level of conscientiousness (High C, also called cautiousness) are focused on doing things right. Usually they are detail oriented and find it easy to follow prescribed guidelines. Typically they strive for accuracy and quality and, therefore, set high standards for themselves and for others. They function best in a structured environment.

Examples:

| | |
|---|---|
| Moses | President Jimmy Carter |
| Elijah | Albert Einstein |
| Mary | General Omar Bradley |
| Luke | David Brinkley |

## S

**STEADY:** People who have a high level of steadiness (High S) are naturally motivated to cooperate with and support others. They are usually patient, consistent, and very dependable. Being pleasant and easygoing makes them excellent team players. They function best in a supportive, harmonious environment.

Examples:

| | |
|---|---|
| Abraham | Pres./Gen. Dwight Eisenhower |
| Nehemiah | Coach Tom Landry |
| Hannah | Perry Como |
| Martha | Mother Teresa |

CP-7

## TYPICAL STRENGTHS

| High "D" | High "I" | High "S" | High "C" |
|---|---|---|---|
| 1. Independent | 1. Verbal | 1. Peacemaker | 1. Analytical |
| 2. Results-Oriented | 2. Outgoing | 2. Good Listener | 2. Organized |
| 3. Confident | 3. Enthusiastic | 3. Patient | 3. Cautious |
| 4. Direct | 4. Optimistic | 4. Productive | 4. Accurate/Detailed |
| 5. Problem-Solver | 5. Fun-Loving | 5. Dependable | 5. Conscientious |

## TYPICAL WEAKNESSES

| High "D" | High "I" | High "S" | High "C" |
|---|---|---|---|
| 1. Impatient | 1. Talk Too Much | 1. Compromise Too Much | 1. Cold |
| 2. Insensitive | 2. Disorganized | 2. Don't Like Change | 2. Unrealistic Standards |
| 3. Dislike Details | 3. Get Too Emotional | 3. Afraid to Confront | 3. Internalize Emotions |
| 4. Poor Listener | 4. Not Time Sensitive | 4. Complacent | 4. Perfectionist |
| 5. Hate Routines | 5. Overlook Key Details | 5. Too Sensitive | 5. Overly Analytical |

## DISC TENDENCIES

| D and I | S and C | I and S | D and C |
|---|---|---|---|
| OUTGOING/GENERALIST | RESERVED/SPECIALIST | PEOPLE-ORIENTED | TASK-ORIENTED |
| control the conversation | listen to others | warm | cold |
| change the environment | maintain the environment | agreeable | tough-minded |
| spontaneous | like time to prepare | relaxed | intense |
| unstructured | structured | feelings-oriented | results-oriented |
| high energy | low energy | trusting | suspicious |
| fast-paced | slow-paced | | |
| initiating | supportive | | |

## PROVIDES FAMILY LEADERSHIP BY

| High "D" | High "I" | High "S" | High "C" |
|---|---|---|---|
| 1. Developing | 1. Verbalizing | 1. Providing Stability | 1. Analyzing |
| 2. Deciding | 2. Networking | 2. Being Compassionate | 2. Organizing |
| 3. Being in Control | 3. Performing | 3. Being a Peacemaker | 3. Being Accurate |
| 4. Initiating Solutions | 4. Being Active | 4. Being Consistent | 4. Following Procedures |

## PERSONALITY GUIDELINES

1. You are much more successful when you operate from your strengths. Understand them and use them.
2. Strengths overdone become weaknesses.
3. Don't expect others to act like you; accept them. God made them different for a purpose.

CP-8

## Comparing Your Husband and Wife Graphs

The graph you developed on page CP-6 describes the natural behavior of both the husband and wife. Study the graph carefully and make note of any DISC dimensions that are plotted two or more blocks apart from one another. This dynamic reveals areas where you and your spouse are most prone to misunderstand one another due to natural temperament differences. The greater the divergence, the more stress you are likely to experience.

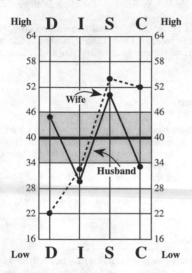

For instance, in the example at left, the wife's graph shows the "D" dimension at 22 (low), but the husband's graph shows the "D" dimension at 45 (balanced). In this example, the husband's natural behavior is more direct, decisive, and bold than his wife's. These two will need to clearly discuss any areas that relate to honoring feelings and completing family projects efficiently.

Also, note that the husband's and wife's C points are separated by three blocks, indicating the wife is more detail-oriented, analytical, and routine-oriented than her husband. He may feel pressure from his wife because he is not as naturally organized as she is. She may feel pressure from his spontaneous decisions.

Notice also that this couple has very similar scores in the High I and High S dimensions. This suggests that both are steady and reliable in their daily habits, and they put a high priority on maintaining harmony in their relationship.

Couples can discover a new dimension in their Christian service by identifying areas of mutual strength that can be utilized by the Lord. If He has blessed you both with a common strength, has He specially gifted you for a reason? Do you know what that reason is?

Further, a new dimension of marital growth can result from learning to work as a team by complementing, not criticizing, one another's weaknesses.

INSTRUCTIONS: Return to page CP-6 and compare your graphs. If the DISC points are relatively close, then your natural behaviors are typically compatible.

If your husband and wife DISC points are significantly separated (two or more blocks) on the graph, the potential for naturally misunderstanding one another rises. Mark the appropriate boxes on the next page and discuss how you each can modify your behavior and make allowances for your partner's shortcomings. Remember, your marriage commitment is not to change your spouse; it is to accept and honor him or her in spite of any weaknesses.

CP-9

293

## Celebrating Your Temperament Differences

If there is a significant difference in your graph points on page CP-6 (two or more blocks), check the applicable dimensions below and use them to help you analyze potential stress areas.

### D Dimension

If your D points are separated by two or more blocks, the High D may be frustrated by the Low D's slowness and lack of directness. The Low D may perceive the High D as pushy, insensitive, or domineering.

To celebrate your differences, High Ds should honor the relational element the Low Ds bring to the marriage, along with their sensitivity to feelings. Low Ds, in turn, should honor High Ds for their decisiveness, force of character, and commitment to defining and reaching family goals.

### I Dimension

If your High I points are separated by two or more blocks, the High I may be frustrated by the Low I's lack of interest in social events, unwillingness to talk, or critical or pessimistic attitude. The Low I, in turn, may be frustrated by the High I's disorganization, lack of attention to detail, emotional outbursts, and constant stream of new ideas.

To celebrate your differences, High I personalities should honor the stability that Low I people bring to the marriages and their need to be alone at times. In turn, the Low I should honor the High I for the contribution to the marriage of creativity, enthusiasm, and positive outlook.

### S Dimension

If your High S points are separated by two or more blocks, the High S may be frustrated by the Low S's impatience, bluntness, insensitivity to people, or lack of follow-through. In turn, the Low S may be frustrated by the High S's sentimentality, naivete, lack of direction, and priority with pleasing others.

To celebrate the differences, the High S should honor the Low S for taking the initiative to make needed changes, for having a high energy level and the ability to complete a task. In turn, the Low S personalities should honor the High S for the steady, calming, and caring influence he or she offers, which makes a house a home.

### C Dimension

If your High C points are separated by two or more blocks, the High C may be frustrated by the Low C's concern for details, lack of discipline, untidy habits, and general disorganization. In turn, the Low C may be frustrated by the High C's cautiousness, unwillingness to take risks, insistence on being right, and sticking to the rules.

To celebrate the differences, the High Cs should honor Low Cs for being able to see the "big picture," being decisive, and having the ability to bring spontaneity to the marriage. In turn, Low Cs should honor High Cs for their contributions of organization, accuracy, and standards to their marriages.

CP-10

294

## BALANCING YOUR PERSONALITY IN YOUR FAMILY

There are three broad characteristics of personality that are especially helpful in evaluating your family dynamics: *leader versus follower, task-oriented versus-people oriented, and detailist versus generalist.* Use the exercises below to identify you and your spouse's natural motivation in each of these terms.

INSTRUCTIONS: Place a mark to indicate where you think you **and your spouse** would fall on each continuum below, *using H for the husband and W for the wife.* Spouses should use different colored writing instruments to distinguish your markings. When you are finished, each line will have four plots—two by you and two by your spouse.

1. Some people are naturally leaders, providing directions to the family by setting goals and delegating tasks. Some are better followers, excelling at offering support and follow-through to the family.

W H

More
Leader ----------------------------------- B ------------------------------------ Follower
Balanced
∧

2. Some people are more task-oriented and concentrate on projects and efficiency in the family. Others are more people-oriented and place the priority with relationships and social events.

H   W

More
Task-Oriented ------------------------------ B ---------------------------- People-Oriented
Balanced
∧

3. Some people like to establish and follow rules and procedures, bringing organization to everything they touch. Others are naturally "big picture" people and prefer more variety and spontaneity.

H  W

More of a
Detailist ------------------------------------ B ------------------------------------ Generalist
Balanced
∧

FOR DISCUSSION AND PRAYER: When each of you has completed the exercise, thoughtfully consider your results and the implications for your family communication. Clarify any areas on the diagrams above where you disagree.

_____

_____

_____

_____

CP-11

## 4. Questions to Ask *Before* Quitting Your Job

What is the main reason I am considering this change?

_____

_____

_____

Have I prayed about it? How is God leading?

_____

_____

_____

What godly counsel have I received?

_____

_____

_____

How does this affect our family goals?

_____

_____

_____

Is this a permanent change or will I return to work later?

_____

_____

_____

Will I be able to keep up with new developments in my field and update my skills regularly in case I do return to the workplace?

_____

_____

_____

Can I afford to quit? Are we in debt? How much?

_____

_____

_____

Can all monthly payments be made from one income?

_____

_____

_____

How will this change affect monthly income?

_____

_____

How will this change affect monthly expenses?

_____

_____

Have we worked out a sample budget for the new income level?

_____

_____

Do I mind delaying the purchase of a larger home, nicer vacations, eating in good restaurants, and buying things we can't afford now on two incomes?

_____

_____

_____

Am I disciplined enough to limit my spending and use of credit cards?

_____

_____

_____

Do we have an emergency fund? access to emergency credit?

_____

_____

_____

What are the pluses and minuses of this change for me? my husband? my children?

_____

_____

_____

Is my husband secure in his job? Is it stable?

_____

_____

_____

What lifestyle changes will be necessary?

_____

_____

Will I enjoy cooking, cleaning, repairing?

_____

_____

Will I miss the company of other adults?

_____

_____

Are there ways I can supplement the income at home?

_____

_____

_____

Will I lose my health insurance? Will my husband's policy cover me and the children?

_____

_____

Will I mind not having my own money to spend?

_____

_____

Would I be interested in homeschooling my children?

_____

_____

## 5. Reading Resources

**BOOKS**

**Home Business**

*Bookkeeping for Beginners*, W.E. Hooper (Beekman Publishers)

*Building a Mail Order Business*, William Cohen (John Wiley & Sons, Inc.)

*Business by the Book*, Larry Burkett (Thomas Nelson)

*Career Opportunities in Crafts*, Elyse Sommer (Crown Publishers)

*Caring for Kids: A Concise Guide to Establish a Successful Day-Care Center*, Tanya Ashworth (Vade Mecum Press)

*Cash in on Your Bright Ideas*, George G Siposs (Universal Developments)

*Cashing in on Cooking*, Nancy Baker (Contemporary Books)

*Cater from Your Kitchen: Income from Your Home Business*, Marjorie P. Blanchard (Bobbs-Merrill)

*Catering Handbook*, Hal and E. Weiss (Hayden Book Co)

*Climb Your Own Ladder: 101 Home Businesses That Can Make You Wealthy*, Allen Lieberoff (Simon & Schuster)

*Complete Guide to a Profitable Career*, Robert E. Kelley (Charles Scribner's Sons)

*Complete Do-It-Yourself Guide to Picture Framing, A*, Lista Duren (Houghton Mifflin Co.)

*Computer Freelancers Handbook: Moonlighting with Your Home Computer*, Ardy Friedberg (New American Library)

*Cooking Business*, Janet Shown (Live Oak Publications)

*Crafts Business Encyclopedia, The*, Michael Scott (Harcourt Brace Jovanovich)

*Creative Cash*, Barbara Brabec (Betterway Publications)

*Disciplines of the Beautiful Woman*, Anne Ortlund, (Word)

*Do What You Love, the Money Will Follow: Discovering Your Right Livelihood*, Marsha Sinetar (Paulist Press)

*Earn Money at Home*, Peter Davidson (McGraw-Hill)

*555 Ways to Earn Extra Money*, Jay Conrad Levinson (HR&W)

*Franchises You Can Run from Home*, Lynie Arden (John Wiley & Sons, Inc.)

*Freelance Foodcrafting: How to Become Profitably Self-Employed in Your Own Creative Cooking Business*, Janet Shown (Live Oak Publications)

*Free Help from Uncle Sam to Start Your Own Business*, William Alarid and Gustav Berle (Puma Publishing)

*Home Filing Made Easy!*, Mary E. Martin and J. Michael Martin (Dearborn Financial Publishing Inc.)

*Home Office and Workspaces*, from editors of Sunset Books and *Sunset* Magazine (Lane Publishing Co)

*Homemade Business: A Woman's Step-by-Step Guide to Earning Money at Home*, Donna Partow (Focus on the Family)

*How to Win Customers and Keep Them for Life*, Michael LeBoeuf (Berkley Books)

*How to Start and Run a Profitable Home Typing Business*, Barbara Aliaga (ISC Press)

*How to Become a Successful Consultant in Your Own Field*, Hubert Bermont (Bermont Books)

*How to Make Money Writing Fillers*, Connie Emerson (Writers' Digest Books)

*How to Open and Operate a Bed and Breakfast Home*, Jan Stankus (The Globe Pequot Press)

*How to Write Articles That Sell*, Perry Wilbur (John Wiley & Sons, Inc.)

*How to Set Up and Run a Successful Typing Service*, Donna Goodrich (John Wiley & Sons, Inc.)

*How to Be a Freelance Photographer*, Ted Schwartz (Contemporary Books)

*How to Run Your Own Home Business*, Coralee Smith Kern and Tammara Hoffman Wolfgram (VGM Career Horizons)

*How to Succeed as an Independent Consultant*, Herman Holtz (John Wiley & Sons, Inc.)

*How to Get Rich in Mail Order*, Melvin Powers (Wilshire Book Co.)

*How to Master the Art of Selling*, Tom Hopkins (Warner Books)

*How to Earn $25,000 a Year or More Typing at Home*, Anne Drouillard and William F. Keefe (Frederick Fell)

*How to Start Your Own Secretarial Services Business at Home*, S.G. Kozlow (SK Publications)

*How to Write a Children's Book and Get It Published*, Barbara Seuling (Charles Scribner's Sons)

*How to Start and Operate a Mail Order Business*, Julian L. Simon (McGraw Hill)

*The Job-Sharing Handbook*, Barney Olmsted and Suzanne Smith, (Ten Speed Press)

*Jewelry Maker's Handbook*, Iva Geisinger (Gembooks)

*Life You Can Love, A*, Diane Eble (Zondervan)

*Making Money with Your Home Computer*, Dana Cassell (Dodd Mead and Company)

*Mothering and Managing a Typing Service at Home*, Carla Culp (MHBN Publications)

*Naturally Gifted: A Self-Discovery Workbook*, Gordon Jones and Rosemary Jones (InterVarsity Press)

*101 Best Businesses to Start*, Sharon Kahn/Philip Lief Group (Doubleday)

*1001 Businesses You Can Start from Home: The World's Most Complete Directory of Part-Time and Full-Time Business Ideas, Including*

*Start-up Costs, Marketing Tips, Sources of Information*, Daryl Allen Hall (John Wiley & Sons, Inc.)

*Organizing Your Workspace: A Guide to Personal Productivity*, Odette Pollar (Menlo Park, CA: CRISP Publications)

*The Part-Time Professional*, Diane S. Rothberg and Barbara Ensor Cook, (Acropolis Books Ltd)

*The Part-Time Solution*, Charlene Canape (Harper & Row)

*Professional Food Preparation*, Margaret Terrell (John Wiley & Sons, Inc.)

*Profitable Part-Time Freelancing*, Clair Rees (Writer's Digest Books)

*Secrets of a Successful Freelance Writer*, Bob Bly (Henry Holt)

*Small-Time Operator* (building a business around your interests), Bernard Kamoroff (Bell Spring Publishing)

*Start Your Own At-Home Child Care Business*, Patricia Gallagher (Doubleday)

*Start Your Own Bed and Breakfast Business*, Beverly Mathews (Pocket Books)

*Start and Run a Profitable Craft Business*, William B. Hynes (ISC Press)

*Starting and Operating a Clipping Service*, Demaris C. Smith (Pilot Books)

*Successful Direct Marketing Methods*, Bob Stone (Crain Books)

*Successful Free Lancing*, Marian Faux (St. Martin's Press)

*Teaching Needlecraft*, Rosemary Cornelius/Peg Doffek/Sue Hardy (VanNostrand Reinhold)

*The Time Minder: Making Time Work for You*, Ruth Wagner Miller (Chappaqua, NY: Christian Herald Books)

*The Time Trap: How to Get More Done in Less Time*, R. Alec Mackenzie (AMACOM)

*The Truth About You,* Arthur F. Miller and Ralph T. Mattson (Ten Speed Press)

*Turn Your Kitchen into a Goldmine,* Alice Howard (Harper & Row)

*Women and Home-Based Work: The Unspoken Contract,* Kathleen Christensen (Henry Holt and Company)

*Women's Work-at-Home Handbook: Income and Independence with a Computer* (Bantam Books)

*Word Processing Profits at Home,* Peggy Glenn (Aames-Allen Publishing Co)

*The Work-At-Home Sourcebook: How to Find "At Home" Work That's Right for You,* Lynie Arden (Live Oak Publications)

*Working at Home: The Dream That's Becoming a Trend,* Lindsey O'Connor (Harvest House)

*Working from Home,* Paul and Sarah Edwards (Jeremy P. Tarcher, Inc.)

*You Can Make Money from Your Arts and Crafts,* Steve and Cindy Long (Mark Publishing)

**Homeschooling**
(See the end of Chapter 16.)

<u>Perspective</u>

*The Best Jobs in America for Parents Who Want Careers and Time for Children Too,* Susan Bacon Dynerman and Lynn O'Rourke Hayes (Rawson Assoc)

*Children at Risk,* James Dobson, Gary Bauer (Word)

*Debt-Free Living,* Larry Burkett (Moody Press)

*Decision Making and the Will of God,* Garry Friesen with J. Robin Mason (Multnomah Press)

*Don't Miss Your Kids,* Charlene Ann Baumbich (InterVarsity Press)

*Home by Choice,* Brenda Hunter (Multnomah)

*Home Filing Made Easy!*, Mary E. Martin and J. Michael Martin (Dearborn Financial Publishing Inc)

*Juggling: The Unexpected Advantages of Balancing Career and Home for Women and Their Families*, Faye Crosby (MacMillan, Inc.)

*A Life You Can Love: A Guide for Discovering Your Personal Style and Designing Your Life Around It*, Diane Eble (Zondervan)

*Love for a Lifetime*, James Dobson (Questar)

*Motherhood As Metamorphosis*, Joyce Block (The Penguin Group)

*Mothers of Many Styles*, Janet Penley and Diane Stephens (Penley & Associates)

*The Myth of the Perfect Mother*, Kimberly Converse and Richard Hagstrom (Harvest House)

*No More Lone Ranger Moms*, Donna Partow (Bethany House Publishers)

*Part-Time Professional*, Diane S. Rothberg and Barbara Ensor Cook (Acropolis Books)

*The Part-Time Solution*, Charlene Canape (Harper & Row)

*A Season at Home: The Joy of Fully Sharing Your Child's Critical Years*, Debbie Barr (Zondervan)

*Sequencing: Having It All But Not All at Once*, Arlene Rossen Cardozo (Atheneum)

*Solving the Work/Family Puzzle*, Bonnie Michaels and Elizabeth McCarty (Business One Irwin)

*Sometimes I Feel Like Running Away from Home*, Elizabeth Cody Newenhuyse (Bethany House)

*Staying Home: From Full-Time Professional to Full-Time Parent*, Darcie Sanders and Martha Bullen (Little, Brown and Co)

*Staying Home Instead: Alternatives to the Two-Paycheck Family*, (revised edition), Christine Davidson (MacMillan)

*Tyranny of the Urgent*, Charles Hummel (InterVarsity Press)

*Using Your Money Wisely*, Larry Burkett (Moody Press)

*What Good Parents Have in Common*, Janis Long Harris (Zondervan)

*The Word on Finances*, Larry Burkett (Moody Press)

*Working Moms: From Survival to Satisfaction*, Miriam Neff (NavPress)

*Your Finances in Changing Times*, Larry Burkett (Moody Press)

*Your Work Matters to God*, Doug Sherman and William Hendricks (NavPress)

## Personality Evaluation

*Do What You Are: Discover the Perfect Career for You Through the Secrets of Personality Type*, Paul D. Tieger and Barbara Barron-Tieger (Little, Brown and Co)

*Finding the Career That Fits You*, Lee Ellis and Larry Burkett (Moody)

*Gifts Differing*, Isabel Briggs Myers with Peter B. Myers (Consulting Psychologists Press)

*How to Find Your Mission in Life*, Richard Bolles (Ten Speed Press)

*How to Get Along with Almost Anyone*, Norman Wright (Word)

*How to Win Friends and Influence People*, Dale Carnegie (Simon & Schuster)

*It Takes All Types!* Alan Brownsword (Baytree Publications Co)

*Personality Plus*, Florence Littauer (Revell)

*Personality Puzzle*, Florence and Marita Littauer (Revell)

*Please Understand Me: Character and Temperament Types*, David Keirsey and Marilyn Bates (Prometheus Nemesis)

*Spirit-Controlled Temperament*, Tim LaHaye (Tyndale House)

*The Three Boxes of Life and How to Get Out of Them*, Richard Bolles (Ten Speed Press)

*The Two Sides of Love*, Gary Smalley and John Trent (Focus on the Family)

*Understanding How Others Misunderstand You*, Ken Voges and Ron Braund (Moody Press)

*Unlocking Your Sixth Suitcase*, John Bradley and Jay Carty (NavPress)

*What Color Is Your Parachute?*, Richard Bolles (Ten Speed Press)

*Your Career in Changing Times*, Lee Ellis and Larry Burkett (Moody Press)

<u>Saving Money</u>

*Best of the Cheap-Skate Monthly*, Mary Hunt (St. Martin's Press)

*The Complete Financial Guide for Single Parents*, Larry Burkett (Victor Press)

*The Complete Home Shopper*, Sue Goldstein (McGraw-Hill)

*The Complete Financial Guide for Young Couples*, Larry Burkett (Victor Press)

*Debt-Free Living*, Larry Burkett (Moody Press)

*Financial Planning Workbook*, Larry Burkett (Moody Press)

*Guide to Off-Price Shopping*, Sue Goldstein (McGraw-Hill)

*Helpful Hints for Hard Times: How to Live It Up While Cutting Down*, Hap Hatton and Laura Torbet (Facts on File Publications)

*How to Manage Your Money*, Larry Burkett (Moody Press)

*Living Smart, Spending Less*, Stephen and Amanda Sorenson (Moody Press)

*Money-Saving Tips for Good Times and Bad*, Walter B. Leonard (Consumer Reports Books)

*Raising Happy Kids on a Reasonable Budget*, Patricia Gallagher (Better Way Books)

*Tightwad Gazette, The*, Amy Dacyczyn (Villard Books)

*Using Your Money Wisely*, Larry Burkett (Moody Press)

*Your Finances in Changing Times*, Larry Burkett (Moody Press)

## NEWSLETTERS

*Entrepreneur: The Small Business Authority* and *New Business Opportunities: The Business Start-Up Magazine*, 2392 Morse Ave, Irvine CA 92714

*HomeWork*, Home & Family Business Fellowship Int., PO Box 2250, Gresham OR 97030

*Moms Inc.*, Fast Forward, 3890 Cone Ave, Rochester Hills MI 48309-4374

*Working Options*, Crescent Plz Ste 216, 7700 Leesburg Pk, Falls Church VA 22043 (703) 734-7975

Larry Burkett, founder and president of Christian Financial Concepts, is the best-selling author of over 40 books on business and personal finances. He also hosts two radio programs broadcast on hundreds of stations worldwide.

Larry holds degrees in marketing and finance, and for several years served as a manager in the space program at Cape Canaveral, Florida. He also has been vice president of an electronics manufacturing firm. Larry's education, business experience, and solid understanding of God's Word enable him to give practical, Bible-based financial counsel to families, churches, and businesses.

Founded in 1976, Christian Financial Concepts is a nonprofit, nondenominational ministry dedicated to helping God's people gain a clear understanding of how to manage their money according to scriptural principles. While practical assistance is provided on many levels, the purpose of CFC is simply to bring glory to God by freeing His people from financial bondage so they may serve Him to their utmost.

One major avenue of ministry involves the training of volunteers in budget and debt counseling and linking them with financially troubled families and individuals through a nationwide referral network. CFC also provides financial management seminars and workshops for churches and other groups. (Formats available include audio, video, video with moderator, and live instruction.) A full line of printed and audio-visual materials related to money management is available through CFC's materials department (1-800-722-1976).

Career Pathways, another outreach of Christian Financial Concepts, helps teenagers and adults find their occupational calling. The Career Pathways "Testing Package" gauges a person's work priorities, skills, vocational interests, and personality. Reports in each of these areas define a person's strengths, weaknesses, and unique, God-given pattern for work.

For further information about the ministry of Christian Financial Concepts, write to:

Christian Financial Concepts
PO Box 2377
Gainesville, Georgia 30503-2377

*Editing:*
Adeline Griffith
Christian Financial Concepts
Gainesville, Georgia

*Text Design / Typesetting:*
Joe Ragont Studios
Rolling Meadows, Illinois

*Jacket Design:*
The Puckett Group
Atlanta, Georgia

*Printing and Binding:*
Lake Book Mfg.
Melrose Park, Illinois

Moody Press, a ministry of the Moody Bible Institute,
is designed for education, evangelization, and edification.
If we may assist you in knowing more about Christ
and the Christian life, please write us without obligation:
Moody Press, c/o MLM, Chicago, Illinois 60610